HITLER AND THE NAZI
CULT OF FILM AND FAME

HITLER AND THE NAZI CULT OF FILM AND FAME

MICHAEL MUNN

Skyhorse Publishing
A Herman Graf Book

Skyhorse Publishing books may be purchased in bulk at special discounts for
sales promotion, corporate gifts, fund-raising, or educational purposes. Special
editions can also be created to specifications. For details, contact the Special
Sales Department, Skyhorse Publishing, 307 West 36th Street, 11th Floor,
New York, NY 10018 or info@skyhorsepublishing.com.

Skyhorse® and Skyhorse Publishing® are registered trademarks of Skyhorse
Publishing, Inc.®, a Delaware corporation.

Visit our website at www.skyhorsepublishing.com.

10 9 8 7 6 5 4 3 2 1

Library of Congress Cataloging-in-Publication Data is available on file.
ISBN: 978-1-62087-727-2

Printed in the United States of America

CONTENTS

INTRODUCTION

The Nazis had a cult for almost everything. Not every cult was necessarily given a name or was recognised as Nazi policy, but Joseph Goebbels acknowledged that cults were a fundamental element of Nazism. To celebrate the occasion of the end of a heroic life, they had a cult of death. To maintain mystical and symbolic rituals Hitler felt were essential to Germanic culture and history, there was the cult of the blood banner. Hitler, identifying with the Roman emperor Nero, indulged in a cult of fire. One might even suggest a cult of suicide existed although most others were unwilling to be a part of it. And to elevate Hitler to the *Führer,* the party embraced the cult of personality.

Hitler was a product of his own making who created his own cult of personality using the forms of media available to him at the time, which, combined with judiciously formulated propaganda, produced and promoted a carefully honed heroic and almost divine public image. By the beginning of the twentieth century the divine right of kings who held their office by the will of God was quickly giving way to other forms of government, some democratic and some dictatorial, and from the latter rose the cult of personality, which took advantage of all the technical accomplishments of the modern world such as photography, sound recording, film and mass publications. Hitler was, alongside Stalin, one of the first to dominate the political stage through technology. But Hitler went further than Stalin in communicating his image because unlike Stalin, Hitler didn't set out to be a politician. He simply wanted to be famous. He tried his hand at being an artist, then a playwright, then a composer of opera. In the end he found he had just one talent – oratory.

It was through his love of art, music, film, theatre and, most of all, opera, and his enthralment with the idea of almost hypnotising his audience with sounds and sights that were inspired by the culture – often very lowbrow – he embraced, that he developed the techniques which resulted in the great geometrical rallies, the night-time torchlight parades, and the Nazification of the German film industry. There was even a Hitler film in the offing, and for a while he intended to play himself. He was, he once confessed, an actor, and he learned to play the part of the *Führer* – how to talk, to stand, to move, to perform. Everything in his public life, and often in his private life as he came to believe his own publicity, was stage-managed. Even the war. He wanted to play the role of a general, and when he tried writing his own script of World War Two, he bombed.

By design rather than as a by-product of his image-building, out of the cult of personality grew his cult of celebrity. He knew no other way to become dictator than by performing. Fame was more important to him than governing, although in his mind they became one and the same thing. Culture and art became politics. Even suicide was a macabre element to his celebrity, his legend and his sense of immortality, which were all irrevocably connected to the final act of his life-long drama; he would write his own ending.

Hitler completely absorbed himself in his cult of celebrity, and his most favoured actors, musicians, writers and other artists could be absorbed into his cult and become great celebrities themselves. All they had to do was promote Nazi ideology. Those that did were permitted to work, and some were pampered and preened into stars, and the public were virtually expected to pay to see the great stars. Artists who didn't support Hitler's ideas were, at best, denied work and, at worst, sent to the camps. Jews never had the luxury of either option. The 'Jewish question' is one of the most deplorable aspects of Hitler's claim to fame.

The German film industry in particular was encapsulated by this cult of celebrity because it was the modern medium of the age. Under the Nazis, cinema became a weapon. Entertainment became policy, and the greatest movie celebrities were advocates for everything Hitler stood for. The extermination of an entire race, played out against the magisterial music of Richard Wagner, whose works were the inspiration for Hitler's new world, became the backdrop for Hitler's own reality show, in which his name was above the title and every celebrity in Germany was a guest star.

The cult of celebrity became the cornerstone of Hitler's Nazism – and Hitler loved celebrities, as did his publicist Joseph Goebbels, who ran the German film industry. Despite all their assertions and pretensions about art and culture, these arbiters of taste used their cult for their own sexual obsessions. Starlets and beautiful actresses were as much a sexual commodity in Nazi Germany as they were in Hollywood.

In Aryan Germany, Hitler governed with theatrical tricks. In ancient Rome the emperors gave the people the spectacle of the games to make them love the Caesars, and, taking his cue from them, Hitler gave his people the spectacle of Nazi culture and became their beloved *Führer*. At the heart of his style of government, backed by military and paramilitary might, was his Nazi cult of celebrity. He had nothing else to offer. In the end his obsession with fame led him into grand illusions that were merely delusions, and resulted in the deaths of around sixty million people.

CHAPTER ONE

CELEBRITY, SEX AND DEATH

If Hitler had nothing better to do, and usually he didn't, he could be found at Berlin's *Universum Film AG* – better known as UFA, Germany's largest film studio at Babelsberg, which was just outside Berlin, near Potsdam – mingling with the stars. A film director at UFA, Alfred Zeisler, recalled that Hitler visited the studio very frequently. He loved to watch scenes being filmed, and he asked about new plots and new talent, and also about the technical aspects of film-making. Zeisler said that Hitler had a very good grasp of the film-making process and asked extremely intelligent questions about some of the technical problems involved. Hitler also enjoyed coming to the studios to have lunch or dinner in the restaurant of the Film Institute, where actors and actresses gathered.[1]

It wasn't as though Hitler didn't have enough to occupy his mind in 1933, having, that year, become Germany's *Führer*, but he cared nothing for politics, or for governing Germany. He had ministers to do all that. Hitler was obsessed with celebrities. And he knew that of them all, he was the greatest celebrity.

The most important thing he could do every day was satisfy his starstruck craving by being among his favourite film stars, and if it so happened that he couldn't escape from the Reich Chancellery, he would get on the phone to the studio, as Zeisler recalled, to find out about films being made, and the actors in them, or just for general news about what was happening at the studios. Zeisler often wondered when Hitler had the time to devote himself to affairs of state because he spent so much time either at the studios, or on the telephone, or looking at films – there seemed little time left for anything else.

At the Berghof, Hitler's mountain retreat, his young mistress Eva

Braun was left to her own devices while he was away working, or so he claimed, though he did very little real work as Chancellor of Germany. Eva was a good actress and might have actually been happy if Hitler had allowed her to actually be an actress, but he forbade her that pleasure. 'I heard she wanted to be in films. Hitler said no,' recalled German actor Curd Jürgens. 'He didn't want his girlfriend to be a film star, but he wanted to have film stars to be his girlfriends.'[2]

Fringe benefits came with being the *Führer*. It was well known among the film community, where secrets were kept through fear, that he enjoyed the company of beautiful starlets. Hitler frequently called Alfred Zeisler at the UFA studio to ask for young starlets to keep him company in the Reich Chancellery. Zeisler duly sent them along, often in pairs, and was naturally very curious about what actually happened in the Reich Chancellery between Hitler and the pretty young women he sent, so one day in 1934 he asked two chorus girls he had procured for the *Führer* what had taken place the previous evening. They told him all that happened was that Hitler sat and bragged the whole evening, telling them how he was going to annex Austria and was going to build up the biggest army in the world and then reinforce the Rhineland. The girls said they thought Hitler 'extremely odd'. Zeisler concluded that Hitler's only intention was to impress the girls with his greatness and power.[3]

Zeisler's claims that he provided Hitler with female stars for company are given some credence by Walter C. Langer,[4] who in his famous psychological study of Hitler said Hitler often requested the studios to send over actresses whenever there was a party in the Chancellery. He seemed to get 'an extraordinary delight' in fascinating these girls about what he was going to do in the future, and he also reeled out 'the same old stories' of his past. He enjoyed impressing the girls with his power by ordering the studios to give the girls better film roles. Like a real movie mogul, he often promised them that he would personally see to it that they were given starring roles. Langer reported that men who, like him, have associations with 'women of this type' did not go beyond that point; i.e., to have sexual intercourse with them.[5]

These encounters with stars and would-be stars, at the studio or in some secret room in the Reich Chancellery, would seem to indicate that Hitler veered erratically from being a starstruck fan to some kind of impotent despot who wanted to impress and scare little girls; he was certainly known to form attachments to much younger women than himself who were vulnerable and whom he could dominate.

It all came down to power. Just having lunch with the stars was more than him being a fan having fun – which was certainly part of it – but it was a demonstration of his power; Germany's biggest stars – and this also applied to musicians, writers and other artistes – for whom millions would kiss the ground they walked on all demonstrated their devotion to him, either through sincere admiration or out of fear, and their endorsement of him helped enormously to win the endorsement of the country long before John F. Kennedy was being elevated to the White House in 1961 by Frank Sinatra and his Rat Packers and other celebrities. Since then the world of politics has become a platform for celebrities, and the politicians themselves have become celebrities. In 1933, Hitler was doing all that. He had only to command celebrities to attend massive public events where he was the star attraction, or to functions where he could impress or bore them with one of his famous monologues about his latest plans, and they duly complied. That was a price they paid for the privilege of enjoying all the perks of Hitler's cult of celebrity.

The power he had over the young starlets is apparent. And probably not as harmless as it might have seemed to the two chorus girls who only had to endure Hitler's boastings. One famous actress endured much more, and paid the ultimate price.

In 1937 Germany was shocked by the news that actress and singer Renate Müller had died at the age of just thirty-one. Her body was found on the pavement outside a hotel on 7 October. She had fallen from the third-storey window of a hotel, and died instantly.

The blue-eyed beauty had starred in more than twenty German films, including *Viktor und Viktoria* in 1933, which was one of her biggest successes – and was remade in 1982 as *Victor Victoria* with Julie Andrews. Renate Müller was regarded by the National Socialists as an ideal Aryan woman and, in light of Marlene Dietrich's defection to Hollywood, was courted and promoted as one of Germany's leading film actresses.

She was already a star when Hitler came to power, and was pressured by Joseph Goebbels, who, as President of the *Reichskulturkammer,* which presided over the German film industry, to appear in some of his personally commissioned pro-Nazi anti-Semitic films. She resisted, so he put her under surveillance by the Gestapo, who established she had a Jewish lover. She finally gave in to Goebbel's demands, and in 1937 she starred in the blatantly anti-Semitic *Togger*.

Her death was officially classified a suicide. The exact details of her death and the minutes leading up to it have become a matter of much conjecture. Several Gestapo officers were seen entering the hotel shortly before she died, and it was suggested either that she was murdered by Gestapo officers who threw her from a window, or that she panicked when she saw them arrive and jumped. Goebbels wanted the public to believe she had been emotionally unstable and had a drug addiction.

Theories for her possible murder include her lack of cooperation with Goebbels, her love affair with a Jew, and the regime's fear that she was going to turn traitor and leave Germany as Dietrich had done. What is certain is that there was a cover-up about her death. The absolute truth will never be known, and her death remains as much of a mystery in the annals of the German film world as Marilyn Monroe's has in Hollywood. Renate's sister Gabriele always maintained that her death was due to post-operative complications on her knee, but that never explained how her body came to be on the pavement.

Almost the moment Renate Müller's body was discovered, Goebbels realised he had a public relations disaster on his hands.

The first story that went out over the radio was that the cause of her death was epilepsy and that she had fallen from a window of a hospital. At some point, this hospital became a hospital for the mentally sick, suggesting Müller was mentally ill, or had had a breakdown. Goebbels spread rumours that she had become addicted to morphine, and was an alcoholic. The true story, of the fall from the hotel window, was only revealed later.

Goebbels saw to it that her funeral at the *Parkfriedhof Lichterfelde* on 15 October was held in private, and her adoring public was barred. Her possessions were confiscated and sold even though her parents and her sister were alive. Some years later, according to unconfirmed reports, they were all buried in the same grave as Renate, suggesting the family were all silenced.

Without resorting to possible murder, terrorisation and extortion, Goebbels acted much in the same way as Hollywood mogul Adolph Zukor once did when one of his top directors at Famous Players, William Desmond Taylor, was found murdered in 1922. Zukor ordered a cover-up so that the police were unable to ever charge anyone because Zukor knew that the identity of the killer – which became an open secret in Hollywood – would reveal facts about Taylor's life which he wanted to keep from the public because of the shocking scandal it would cause. It seems likely that, for similar reasons, Joseph Goebbels, playing the part of the amateur movie mogul, did the same when Renate Müller died; she might have known some of Hitler's most deviant secrets.

The full truth about her last years and death has never been fully uncovered, and there has been much unconfirmed information and clearly designed misinformation, as was the case with Monroe. Müller might have had a breakdown in 1933 due to the stress of trying to keep her weight down, and illness might have interrupted filming in 1934 – it was said to be epilepsy – but despite reports that her career was sporadic from then on due to whatever illness she might have had, she actually starred in four films during 1935 and 1936, and her last film in 1937, *Togger*, commissioned by Joseph Goebbels.

Albert Zeisler knew of Müller's secret. On one occasion when Hitler called and asked Zeisler for the company of a pretty actress, possibly in 1935, or before, he sent Renate Müller. Quite why Zeisler chose her isn't clear but it is very likely that Hitler asked for her. Whether she went under duress or from sheer admiration for Hitler isn't obvious; according to Zeisler, she was prepared to have sexual relations with Hitler.

At the Reich Chancellery, Hitler took great delight in telling her that he had made a thorough study of medieval torture methods and was modernising them with the intention of introducing them to Germany. He described these methods to her – methods which were later adopted by the Gestapo – in such explicit detail that she was horrified to the point where she felt her 'flesh creep'.[6]

Renate did her best to seduce him without success; she told Zeisler that he seemed uninterested in sex. However, on another occasion, he seemed to become excited and she thought they would finally make love, but instead he jumped to his feet, raised his arm in the Nazi salute and bragged that he could hold his arm that way for an hour and a half without tiring, unlike Göring, who, Hitler said, could not hold out his arm even for twenty minutes.

She arrived one morning at the studio in a very depressed state and when Zeisler asked her what was troubling her she told him she had been with Hitler at the Reich Chancellery that night and she had been sure they were going to have sexual intercourse. They had got as far as undressing, but then Hitler fell to the floor and begged her to kick him. She resisted but he pleaded with her and condemned himself as unworthy and grovelled on the floor in an agonising manner. As disgusted as she was, she gave in and kicked him, which excited him. He begged for more and, masturbating, said it was better than he deserved and that he was not worthy to be in the same room as she. When he was satisfied, he suggested they got dressed, and he thanked her warmly for a pleasant evening.[7]

This tale has been often regarded as pure fiction by some historians because Zeisler hated Hitler for making him leave Germany after he refused to make films that would promote Nazi ideology.

While it certainly appears to be almost too sensational, presenting a clichéd image of a mad dictator who can only enjoy perverse sex, Hitler did struggle with a compulsion to completely degrade himself whenever he felt some kind of affection for a woman. Nazis Ernst Hanfstaengel, Otto Strasser and Herman Rauschning all reported that whenever Hitler was smitten with a girl, even in company, he tended to 'grovel at her feet in a most disgusting way'.[8]

Like almost all the girls Hitler was attracted to, Renate Müller was blonde. Zeisler recalled 'another tall blonde called Loeffler' who became involved with Hitler, but after a while she ran off with a Jewish man and lived in Paris, which upset Hitler so much that for some time he did not even bother calling the studio to ask for girls.[9]

For years, Hitler's sexuality has been a matter of debate and disagreement. Suggestions that Hitler was homosexual appear to be unfounded but may well have been based on what was observed as his feminine characteristics – his gait, his mannerisms and even his choice of art as a profession were once interpreted as feminine manifestations. With the possible exception of Heinrich Hoffmann, the Nazi Party's official photographer, and Hitler's personal adjutant, no one knew the nature of his sexual activities, causing much conjecture in party circles, with some believing that he was sexually 'normal' while others suggested that he was immune to sexual temptation. Others thought he was homosexual because many of the party's inner circle in the early days were known homosexuals. Rudolf Hess was known as 'Fraulein Anna'. For a long time Hitler ignored the fact that many in the SA leadership were homosexuals, including Ernst Röhm. Röhm was well aware that Hitler was attracted to the female form, and one time remarked in Hitler's presence, 'He is thinking about the peasant girls. When they stand in the fields and bend down at their work so that you can see their behinds, that's what he likes, especially when they've got big round ones. That's Hitler's sex life.'[10]

Hitler preferred to look rather than touch, and he also enjoyed the pornography his official photographer Heinrich Hoffmann made available to him. Ernest Pope claimed Hitler frequently visited *The*

Merry Widow, in which an American actress played the lead. 'I have seen Hitler nudge his *Gauleiter* and smirk when Dorothy does her famous backbending number in the spotlight.' Hitler watched through opera glasses and sometimes had command performances for his private benefit.[11]

What is clear is that Hitler was unable to have a normal relationship with women. It seems almost too clichéd to suggest that the man who delighted in the sadistic torture of his enemies and had not an ounce of compassion for those he sent to their deaths was also a voyeur and a masochist in need of punishment from pretty girls.

If it is true what Zeisler claimed about Renate Müller being coerced into inflicting pain upon Hitler, it would appear to shed light on her death. What is also apparent is that she had been seeing Hitler for around two years because Zeisler, who had effectively pimped for Hitler by sending her to him, left Germany in 1935, two years before she died, although she might have ended her association with Hitler, or attempted to, during or before 1937. But whether she killed herself because she was literally driven insane by being forced to indulge in his S&M games, or because she had to be done away with to keep her from going public with revelations of her bizarre association with him – in Hitler's Germany superinjunctions were usually imposed with deadly force – her death can also be theoretically linked to Hitler because of the history of Hitler's women committing or attempting suicide, or even murder. But what was it about Hitler that did this to the women closest to him?

He was deranged – that is without question. To be drawn into close proximity with him in any kind of emotional or physical way must have caused people who were vulnerable or dependent upon him in some way to lose their sense of normality and even become severely unbalanced. He certainly was not sexually conventional, and, by inflicting sexual activities so extreme upon others as he appeared to do to Renate Müller – and must have done to others – he must have contributed to them being driven to the edge of their own limits of normality and sanity. There also remains the possibility that some of these women, knowing of his sexual deviances, were a threat to him, and murder can't be completely discounted, especially in the case of Renate Müller.

In Hitler's cult of celebrity, as in showbusiness anywhere in the world, celebrity and sex went hand in hand. But in his case, celebrity also went hand in hand with terror and death. His cult of celebrity was like a vortex into which anyone wanting success in their chosen field, whether it was drama or music, painting or writing, was sucked without mercy. It's known that Hollywood can be cruel, but Hitler's cult of celebrity was devastating for all, including Hitler himself. It was as though he couldn't control it or himself; he was driven by one overwhelming and unhinged desire – to get to the top.

CHAPTER TWO

IN THAT HOUR

One evening in the autumn of 1905, in Linz, the third biggest city in Austria, sixteen-year-old Adolf Hitler met August Kubizek, older by nine months. Their friendship was formed by their mutual love of music and opera, and, dressed in their finest clothes, they went almost every evening together to the opera or the theatre. As well as sharing a love for the opera, they also shared an ambition to be famous; Kubizek dreamed of becoming a great musician. Hitler had come to Linz in the hope of being accepted for a place at the city's Academy of Fine Arts.

When it came to pop music, the teenage Adolf Hitler was a fan of the operettas of Johann Straus and Franz Lehár, and in later years he would enjoy Liszt, Brahms, Beethoven and Bruckner,[12] but he considered Richard Wagner to be the supreme artist, a genius, someone to emulate.[13] Hitler was simply wild about Wagner.

Kubizek and Hitler saw operas by the Italian masters Donizetti, Bellini and Rossini, and the works of Puccini and Verdi, but Hitler considered the music inferior in every way because they were not German. 'For him, a second-rate Wagner was a hundred times better than a first-class Verdi,' said Kubizek, who did not agree but always gave in to Hitler's insistence that they forgo Verdi at the Court Opera to see Wagner at the more lowbrow Popular Opera House. 'When it was a matter of a Wagner performance,' wrote Kubizek, 'Adolf would stand no contradiction.'[14]

In death, Richard Wagner remained the most popular composer of the era, and Hitler was just one of thousands who flocked to hear the works of the master of Bayreuth performed at the Hofoper in Vienna during the early years of the twentieth century. Hitler and Kubizek went to all of Wagner's operas that were performed at the Court Opera in Linz, one of the best opera houses in Europe. During Hitler's time in Vienna, from 1905 to 1913, Wagner's operas were performed at the Court Opera no fewer than 426 times.[15]

When one day Hitler and Kubizek heard a piece by Verdi being played by a street organ-grinder, Hitler told his friend, 'There you have your Verdi. Can you imagine Lohengrin's Grail narration on a barrel organ?'[16] Wagner's *Lohengrin* was the first opera Hitler ever saw, and he had been caught up in the saga of the mysterious knight of the grail sent to rescue the condemned maiden Elsa, only to be ultimately betrayed by her. *Lohengrin* always remained one of his favourite Wagner operas.[17]

Seeing a Wagner opera was not just a visit to the theatre for Hitler but 'the opportunity of being transported into that extraordinary state which Wagner's music produced in him, that escape into a mystical dream-world,' said Kubizek.[18] Hitler recalled, 'When I hear Wagner, it seems to me that I hear rhythms of a bygone world.'[19] American journalist Frederick Oechsner, after meeting Hitler years later, reported that when Hitler listened to Wagner's music, he saw 'grimaces of pain and pleasure contort his face, his brows knit, his eyes close, his mouth contract tightly'.[20]

It was not merely the music that inspired and shaped Hitler. He was aroused by the drama of the opera, and by the heroes he dreamed of becoming. To be able to identify with a hero of drama, whether in opera, books or films, has always been a factor in successful creative and artistic works, from Homer to Harry Potter. To create an identity between an audience and a James Bond or a Shirley Valentine or a Billy Elliot is part of what makes drama work on its most basic level, by drawing an audience into its story and compelling them to suspend disbelief. But Hitler became increasingly unable to break off from that disbelief when the curtain fell, and very quickly he came to believe that it really could all become reality and that Wagner was telling him he had some predestined role to play in the future.

Wagner conjured up the sounds and images of Germanic myth, of gods and of the monumental struggle for deliverance and salvation, of death and triumph. Wagner's heroes – Siegfried, Rienzi, Stolzing and Tannhäuser – were all outsiders in conflict with the unbending status quo governed by tradition. Hitler was enthralled by the themes common to Wagner, sacrifice, betrayal, redemption and heroic death. Wagner's heroes overcame all adversity to achieve greatness, and that appealed to Hitler, who fantasised that he could live like a Wagnerian hero,[21] but more than that, he wanted to become a *new* Wagner; that is, a supreme artistic and philosophical genius, which was his view of Wagner.

When Wagner's first masterwork, *Rienzi, der Letze der Tribunen* (*Rienzi, the Last of the Tribunes*), was performed in Linz, either in 1905 or 1906, the two friends went to see it. It proved to be a turning point in the life of the young artist. *Rienzi*, set in medieval Rome, tells of a tribune who defeats the nobles attempting to raise a rebellion against the people's power. The Church turns against him and he is forced to make a final stand in the capitol, which the people burn down around him.

Hitler was carried away by the sounds and sights portrayed in *Rienzi*. As though delivered of a personal and divine revelation through the musical genius of Wagner, he left the theatre in a state of near ecstasy and led Kubizek up the slopes of Freinberg, a mountain outside Linz, there to expound on the significance of what they had just seen. And, as if he had been charged to fulfil some kind of Wagnerian prophecy, Hitler told Kubizek 'in grandiose, compelling images' what his own future and that of his people was to be.

While scholars, historians and biographers dispute some of the details in Kubizek's account, something unusual and pertinent to history certainly happened that night in Linz which set Hitler on the long as yet unforeseeable journey that would result in acts of unspeakable evil and the deaths of millions.

Part of the problem with Hitler was his inability to distinguish between reality and fantasy. When he and Kubizek bought a lottery ticket, Hitler immediately began planning the fine house he would build for himself and Kubizek on the bank of the Danube with the winnings. He spent weeks deciding on the decor and choosing furniture, and deciding their life of leisure would include a middle-aged female housekeeper; then when he didn't win, he flew into a fury, unable to comprehend his failure to hold the winning number.[22] Although he didn't win the lottery prize, he never gave up his dream of living in luxury and being known the world over. It didn't really matter to him what he was known *for*.

In the early twentieth century, fame could not be won on TV talent shows, or by living for several weeks in a televised house, or by kissing-and-telling, or by being a politician or a footballer, or just by being famous for being famous. In the twenty-first century, celebrity culture has become the obsession of the age, but the cult of celebrity that the Nazis seeded and grew began with Hitler himself. Yet in the beginning Hitler had nothing going for him but his own fantasies, fed by Wagner's music.

All music has the potential to affect the emotions; to bring memories to the surface, stirring up both nostalgia and experiences best forgotten; to inspire artistic endeavours. When film director Quentin Tarantino listened to music from spaghetti Westerns as a youth, he envisioned new scenes, new plots to go with the music, resulting in films such as the two *Kill Bill* movies. Film music, like the opera, is designed to affect the senses, which is why some film actors like to have music played before and even during the filming of a scene. When making *Once Upon a Time in America*, Robert de Niro liked to hear Ennio Morricone's music, already scored and recorded, played over the scene to help him find the mood and tone of the moment to affect his performance.

Film composers are also heavily influenced by Wagner. Ennio Morricone repeated *Ride of the Valkyries* in *My Name Is Nobody*, and Hans Zimmer sampled and emulated Wagner in his *Gladiator* score, especially in scenes which reminded him of moments from *Triumph of the Will*, Leni Riefenstahl's spectacular film of the 1934 Nazi Party congress in Nuremberg, which was attended by more than 700,000 Nazi supporters.

The art of film scoring evolved directly from Wagner's use of leitmotivs by which individual characters have their own themes, a contrivance used precisely because of its subtle emotional effect on an audience. Critic Theodor Adorno wrote that Wagnerian leitmotiv 'leads directly to cinema music where the sole function of the leitmotiv is to announce heroes or situation so as to allow the audience to orient itself more easily.'[23] It was Wagner's use of leitmotivs which made his music so powerful, evocative and influential, on composers and listeners alike.

Music can also create fanaticism. During the late 1940s girls screamed, cried, swooned and fainted in sexual ecstasy at the sight and sound of Frank Sinatra. In the 1960s it happened all over again with the Beatles. Fans of singers, bands and musical artists of every kind can often respond with extreme fanaticism to the works of those they idolise. They come to know everything there is to know about their idols. They have images of their idols to worship. For many, it becomes almost a religion, a fact not lost on someone who observed this phenomenon from the closest vantage point: 'For some reason celebrities of a certain kind are treated as messiahs whether they like it or not; people encapsulate them in myths that touch their deepest yearnings and needs,' wrote Marlon Brando.[24]

Hitler said, 'For me, Wagner is something godly, and his music is my religion. I go to his concerts as others go to church.'[25] Wagner literally became a religious experience for Hitler.[26] But even such extreme devotion does not necessarily turn the most fanatical of admirers into a Hitler. Yet that's what happened to young Adolf.

He knew just about everything there was to know about Wagner's life and work, and he boasted that he had read everything the master had written,[27] which included all of Wagner's anti-Semitic articles. Wagner hid behind a pseudonym when he wrote his first anti-Semitic essay, 'Das Judenthum in der Musik'[28] (originally translated as 'Judaism in Music' but better known as 'Jewishness in Music'). In the article, he attacked Jewish contemporaries Felix Mendelssohn and Giacomo Meyerbeer, and claimed Jews were a destructive and alien aspect in German culture – Germans 'felt instinctively repelled by any actual, operative contact with them'.

He argued that Jews had no connection to the German spirit and so Jewish musicians were only capable of producing shallow music intended only to achieve financial success rather than be a genuine work of art. 'Only one thing can redeem [Jews] from the burden of your curse,' he wrote. 'The redemption of *Ahasverus* – total destruction.'[29]

Not everyone saw anti-Semitism in Wagner's operas, but that was because he disguised it well, so he wouldn't offend his Jewish patrons or the Jewish conductors and performers. When he reprinted 'Das Judenthum in der Musik' in a pamphlet with an extended introduction under his own name in 1866, it led to public protests at the first performances of *Die Meistersinger* in Vienna and Mannheim when the character of Beckmesser was recognised as a mocking depiction of a Jew.[30]

Wagner never explicitly identified Beckmesser or any other character in any of his operas as being Jewish, but Wagner intended to create certain characters as Jewish representations, such as Klingsor in *Parsifal* and Mime in the *Ring*, a fact not lost on some of his peers. Gustav Mahler, Wagner's Jewish contemporary and admirer, wrote, 'No doubt with Mime, Wagner intended to ridicule the Jews with all their characteristic traits – petty intelligence and greed – the jargon is textually and musically so cleverly suggested; but for God's sake it must not be exaggerated and overdone.'[31]

Hitler understood the racist overtones and was particularly inspired by the message of *Parsifal*, Wagner's last opera and arguably his most racist. Hitler believed that by stripping away all the 'Christian embroidery and Good Friday mystification', the drama's true context is revealed: Wagner does not praise Christian beliefs, but 'pure noble blood'. To Hermann Rauschning – who was close to Hitler during his rise to power, especially the years 1932–1934 – he explained, 'The king is suffering from the incurable ailment of corrupted blood.' Corrupted blood was racial impurity. Hitler went on, 'I have the most intimate familiarity with Wagner's mental processes. At every stage of my life I come back to him ... If we strip *Parsifal* of every poetic element, we learn from it that selection and renewal are possible only amid the continuous tension of a lasting struggle.'[32]

Hitler's analysis corresponds with the interpretation of Paul Lawrence Rose, who wrote of the manifestations of Wagner's racial ideology. 'Wagner intended *Parsifal* to be a profound religious parable about how the whole essence of European humanity had been poisoned by alien, inhuman, Jewish values. It is an allegory of the Judaisation of Christianity and of Germany – and of purifying redemption.' He wrote that *Parsifal* 'preached the new doctrine of racial purity... In Wagner's mind, this redeeming purity was infringed by Jews.'[33] No wonder Hitler proclaimed that he made his religion from *Parsifal*.[34]

Wagner had many Jewish friends and colleagues, and he even described his friendship with the French Jew Samuel Lehrs as 'one of the most beautiful friendships of my life.'[35] Yet Wagner was influenced by the writings of racialist Arthur de Gobineau, whose *An Essay on the Inequality of the Human Races* he read in 1880;[36] in his own writings of his final years Wagner reflected Gobineau's theory that Western society was doomed, being of miscegenation between 'superior' and 'inferior' races.

He noted in his diaries, as recorded by his wife Cosima, 'All Jews should be burned at a performance of Nathan the Wise',[37] and wrote of 'cursed Jew scum'.[38] He wrote to Franz Liszt, Cosima's father: 'I have cherished a long repressed resentment about this Jew money-world, and this hatred is as necessary to my nature as gall is to blood.'[39]

Hitler knew well of Wagner's outspoken anti-Semitism, and believed what Wagner said was true, and that the music he wrote was the work of a prophetic genius. Wagner's anti-Semitism, his mantras, his music and the spectacle of the operas all played important roles in Hitler's future Germany.

Hitler was in awe and envy of Wagner's fame – of his celebrity. After death, Wagner lived on in his music and his fame. It was a form of immortality, and that appealed to Hitler, along with the other trappings of fame – wealth, adulation, admiration. Hitler wanted all that and became convinced that he could have it all, that it was his for the taking, that his destiny had been revealed to him by his god Wagner.

Wagner was more than a composer: he was a national hero and powerful political force. Writers, philosophers and politicians testified to his profound influence. Such was the adulation from King Ludwig II of Bavaria, he helped to finance the Bayreuth *Festspielhaus*, which was designed specifically by Wagner for the performance of his operas. Wagner had been thinking about a festival since 1850, and it became the world-famous Bayreuth Festival. Wagner societies were springing up everywhere and were promoted in the German-nationalistic *Bayreuther Blätter*. From the opening of the festival in 1876, anti-Semitism and racism were embedded in the Bayreuth opera.[40]

The relationship between Hitler and Wagner's music has long been recognised as a major factor in Hitler's life and career.

His background, the influences in his early years, and indeed his personality traits, simply gave him a particular predisposition to have his fantasies and delusions ignited by a night at the opera. He wanted to be famous, he wanted to be wealthy, he wanted to show the bourgeois he wasn't to be rejected. Wagner's operas, particularly *Rienzi* and also *Lohengrin*, told him, like a personal revelation – through the power of the emotion of the music and the drama and his own overwhelming idolisation of Wagner – that not only could he achieve all those things but that he was destined to bring them all to pass.

To a great degree, Wagner's music made Adolf Hitler into the monster he became. It was the catalyst for what was to come, and the driving force throughout Hitler's life. A vision had transformed him – one might say *transfigured* him in an almost religious sense. Years later, in Bayreuth in 1939, Kubizek met Hitler again and reminded him of the night they first saw *Rienzi*. Hitler was prompted to tell his hostess Winifred Wagner, daughter-in-law of the maestro, 'In that hour, it began.'[41]

CHAPTER THREE

IMPURITY OF THE BLOOD

Music and drama alone could not create a Hitler. There had to be some form of madness that gave him a predisposition to the influence of Wagner, and to his unrealistic dreams of fame and fortune. The answer may well lie in his genes. His father was Alois Hitler, and his mother was Klara Pölzl. Klara wasn't just Alois's wife, but his foster daughter too. As if that were not a bizarre enough circumstance, Klara's mother's name was Hitler, and that was because Alois and Klara shared a common ancestor – his grandfather, her great-grandfather. Klara was a first cousin once removed to Alois.

Alois Hitler of the Austrian Finance Ministry and his first wife Anna Glassl-Hoerer (she was fifty when they married, he thirty-six) had fostered Klara when she was sixteen, after Anna became invalided by sickness and he inherited a large sum of money from his mother's estate. Through an affair he had with Franziska Matzelsberger he had a son, Alois Junior, and a daughter, Angela, and after Anna died, he married Franziska. When she became seriously ill, Klara took care of her and the two children. Franziska died on 10 August 1884.

Alois wasted no time in seducing Klara – there is the suggestion he raped her – and she became pregnant. They married on 7 January 1885, and she gave birth to a son, Gustav, on 17 May 1885, nine months after Franziska died. A daughter, Ida, followed on 23 September 1886, or so it is alleged; there was the suspicion that Ida was an 'imbecile' and may have been kept hidden from public view. A third child, Otto, was born and died in 1887. According to William Patrick Hitler, the son of Adolf's half-brother Alois Jr, another illegitimate child had been born to the couple earlier, but no record of it exists.[42]

On 20 April 1889, Adolf Hitler was born in Ranshofen, a village annexed to the municipality of Braunau am Inn, Upper Austria. His family moved to Kapuzinerstrasse in Passau, Germany when Adolf was three. Living in Passau for a mere two years as an infant was enough to imbue the boy with a German accent.

Alois Jr disliked his younger half-brother, who he felt was spoiled by his mother. As adults the half-brothers were never close, and when Adolf came to power, he and Alois Jr had practically no contact with each other. Hitler did not mention Alois Jr in *Mein Kampf,* and he allegedly had him sent to a concentration camp in 1942, although there is no record of that happening except in a dubious newspaper report.[43] However, Alois Jr's son Heinz died in a Soviet prison in 1942 after being captured on the Eastern Front during the war, which might have led to the conclusion that it was Alois Jr who had been sent to a concentration camp. Alois Jr actually died in Hamburg in 1956.

Two more children were born to Klara and Alois – Edmund on 24 March 1894, and Paula on 21 January 1896. Edmund died of measles on 28 February 1900. Paula was said to be a little on the 'stupid side',[44] and as an adult she called herself 'Frau Wolf' and was described by a neighbour as 'very queer'.[45] The family doctor, Eduard Bloch, believed that Klara and Alois had another daughter called Klara, slightly older than Adolf, whom they hid away because she was an 'imbecile', although Dr Bloch may have actually seen the supposedly dead Ida; in either case, there is the strong possibility that the Hitler family had at least one daughter who was mentally disabled.[46]

With the loss of so many children, one daughter on the 'stupid side', and another possible daughter an imbecile – and one who would become the personification of evil – there would seem to be what American psychiatrist Walter C. Langer classified 'a constitutional weakness' in the Hitler family, and a question of the 'purity of the blood',[47] that was the result of an incestuous relationship between Alois and Klara. If there was impurity of the Hitler blood, Adolf was infected.

Adolf was the focal point of Klara's life and she lavished all her affection on him, until Edmund was born and changed all that. Two years after that, baby sister Paula provided him with further competition for his mother's attention and affection. Adding to his misery at home was his father's domineering temperament which, according to William Patrick Hitler, led to beatings for all the family, including Klara. On one occasion he beat Alois Jr into unconsciousness, and another time beat Adolf and left him for dead. Alois Sr was a drunkard who spent much of his time in the taverns, returning home to beat Klara, the children and even the dog. Adolf hated his father, and became ever more dependent on his doting mother's affection.

Adolf's schooling suffered as his father's work kept the family moving from one place to another. He enjoyed his time at a Catholic school in an eleventh-century Benedictine monastery cloister from the age of eight, and was so impressed and intrigued by the religious life there that he decided to become a priest. What inspired him most of all was the theatricality of worship; he enjoyed the opportunity 'to intoxicate myself with the solemn splendour of the brilliant church festivals'.[48] He was expelled when caught smoking, and he developed a hatred for the monks but retained his delight in religious ceremony, which was later manifest among all the theatrical elements of his style of leadership and government.

He constantly fought with his father and teachers, and he lost interest in his lessons. The only subjects in which he excelled were freehand drawing and gymnastics, subjects that required no preparation or thought. He was becoming the kind of person that can be found among psychiatric patients, according to Walter C. Langer, who are actually very intelligent but refuse to work, and who are bright enough to understand the fundamental principles without exerting themselves, giving the impression of knowing something without ever actually studying, and glossing over superficial knowledge with glib words and terminology.[49]

Hitler possessed no great intellect and read lowbrow books such Karl May's Wild West stories. He came to school with Bowie knives and hatchets, and tried to get the other boys to play at being

Indians. He always wanted to be the chief, but none of the other boys considered him someone with leadership qualities and ostracised him.[50] He slipped more and more into his own fantasy world in which he was the leader. The problem was, he had no followers.

He became bitter and mutinous, and took an obsessive interest in German nationalism as a means of rebelling against his father, who was proud to serve in the Austrian government. Most who lived near the Austrian–German border considered themselves German-Austrians. Alois favoured Austria over Germany, but Adolf took the opposite view. He transferred his love for his mother to Germany, which, being young and vigorous and holding the promise of a great future under the right circumstances, became a symbol of his ideal mother. Austria became a representation of his father – old, exhausted, and decaying from within. While most Germans referred to Germany as the 'fatherland', Hitler often referred to it as the 'motherland'.[51] In defiance of the Austrian monarchy as well as his father, Hitler refused to join in singing the Austrian imperial anthem and sang instead the German anthem, *Deutschland über Alles*.

After Alois died on 3 January 1903 from a stroke, Adolf's behaviour became more disruptive. In 1906 he was expelled from the *Realschule* in Steyr because he used his school certificate upon completion of his second year as toilet paper; he received a dressing down that was probably the most humiliating experience of his life.[52] He vowed never to return to school and returning to live with his mother and sister Paula in Linz, he dedicated himself 'wholly to art'; drawing, watching his first movies[53] and going to the opera. He wrote that these were 'the happiest days which seemed to me almost like a beautiful dream'[54] – they were days spent in idleness, which is how he wanted to spend the rest of his life, and he thought he could achieve that by becoming an artist.

Aged eighteen, he went to Vienna for the first time, and was impressed by the architectural splendours of the bourgeois city, describing the parliament building 'a Hellenic marble on German soil' which he painted in watercolours. He even managed to sell some of his work. He was 'full of confident self-assurance'[55] when in October 1907 he applied to the Academy of Art. He failed because his sample drawing was graded 'unsatisfactory';[56] the director of the academy advised him to study architecture. Hitler described this whole experience as 'an abrupt blow',[57] but still had every intention of becoming an artist – or doing nothing at all.

On 21 December 1907, Klara died from breast cancer. Hitler returned to Linz and created a lasting impression of his beloved mother by sketching her in death. His intense grief was brightened when Magdalena Hanisch, who owned the house where his mother had lived and died, wrote a letter of recommendation to Alfred Roller, one of Germany's finest stage designers, who worked at the *Hofoper* and taught at the Vienna Academy of Arts and Crafts, describing Hitler as 'an earnest, aspiring young man', and that he 'has in mind a serious goal'. Roller replied that he would be happy to meet with the young man[58] and, imagining that he would become a set designer for plays and operas under the tutorage of Alfred Roller, Hitler arrived back in Vienna in February 1908.

What actually took place between Hitler and Roller is unknown. Their letters were carefully preserved by the Third Reich, but Hitler remained forever silent on the matter, probably because Roller most likely did little more than encourage Hitler to study and work hard, anathema to Hitler, who scorned the very idea that a man must work to live. All he really wanted to do was live the life of an artist and remain free to indulge in music and opera.

He applied to the academy again; he could only qualify for his orphan's pension if he was engaged in a formal course of education. He also lived on his father's inheritance and his mother's legacy. Kubizek came to Vienna to study at the Conservatory of Music, and they shared a single dreary rented room. Hitler rarely rose from bed before noon and then spent afternoons visiting museums and libraries, and in the evenings went to the opera; he saw *Tristan and Isolde* up to forty times.[59]

He sketched buildings and wrote a thesis on his concept of an ideal German state. He studied Wagner's life, work, philosophies and anti-Semitic proclamations. He would later recall the sensation of hearing the funeral march from *Götterdämmerung* for the first time, and of the anti-Semitic feelings it stirred within him:

> I first heard it in Vienna. At the Opera. And I still remember, as if it were today, how madly excited I became on the way home over a few yammering Yids I had to pass. I cannot think of a more incompatible contrast. This glorious mystery of the dying hero and this Jewish crap.[60]

Götterdämmerung – Twilight of the Gods – is the last in Wagner's cycle of four operas, *Der Ring des Nibelungen* (*The Ring of the Nibelung*, or sometimes just called *The Ring*), concluding the story of Siegfried and Brünnhilde and how she betrays him, leading him to his death the only way he can be killed – by a spear in his back. When she rides her horse into his funeral pyre, the world and Valhalla go up in flames, and all gods and heroes die in the fire – the twilight of the gods, *Götterdämmerung*.

Hitler was to become obsessed with the whole concept of *Götterdämmerung*, and how he would one day follow Siegfried into the flames that would end the world at whatever cost to all others. That's how powerful an influence Wagner was on Hitler. Death, he concluded, was to be celebrated: his cult of death would pervade his life and career. And it would be consummated in fire, resulting in what might be called a Nero complex – a desire to see all he ruled razed by fire so he could rebuild it.

Failing as an artist, Hitler imagined he could write a Wagnerian opera; he had to emulate the man he considered the supreme artist in every way. He knew that among Wagner's papers had been found an unfinished piece, *Wieland the Smith*, and Hitler announced to Kubizek that he would complete it.[61] With no musical training, he created melodies by finding the notes on the piano, which Kubizek wrote down.

Wieland the Smith is an Icelandic legend about King Nidur, who is driven purely by avarice to rape his daughter, kill his sons, and drink from cups fashioned out of their skulls. Hitler wrote erupting volcanoes, Icelandic glaciers, and valkyries riding through the clouds. He considered himself to be a new Wagner, and his imagination knew no bounds, but his talent and patience did; the opera was never finished. Failing to become the new Wagner, he decided fame and fortune instead awaited him as a playwright, and he took to writing a stage drama using ideas from Germanic sagas. Kubizek noted that when writing plays, Hitler imagined 'the most magnificent staging', and was impressed by the 'enormous pomp' which put all that Wagner had ever created for the stage 'completely in the shade'. But, like his opera, Hitler's plays also came to nothing. His thoughts returned to painting, and in September 1908 he submitted paintings to the academy once more. Again he was rejected, and he found himself slipping into an identity crisis, fearing he could never emulate Wagner the genius and supreme artist in any way whatsoever.

Driven by his rejection at the hands of the establishment, his persona took on a new dimension. Kubizek observed that he was given to sudden and vehement fits of despair, intense aggression and an apparent unrestrained facility for hatred. Humiliated, he withdrew into isolation, without any explanation moving out of the apartment he shared with Kubizek and into one alone where he could rant inwardly at the bourgeois world that had turned against him.

He continued to frequent the opera and the theatre and, despite his growing hatred for the bourgeois, he dressed as though he were one of them, affecting an air of superiority to show the working class that they were beneath him. His bearing and care with his words were all an act, a skill he would hone to considerable effect in later years, not as an actor but as a politician, although to him the difference between the two vocations was blurred. His reason for putting on such a performance at this time was his need to belong to a better class, even though he inwardly detested such people; although he would later claim that he was, in these years, a revolutionary both artistically and politically, he did not actually decry bourgeois values but rather continued to hunger after them.

Despite his young age, he remained unswayed by and even

unaware of modern trends in music, and eschewed the works of
Richard Strauss and Gustav Mahler, always preferring Wagner as
well as Anton Bruckner. He considered anything modern, including architecture, simply unappealing; in regard to politics he had
no strong opinions, especially of the revolutionary kind; thus he
avoided artistic and political oppositions of the time, and concen-
trated on becoming a *Herr*. But all he became was increasingly bitter.

The common theme in Wagner's operas was that of the
outsider, and that's exactly how Hitler came to see himself. Like
Wagner, Hitler was an academic failure, an anti-Semite and a
vegetarian. Hitler came to consider that he, Wagner and the
white knight were all a reflection of each other. Over the years
Hitler would find even more to compare himself to Wagner. The
composer held a life-long grudge against Paris for his early disappointments and envisioned the city being destroyed by flames. For
Hitler, Vienna would be his city of disappointments, and when,
in 1944, he was asked to provide additional anti-aircraft units to
defend Vienna against Allied bombers, he refused and said that
Vienna must find out what bomb warfare was like.

Hitler took inspiration from Wagner's immovable conviction of
his vocation, and he convinced himself that he and Wagner shared
the same kinds of rejections. Since Wagner had overcome then, so
too would Hitler. He came to believe Wagner was a prototype of
himself, and was thus Wagner's successor. He later declared, 'With
the exception of Richard Wagner, I have no forerunner,'[62] and he
described Wagner as 'the greatest prophetic figure the German
people has had' and said that he was overcome by 'a literally hyster-
ical excitement' when he realised his own psychological kinship
with the great composer.[63]

Beset with a growing hatred for the bourgeois world he was so
desperate to be a part of but which he considered had rejected him,
he sank into a world that existed only in his mind, with a Wagner
score, but which he could not contain as a simple private fantasy.
For him it had to become reality, and over time his life became a
creation of delusions.

CHAPTER FOUR

HIS GREATEST ROLE

Hitler moved from one residence to another, and on at least one occasion when filling in a resident's information form, he listed his occupation as 'writer'. His inheritance dwindling, he existed largely on his orphan's pension, which he claimed by asserting that he was attending the academy. He had become a miserable wretch without friends, despising the upper classes, and had grown pale with sunken cheeks. In December 1908 he moved into a men's refuge for the homeless in Meidling, and insisted on describing himself as an 'academician and an artist'.[64] At the home he became friends with Reinhold Hanisch for a brief period of about seven months, and they went into partnership, with Hanisch selling to picture dealers and picture framers Hitler's reproductions of postcards and lithographs of Viennese scenes which he painted in watercolours. They did quite well and split the proceeds fifty-fifty. Back in the men's home, Hitler was the cause of trouble, sometimes engaging in heated exchanges about Jews, Slavs and the Social Democratic Party.

There were many anti-Semitic influences upon Hitler, and all Germany, due to a general anxiety among the bourgeois of Jews and a belief in the theory of the master-race that was endemic throughout the German empire. Hitler read a magazine, *Ostara* (named from the German goddess of spring), published by defrocked monk Jörg Lanz von Liebenfels, who used the magazine to promote his anti-Semitic and *völkisch* theories. Hitler visited von Liebenfels where he lived in Werfenstein Castle in Lower Austria, over which flew the swastika and from where, with the aid of some wealthy industrialists, von Liebenfels founded the *Ordo Novi Templi* (Order of the New Templars).[65]

Hitler also read the many cheap anti-Semitic pamphlets published in Vienna in which a Germanic hero appeared – a white knight – a symbolic figure which rode straight out of Richard Wagner's operas. It must have come to him like a sign. Hitler referred to Martin Luther, who wrote *On the Jews and Their Lives*, in *Mein Kampf*, as a great warrior, a true statesman and a great reformer alongside of Frederick the Great and Richard Wagner. Hitler also accepted Wagner's view of Social Darwinism – the survival of the fittest – and it became his mantra. He even emulated Wagner's style of grammar and syntax in his own eventual writings.

In Wagner's terms, and therefore Hitler's, it all came down to a matter of black versus white, good versus evil, purity versus corruption, all expressed in Germanic terms such as the mystique of blood purification – as in *Parsifal* – and conflict between Siegfried and Hagen, bloody, sexual, pagan dramas told through music and bound up in staged spectacle that became Hitler's church and where he found the 'granite foundations' for his own mystical view of the world.

His fears, thoughts and inspirations were all magnified into grandiose ideas, fanned by the flames of Wagner's blazing compositions, stunning visual concepts, and the smouldering embers of anti-Semitic subtext, for, as Hanisch wrote, 'In music Richard Wagner brought him to bright flames.'[66]

He displayed little interest in politics, but was mesmerised by the sight of workers marching four abreast through the streets under the red Communist flag; Communism was a threat to the upper-class Viennese way of life which he coveted and yet despised. He stood with bated breath, watching 'the human snake wind past' until, two hours later, he made for home, 'a victim of fear and depression', and he realised that this was the intended effect of the men marching as one, creating a shape as if it were one complete animal which intimidated the outsider while encompassing the insider. He was uninterested in the political purposes being demonstrated, but had been hugely impressed by the theatrical effect of the march and, upon his return home, spent many hours pondering ways that he might be able to control an audience.[67]

He pondered, dreamed and fantasised, but was otherwise generally inactive. Hanisch noted that Hitler 'was never an ardent worker, was unable to get up in the morning, had difficulty getting started, and seemed to be suffering from a paralysis of the will.'[68] He managed to find a job in the office of a construction company, but even there his fantasies kept him busier than the work itself as he imagined he was an architect, sketching his first plans for the reconstruction of Berlin. Everything he imagined and designed had to be on a grandiose scale because that's how Wagner did things.

Wagner had always tried to make every next project bigger, more spectacular and even more breathtaking than before. After *Rienzi*, he composed a choral work for 1,200 male voices and a hundred-strong orchestra. He believed in the ability to hypnotise his audience en masse, not simply with music but with spellbinding visuals and spirit-soaring tales from legend. Hitler would eventually learn to use all of these techniques in his speeches and the mass rallies so that he too could hypnotise his audiences en masse, incorporating and magnifying the marching animal effect that intimidated the outsider while encompassing the insider.

But politics were not on Hitler's mind, only art, and yet he began to see what Wagner believed, that art was the purpose of life and that the artist made the crucial choices wherever 'the statesman despairs, the politician gives up, the socialist vexes himself with fruitless systems, and even the philosopher can only interpret but cannot prophesy.'[69] Wagner prophesied that the state would be elevated to the stature of a work of art, and Hitler saw that prophecy fulfilled by conceiving the most vivid and theatrical aspects of the Third Reich: vast columns of marching soldiers with flags and banners, torchlight parades, and stirring Wagnerian music. Even his oratories were spoken operas. It was as though the whole political spectrum of Hitler's career existed purely for him to stage his own grand operas.

But he achieved all of that not for the sake of good government but only so he could perform and be celebrated as a great artist. The problem was, he had yet to discover what it was that would lift him to the lofty heights of celebrity, and he was brought back down to earth when he lost his job and became a mere construction worker, forced to work with the lower classes he wanted to avoid.

He maintained his sense of superiority by keeping apart from them, but when he became drawn into their political wrangles the many Communists among them threatened to throw him off the scaffolding, leading him to the conclusion, as he wrote in *Mein Kampf,* that the simple solution to dealing with those who disagreed was 'bashing in the head of anybody who dared to oppose'. Hitler concluded, 'The masses love a commander more than a petitioner,' and the masses see only 'the ruthless force and brutality of its calculated manifestations to which they always submit in the end'. Terror at work, in the meeting halls and at mass rallies 'will always be successful unless opposed by equal terror'.[70]

He believed:

The psyche of the broad masses does not respond to anything weak or half-way. Like a woman, whose spiritual sensitiveness is determined less by abstract reason than by an indefinable emotional longing for fulfilling power and who, for that reason, prefers to submit to the strong rather than the weakling – the mass, too, prefers the ruler to a pleader.[71]

In the years ahead, he would add terror to his campaign of theatrical government to advance his growing cult of celebrity until, at the height of his power, it would be led more by fear than art for art's sake. In August 1910 Hanisch sold Hitler's painting of the Vienna parliament for ten crowns. Hitler believed it was worth fifty and accused Hanisch of pocketing forty crowns, so had him arrested; Hanisch was sentenced to seven days in jail. In 1938, Hitler, afraid of the damage Hanisch could do to his political career – because he knew the truth about Hitler's squalid existence – he had him tracked down and murdered.[72]

Around the end of 1910 and the start of 1911, Hitler received a considerable sum of money from an aunt, Johanna Pölzl; yet he continued to drift aimlessly. In his mind, destiny would intervene, so he needed to do nothing to help himself but just continue living among the homeless men of Vienna until his time came. But that may well have been the perfect excuse for him, for he was simply lazy. It was an excuse and a dream that never went away, even through the years when he held the fate of the world in his hands and played with it like it was a prop in the hands of an actor living his own fantasy as Wagner's white knight.

In May 1913, at the age of twenty-four, Hitler finally moved out of the men's home and away from Vienna. He had to leave the city to escape the Austrian military draft when he was summonsed. Withdrawn and friendless, he went to Germany and arrived in Munich, a city considered the centre of art and science in Germany.

He spent his time in cafés reading newspapers and sketching, and in taverns where he made casual and often temporary acquaintances who were happy to join him in denouncing the volatility of the Dual Monarchy and the calamitous outcome of the German–Austrian Alliance, as well as the evils of Slavs, Jews and anything they considered anti-German. He was known to shout suddenly if something was said that excited him, and he enjoyed making political predictions in prophetic tones.

He was certainly among the cheering crowd in Odeonsplatz in Munich on 1 August 1914 when the state of war was declared. Many, including Hitler, saw the war as renewal for Germany.

He enlisted in the German army and not the Austrian, and was assigned to the 16th Bavarian Reserve infantry regiment and served as a courier. He was never promoted above corporal because his superiors felt he lacked the qualities of leadership. He was aloof, and kept his distance from his comrades, who considered him an oddity. His officers, however, found him reliable and obedient.

In December 1914 he was awarded the Iron Cross Second Class, and in May 1918 a regimental certificate for bravery in the face of the enemy. In August that year, he also received the Iron Cross First Class, which was rarely awarded to enlisted men. The precise reasons for these awards are not known and Hitler never explained, preferring to remain silent on the matter – possibly because his regimental adjutant, Hugo Gutmann, who proposed these decorations, was Jewish. He concluded that behind all of this, and the war itself and all its causes, were the Jews.

Like many German soldiers, he considered that the old leadership had failed and the social order they were all defending, and that many were dying for, was crumbling from within. He attracted attention from his comrades by 'philosophising about political and ideological questions in the crude manner of ordinary folk'. The catalyst for his series of oratories might be seen in an anecdote told by Reinhold Hanisch, who claimed that around 1910 he and Hitler went to see the film *Der Tunnel*, in which one of the main characters was a popular orator. He and Hitler emerged 'altogether overwhelmed' from the movie, and 'henceforth there were eloquent speeches in the Home for Men.'[73]

The anecdote is false: *Der Tunnel* had not yet been made when Hanisch was Hitler's companion, being released in 1915. However, it is very likely that Hitler saw it while rehabilitating in Germany, and the 'eloquent speeches' might well have begun in Berlin. If this was Hitler's inspiration to become an orator, he might have acquired his exaggerated style of arm-waving and chest-thumping by emulating the larger-than-life style used in the silent film to suggest passion and verve – a would-be political speaker performing like a silent screen actor.

While convalescing in the Pasewalk hospital in Pomerania after being blinded by poison gas, he learned, on 10 November 1918, that the war was lost, the House of Hohenzollern had fallen, and a republic had been proclaimed in Germany which was submitting to all and any conditions laid down by the former enemies.

On 28 June 1919 Germany was forced to sign the Treaty of Versailles, which cited Germany's responsibility for the war, along with Austria and Hungary. Germany had to agree to relinquish several of its territories, demilitarise the Rhineland, and disarm. Economic sanctions were imposed and heavy reparations levied. A number of countries were involved in negotiating this treaty, but most dropped out; in the end it was the result of demands made by Britain, France and the United States.

Germany was now gripped by revolution as Communist groups and other left-wing organisations attracted disillusioned Germans, and a soviet was established in Munich. The new German Republic, under the Social Democrats and the army, sent units of paramilitary soldiers into Munich to quell the red revolution. Hitler was among those mistakenly arrested and questioned, but he was released when he was recognised by officers who knew him.

He supplied information to the tribunals set up by the Second Infantry Board and helped to trace soldiers who had participated in the soviet regime. For his services, Hitler was posted to the propaganda department of the Group Command, where he attended lectures given by Gottfried Feder, an economist who developed hostility towards wealthy bankers during the war, writing a 'manifesto on breaking the shackles of interest' (*Brechung der Zinsknechtschaft*). He was an excellent speaker, and inspired, Hitler became active in hosting discussions, as noted by historian Karl Alexander von Miller, who one time found his way blocked by a group of men who 'stood fascinated around [Hitler] who was addressing them without pause and with growing passion in a strangely guttural voice'.[74]

Hitler was detailed to an 'enlightenment squad' at Lechfeld camp for returning soldiers, where he gave speeches in which he was able to share their sense of disillusionment and feeling of betrayal. They responded to his condemnation of the Versailles Treaty, which he called 'the shame of Versailles', and he was able to wrap all the country's ills inside a 'Jewish–Marxist world conspiracy'.[75]

He was learning the art of oratory to remarkable effect, discovering that he finally had a talent which not only made him stand out from the crowd, but could well be the tool by which he fulfilled his Wagnerian destiny and which led to his ultimate goal of being famous. He didn't have anything remarkably new to say, stringing together ideas and sayings he had heard or read and presenting them as his own, but his reputation as an orator soon spread, and in September 1919 he accepted an invitation to join the board of the German Workers' Party (*Deutsche Arbeiterpartei* – DAP), the forerunner of the Nazi Party.

Responsible for recruitment and propaganda, he gave his first public oratory for the DAP on 16 October, at a public meeting where he stood for thirty minutes giving a speech that grew ever more furious. By the end, 'the people in the small room were electrified'. In that moment he made a remarkable discovery: 'I could speak.'[76]

What had impressed him so much was not his own ability, which he had been developing and would continue to evolve into the skill that would mould him into the *Führer*, but the resulting ovation, the excitement, the acceptance and the adulation that was suddenly his. That experience was, for him, the most stimulating and exciting sensation of his life, which had to be repeated often, taking him to a physical and emotional exhausting peak, possibly becoming almost a form of sexual release.

He began promoting himself as the 'drummer', paving the way for the Germanic messianic knight who would lead the oppressed people in their struggle against the Bolshevists and the Jews. He lacked the confidence to envelop himself completely in his Wagnerian fantasy by becoming the knight, but was comfortable being the voice crying in the wilderness like a modern-day John the Baptist and promoting a new cult of providence.[77]

He gave countless speeches in beer cellars and on the streets of Munich, and revelled in the applause. He was no longer the outsider who had been callously rejected by the bourgeois. People paid attention to him now. Awkward and often bumbling when trying to express his ideas in private, speaking to the masses gave him a sense of being involved.

Speaking at the *Festsaal* in the *Hofbräuhaus* before almost 2,000 people on 24 February 1920, he condemned the Versailles Treaty, the government, the profiteers, the usurers and the Jews. A week

later the DAP changed its name to the National Socialist German
Workers' Party (*Nationalsozialistiche Deutsche Arbeiterpartei* –
NSDAP) and adopted the swastika as its symbol. From the word
Nationalsozialistiche was to come the abbreviation 'Nazi'.

On 1 April 1920, Hitler left the army and devoted himself to
seizing the leadership of the NSDAP and so shaping the party
according to his own dogma. It would be a gamble, but he felt he
had nothing to lose. It was to be all or nothing, as was often the
case throughout his career, which was now becoming political, and
he in the process was developing a cult of personality – *his* personality. As his fame increased, so did his confidence. Among his early
followers were Rudolf Hess, a recipient of the Iron Cross Second
Class and a pilot with the rank of lieutenant, former air force pilot
Hermann Göring, and army captain Ernst Röhm, who became
head of Nazi paramilitary organisation the *Sturmabteilung* – the SA,
known more commonly as stormtroopers – which protected Hitler
and other party speakers at meetings, as well as literally attacking
political opponents. Also drawn by Hitler's speeches was General
Erich Friedrich Wilhelm Ludendorff, a hero of the First World War
who received the Grand Cross of the Iron Cross and the Pour le
Mérite. He had turned to National Socialism, convinced that the
German army had been betrayed by Marxists and republicans, and
became the party's heroic leader.

From 1922 Hitler often held as many as twelve rallies in a single
evening, and was always the principal speaker. He had become a
star in his own right, and the masses came to these rallies because
they wanted to see and hear Herr Hitler.

Prior to each speech, onlookers and participants were overwhelmed by the parades of banners, the communal singing and the
general histrionic atmosphere, all designed to whip up the people
in preparation for the appearance of their new Messiah. His love
of grand opera was the inspiration for the spectacle of these rallies,
with touches of church ritual. For hours the people would wait for
his arrival in the hall, entertained, stirred and captivated by the
marching music. There would be short speeches by lesser people,

while everyone waited impatiently for the star of the National Socialist Party to arrive. Whispers were purposely to insinuate there might be some reason for his failure to arrive, making tension mount to fever pitch.

Then he would enter with his retinue, and the crowd would erupt with shouts of '*Heil! Heil!*'

All his speeches were structured to open with the denunciation of the government and their actions since 1918. He called those who signed the armistice of 11 November 1918 'November criminals', and he condemned them and the republic for bringing this humiliation upon them; many Germans were in complete agreement. Thousands who were dissatisfied with the republic came to hear him. He launched a verbal attack on whatever group or race seemed appropriate, but his targets were usually Jews and Bolshevists. He had learned how to work up the crowd into a frenzy by this point, and their elated cheering and applause would lift him to a tremendous state of excitement that continued until he had delivered his triumphant call for unity with which he always finished his speech.

His techniques were pure theatre. He learned to seize and interpret the atmosphere and sensations of each occasion. His skill as an orator was such that while he vilified those who had betrayed Germany and condemned all who threatened its racial purity, he had little of substance to offer them by way of solutions, and he used rhetoric that promised more than it could deliver. But he did it all with consummate skill. His body language spoke as loudly as his voice. The wild gesticulating familiar from newsreels was not the physical reaction to apparent mad ranting but carefully choreographed gestures, each the gesture of a character he had seen at the opera.

At some point he even had some tutorage from an actor, not necessarily for the speeches but for all the personas he developed over time, from the serious politician, to the surprisingly witty man in private, to the suddenly furious and raging madman against whom nobody was going to argue. The ranting was often, though not always, an act to ensure that he got his way. As a child he managed this by throwing temper tantrums, which his mother invariably gave in to. By this technique, he came to dominate her, and it worked for him on virtually everyone around him.[78]

Some of his closest associates felt that he induced these rages simply to frighten those about him. Hermann Rauschning recognised his 'technique by which he would throw his entire entourage into confusion by well-timed fits of rage and thus make them more submissive'.[79]

But there were also some genuine rages of a man who would not be questioned, contradicted or argued with, and furthermore would not stand for anything not being the way he wanted or needed it to be. Karl von Wiegand, the German-born journalist who moved to America, reported that among Hitler's staff there was a tacit understanding: 'For God's sake, don't excite the Fuehrer [*sic*] – which means do not tell him bad news – do not mention things which are not as he conceives them to be.'[80] Frederick Augustus Voigt, a British journalist of German descent, observed, 'Close collaborators for many years said that Hitler was always like this – that the slightest difficulty or obstacle could make him scream with rage.'[81]

Those were the kind of rages that he seemed to have no control over, and which became far more frequent in later years, but in earlier years – certainly before the Second World War – he often maintained complete control over his sudden and fierce outbursts.

The rumour among those in German theatre and cinema of the 1930s and 1940s was that he had taken lessons, though no one ever admitted being his drama teacher. There were probably a number of such teachers, but none of them, especially when the Nazi reign was coming to an end, wanted to be named,[82] which was wise because after the war, actors, directors, writers and artists who had worked for the Third Reich's theatre and film industry were all punished according to the seriousness of their crimes and paid the price for profiting from Hitler's celebrity cult.

On one occasion, some years after he had come to power, Hitler was lunching at the Film Institute. Film director Alfred Zeisler recalled that Hitler flew into a rage at someone at the neighbouring table who mentioned the word 'Jew', ranting on for about ten minutes, much to the embarrassment of all the people there. Zeisler's impression of Hitler's tirades was that in the course of such a rage he worked himself into a trance-like state in which he lost contact with his surroundings and enjoyed the uninhibited expression of his feelings. Zeisler believed that Hitler went out of his way at times to find cause to rant and rave, and when he found it he worked hard at increasing its intensity in order to attain this trance-like state.[83]

Those close to him, especially those with musical knowledge, recognised that Hitler understood Wagner's use of leitmotivs, employing repetition, thundering crescendos, and rhythm in his speech which mesmerised audiences. Ernst Hanfstaengl, who played piano for Hitler, wrote that when he played the *Meistersinger* prelude, he noticed that 'whole interweavings of leitmotifs, of embellishments of counterpoint, and musical contrast and arguments, were exactly mirrored in the patterns of his speeches, which were symphonic in construction and ended in a great climax, like the blare of Wagner's trombones.'[84] Hanfstaengl also observed that Hitler's arm movements during his speeches were similar to a conductor using his baton.

From opera, from music and from cinema, Hitler learned how to perform as the *Führer*. It was his greatest role.

CHAPTER FIVE

GOD'S GIFT

Like all who worshipped Wagner, Hitler had to make a pilgrimage to the Bayreuth Festival, which Wagner himself had instituted as a showcase for his own operas; Hitler made his first visit there on either 30 September or 1 October 1923. The Bayreuth *Festspielhaus* contained many architectural innovations to accommodate the large orchestras and allowed Wagner the scope he needed to stage his epic works. Since the festival opened in 1876 with a performance of *Das Rheingold*, it had become the destination for all Wagner pilgrims.

After Wagner's death in 1883, his son Siegfried hosted the festival, aided by his English-born wife Winifred. They had married in 1915 when he was forty-five and she seventeen. He had not wanted to marry at all, but his parents needed their son to provide heirs to the Wagner dynasty, and he carried the genes of genius, being a composer himself who actually wrote more operas than his father had. However, not only was he not the genius his father was thought to be, but marriage was not convenient for his bisexual lifestyle. In the end he gave into his parents' demands, if only to protect himself from journalist Maximilian Harden, who openly accused several public figures of homosexuality, including Prince Philipp of Eulenburg-Hertefeld, who was a friend of Kaiser Wilhelm II. With further names about to be exposed, Siegfried agreed to meet Winifred at the Bayreuth Festival in 1914.

Winifred Marjorie Williams was born in Hastings on 23 June 1897 to writer John Williams and wife Emily. Both parents died before Winifred was two, and she was raised in a series of homes until she was adopted by a distant German relative of her mother, Henrietta, and her husband Karl Klindworth, a musician and friend of Richard Wagner. Winifred was brought up on Wagner and by her mid-teens she knew all of his operas – and she forgot England. Gottfried Wagner said of his grandmother, 'She became 150 per cent German and also 150 per cent Wagnerian. She grew up with that whole ideological world view and that's what she always represented strongly to the outside world.'[85]

Winifred was chosen to become Siegfried's wife, and they married on 22 September 1915. For her, it was the veritable fairytale dream come true: in seventeen years she had gone from being a penniless orphan to being mistress of Bayreuth – that was almost like being a German princess, because the Wagners were royalty to many of the German people, living in a grand mansion, Villa Wahnfried. 'The attitude of the people of Bayreuth to the Wagners was like that of the English to the Windsors,' recalled one of Winifred's neighbours, Pinchas Joeli. 'By Bayreuth standards, Villa Wahnfried was Buckingham Palace. The Wagner family was *the* family of Bayreuth.'[86]

Following their marriage, they had four children in rapid succession: Wieland (born 1917), Friedelind (1918), Wolfgang (1919) and Verena (1920). To the public eye they were a happy family, but for years Siegfried and Winifred had been living their separate lives as Siegfried went back to his old ways, seeking out men. This deeply hurt his wife, who took sole charge of the children. Her rejection by Siegfried and the pressure of running the house and raising the children left their mark on her – and little room for feelings. 'She wasn't warm or tender,' said granddaughter Daphne Wagner. 'I can't remember her ever hugging me.'[87]

When Hitler first visited the Wagners at Villa Wahnfried in Bayreuth he was warmly greeted by Richard Wagner's 86-year-old widow Cosima, who embraced and kissed him. The whole Wagner family welcomed Hitler with open arms, with the exception of Siegfried. Winifred was a frustrated wife, kept in her place by four children, a host of aunts and her mother-in-law, so she was especially warm towards Hitler, who was still young and someone Winifred could easily idolise. He in turn was flattered. Winifred later said, 'I must admit my first impression of him was excellent. His eyes in particular were incredibly attractive. Very blue, large and expressive eyes.'[88]

Also there to welcome Hitler was British author and racial theorist Houston Stewart Chamberlain, who was married to Cosima's daughter Eva. Houston had devoted his life to studying and writing about the work of Richard Wagner. In 1889, the year Hitler was born, Houston had arrived in Germany from England and remained, becoming a German citizen. He immersed himself in the racial theories Wagner preached, which confirmed his own theory that the Roman Empire was brought down by racial impurity. He wrote of the opposition between an Aryan race and a destructive Jewish race, and his 1899 book *Foundations of the Nineteenth Century* expressed his racial theory of the destiny of the superior Aryans to rule inferior races, which had been embraced by Wagner and Cosima. Winifred embraced it too. She was, said her grandson Gottfried Wagner, 'an absolutely militant anti-Semite. She was anti-Semitic and racist with everything that entailed.'[89]

Chamberlain quickly concluded that Hitler was 'God's gift to Germany', and wrote, 'With one blow you have transformed the state of my soul … that Germany, in the hour of her greatest need, brings forth a Hitler is proof of her vitality.'[90] Winifred considered Hitler to be the Messiah of Wagner's prophecy, but Siegfried saw him as 'a fraud and an upstart'.[91]

Hitler was now a star, but only within the Nazi Party. He wanted to be *the* star of the party, and more than that, the star of Germany. Adopting as his maxim 'All or nothing', he and General Ludendorff led the Munich Putsch on 9 November 1923. It was intended to be the start of a revolution. Winifred Wagner was in Munich on that day to see history being made. Gottfried Wagner recalled, 'My grandmother was well aware there was going to be a putsch. She told me many times that she wanted to take a pistol with her and be actively involved.'[92]

With three thousand stormtroopers, Hitler, Ludendorff and Göring marched to the centre of Munich, confident that the army would not open fire on legendary General Ludendorff. But when they came up against a column of police in the narrow Residenzstrasse, a shot rang out – it isn't known who fired the first bullet – and the shooting began. It took just around one minute for the putsch to be crushed. The biggest gamble of Hitler's life up to that point had failed, and it looked like his political career had been brought to an unexpected and humiliating end.

His failure merely strengthened Winifred's fanaticism. She declared publicly, 'I frankly admit that we too are under the spell of this person, that we who stood by him in the days of his good fortune are also loyal to him in his hour of need.'[93]

Awaiting trial in jail, Hitler quickly fell into a depression and talked of suicide. Friends talked him out of it, and his spirits quickly rose when he realised that his trial for treason was an opportunity to make it his stage from which to deliver his 'messianic message'.[94] His friends all pleaded innocent, but he took everyone by surprise by pleading guilty and admitting full responsibility for his actions, proceeding to deliver a speech in which he proclaimed himself as the saviour of the Fatherland.

Many in the court, including the judge, were impressed. So was the Nazi Party, which immediately ejected General Ludendorff from his position as party leader and replaced him with Hitler, who, although in Landsberg Prison, was now in the position he had worked hard to attain, leader of the National Socialists. He was sentenced to five years, but his trial had turned into a personal triumph, and he hung a laurel wreath of victory in his cell. During his imprisonment he wrote *Mein Kampf* (*My Struggle*), expounding his doctrine of anti-Semitism and *Lebensraum* – the 'living space' Hitler would choose for ethnic Germans throughout territories he would one day seize in eastern Europe – all written on stationery that Winifred Wagner sent to him along with food parcels. Writing his book on Bayreuth paper gave the book a parallel with the past – Hitler's life and struggle put down for posterity on paper from the home of the Master.

Wagner remained an overpowering influence on Hitler, right

down to his choice of title for his book. There were a number of words in Wagner's writings that Hitler used, turning them into a code. '*Kampf*' was one of those words, and in Hitler's eyes the word referred to his struggle against Jews and other 'aliens'. '*Wolf*' was another code word, which in the *Ring* operas refers to the god Wotan. Hitler applied the word to himself, and the children of Siegfried and Winifred Wagner called him 'Wolf'. Hitler's wartime sanctuary in Poland became known as *Wolfsschanze* – Wolf's Lair.

Hitler also took the word 'Barbarossa' from Wagner, derived from the words 'barbaric' and 'barbarian', to indicate that the German people could return to their barbarous roots, free of conscience to wage war and havoc, which was not a negative but a positive. Barbarossa would become the code word for the invasion of Russia.

As he wrote *Mein Kampf*, he listened to Wagner on the gramophone he was permitted in his room. At this time Winifred Wagner, recalling her father-in-law's *Die Walküre* when Siegmund pulls the sword out of the ash tree, predicted that Hitler was the man who would 'pull the sword out of the German oak' and save Germany from Jewish corruption.[95]

In 1925 Hitler attended the Bayreuth Festival for the first time. He later remembered, 'The next morning Mrs Wagner brought me flowers. I was thirty-six years old and the sky was full of violins.' The attraction was mutual. In 1934 Helga von Dolega Kozierowski was a guest at Villa Wahnfried when she saw a photo of Hitler, taken in the 1920s, hanging in the dining room. 'How long has it been there?' she asked Winifred Wagner. 'For ages,' Frau Wagner replied. 'He belongs there.'[96] Bayreuth was Hitler's spiritual home, the *Festspielhaus* the temple where he worshipped his god.

Hitler now resolved to avoid open violence, saying, 'If we can't outshoot our opponents, we must overwhelm them by force of numbers. We must win support instead of spreading terror.'[97] He presented himself as a respectable citizen, and began wearing dark suits and surrounding himself with children in white, emulating Jesus – 'Suffer the little children to come unto me.' He was still working on his style, often imitating the mannerisms of the military leaders to impress the lower ranks, and took to carrying a riding crop and wearing jodhpurs to emphasise his authority. He also had an eye for young women.

Nothing is more sexually attractive than power, and since Hitler could never have been described as a handsome man, his sex appeal lay in his power. For most older, less celebrated men, a younger woman is just a fantasy, but for those who have fame, wealth and, above all, power, it's a reality, and for Hitler, a celebrity of his own making, younger women were readily available.

He was wearing jodhpurs and carrying his crop when he met a very pretty girl, Maria Reiter, in Kurpark, a Berchtesgaden park (in 1927 or 1928). She was sixteen, he thirty-seven; he was walking his dog, she hers. They stopped and talked. He liked her 'fresh Nordic charm'. She worked in a shop in Obersalzberg, one of Hitler's favourite retreats. He asked her out, and she said yes. She told her sister, 'He cuts a fine figure with those riding breeches and that riding crop.'[98]

They began taking long rides in his Mercedes. He called her 'Mimi', and at his request she called him 'Wolf'. He told her that he wanted to marry her and have blond children, but first he had to save Germany. They continued to meet in his Munich apartment and dreamed about their future together.[99]

She later recalled how he impressed upon her that he wanted her 'to be his wife, to found a family with her, to have blonde children, but at the moment he had not the time to think of such things. Repeatedly Hitler spoke of his duty, his mission.'[100] He told her to wait, and then they would eventually be together. It was Hitler's first known love affair.

Hitler was supposedly attracted to Winifred Wagner, although whether he was in love with her is speculation. Winifred was an important person in Germany, and she had the family link to Richard Wagner. But she was not of Wagner's blood, and she was older than Maria by fourteen years. It must have been a dilemma for Hitler to choose between the two, although Winifred was politically more desirable. Marrying her would be like marrying nobility. But Maria was more attractive and much younger.

He was sexually drawn to teenage girls – as are many men who achieve celebrity status, who not only attract women much younger than themselves but are easily drawn to them *because* they make themselves available. This has been evident in the world of 'celebrity' through the decades. Among film stars, rock stars, sports stars, and celebrities of every kind, there have always been men who, regardless of their mature years, have publicly or privately enjoyed romantic and sexual relationships with teenage girls – Charlie Chaplin, Errol Flynn, Bill Wyman and Tony Curtis are among those who have at some point in their lives shown a predilection for teenage girls. Maria Reiter was completely captivated by her older lover, but while he was flattered and excited by the attention she gave him, he ignored her for months, plunging her into a deep depression. He was spending time with other young women. One of them was Henriette 'Henny' Hoffmann, the daughter of Heinrich Hoffmann.

Alfred Zeisler was aware of what he considered a 'strange relationship' between Hitler and Hoffmann, and was 'under the impression' that Hoffmann supplied Hitler with pornographic pictures.[101] When Heinrich Hoffmann's wife, Therese, died, the Hoffmann home became the scene of frequent parties, and at one such gathering Henny began to talk about her relationship with Hitler, whereupon Hoffmann flew into a rage and fell out with Hitler for a while. The relationship between Hitler and Henny was over.[102]

Hitler hardly seemed the type to be a playboy, and yet because he was rarely without a pretty young woman – sometimes two – to keep him company when it suited him, a playboy is exactly what he was, even if an unconventional playboy. Yet he was hardly a Lothario or a Casanova; he was not renowned as a lover. But despite being not far off middle age, he had no problem finding young women, and he soon had another one. He took an unusually personal interest in his niece Geli Raubal, daughter of his half-sister Angela. Allegations of a sexual relationship between them were made by Otto Strasser, a political enemy of Hitler, which cast doubt on the allegations for some historians. It has never been established whether or not there was anything sexual between Hitler and Geli, but his attention towards her was anything other than normal. Hitler's father had married his cousin, and it might well have been in Hitler's nature to have believed that if it was acceptable for his father and, more importantly, mother to commit something close to incest, then it was acceptable for him to do so too.

Hitler's sexuality has never been conclusively defined. August Kubizek believed Hitler was repulsed by all sexual activity, especially homosexuality and masturbation.[103] But Kubizek was judging only by his observations and couldn't have possibly known what Hitler did in private. Hitler was a voyeur and enjoyed the free pornography that Heinrich Hoffmann supplied. He liked to give the impression that women and sex meant little to him. Karl von Wiegand reported that he 'has a profound contempt for the weakness in men for sex and the fools that it makes them'.[104]

Hitler was terrified of sexually transmitted diseases, and was horrified but fascinated by prostitution,[105] which he saw as an almost exclusively Jewish crime.[106] He preferred women who were submissive – women who were his inferiors. He had no respect for women and often said that if a man went astray it was the woman's fault. He regarded women as being responsible for any man's downfall, yet he believed in an idealistic form of love and marriage, but only if it was possible to find a loyal woman.[107]

He kept an unusually tight rein on Geli, never allowing her to associate with friends unless he or someone he trusted was near her at all times, and making sure she was accompanied on shopping excursions, to the movies and to the opera.

It might be that Hitler took his role as 'uncle' far too seriously and thought of her almost as a daughter whom he had to protect. He didn't make her presence in his life a secret and often had her at his side in public, but whatever his true feelings for her, she gave her affections to Emil Maurice, a founding member of the SS and Hitler's chauffeur. Hitler dismissed him, but later rehired and even promoted him.

Maria Reiter must have been aware of Geli, if only because Hitler was proud to present her in public as his niece, but may have been ignorant of the intense nature of the uncle–niece union. When rumours began spreading about his affair with Maria, he feared he would be hurt politically, and in the summer of 1928 he told her it was over. She tried to kill herself by hanging, but her brother-in-law cut her down and saved her life.

In October 1929, Hitler met a pretty young woman who wanted to be an actress or a model, or just be swept off her feet by a knight in shining armour. Eva Braun, born 6 February 1912 in Munich, came from a respectable Bavarian Catholic family. Eva had an older sister, Ilse, and a younger sister, Margarete, who was always called Gretl.

Eva had the gift of getting her own way because 'she was just too charming. She wrapped everyone round her little finger,' recalled Eva's cousin Gertraud Weisker. 'It was easy for her to get through school without putting in much effort or doing particularly well.'[108] Her dream, like many little girls, was to be carried off by a heroic white knight – in reality, she just wanted someone to take care of her.

She was educated at a *Lyceum*, which in Germany was comparable with the British grammar school or a prep school in the United States. As a teenager she wanted to be chic, to impress, and be the centre of attention. Her one goal in life was to be famous; she would achieve that, eventually becoming the most famous woman in Germany, but not in her lifetime. Traudl Junge, Hitler's secretary in the Berlin bunker where he spent his final months, said that Eva believed 'she would go down in history as the heroic loved one, the *Führer*'s wife.'[109]

She spent a year at a business school in a convent where all the girls were imbued with Catholic finishing touches. She preferred acting to godliness, and thought it might be her road to fame. She had average grades and a talent for athletics. After graduating, she worked for several months as a receptionist at a medical office, then, at age seventeen, took a job as assistant and photographer's model for Heinrich Hoffmann.

In October 1929, at his studio in Munich, Hoffmann introduced her to Hitler. He was twenty-three years her senior. Hoffmann, thinking only of his business, played matchmaker, 'pushing them together, serving Eva Braun up on a silver platter until Hitler took the bait,' said Hitler's caretaker Herbert Döhring.[110] She frequented Hitler's regular inn, where he delivered monologues which she rarely understood, but she allowed herself to be captivated by him; he decided just how close he would allow her to get. 'He had power over her. He exploited that power,' said Gertraud Weisker. Eva allowed herself to be exploited because she was beginning to see him as the white knight she had longed for, which must have enforced his own self-view that he was the white knight of Wagner's operas. The worlds of Hitler's fantasy and Braun's fantasy were colliding.

At times Hitler would declare that he was too old for Eva, and yet he always took a fancy to women young enough to be his daughters. But women, young or old, were the last thing on his mind. He had a career to build. To that end, he needed the help of someone who could be his agent, his publicist, his image maker, his confidant, his right arm, and above all, someone who idolised him to the point of making Hitler into what he most wanted to be: the undisputed, divinely appointed and anointed *Führer*. There was only one man in all Germany who would be born in Hitler's lifetime and possess all the necessary credentials and talent, and the fanatical dedication, to create an Adolf Hitler. His name was Paul Joseph Goebbels.

CHAPTER SIX

HITLER'S PUBLICIST

The first time Hitler met Göring was on 12 July 1925, at a rally in Weimar. Hearing Hitler speak, Goebbels wrote in his diary, 'What a voice. What gestures, what passion. My heart stands still.' He managed to shake Hitler's hand; it was just a fleeting moment but it was a moment of revelation for Goebbels: 'Now I know that he, who leads, is born to be the *Führer*. I am ready to sacrifice everything for this man.'[111]

Like any obsessed fan who buys the autobiography of their latest idol, Goebbels bought *Mein Kampf*, which had just been published. When he finished it, he asked himself, 'Who is this man? Half plebeian, half God! Really Christ, or only John?'[112]

Paul Joseph Goebbels – born 29 October 1897 in the small town of Rheydt, some 15 miles west of Düsseldorf, to devout Catholic parents – had artistic aspirations of his own. He was, unlike Hitler, academically gifted, and studied history, literature, philosophy and art at universities in Freiburg, Würzburg, Munich and Heidelberg. Suffering from an infantile paralysis of the right foot – probably talipes, commonly known as clubfoot – he had spent his childhood largely in isolation from his peers, despite an attempt correct his foot by surgery in 1907: 'Childhood from then on [was] pretty joyless. I could no longer join in the games of others. Became a solitary, lone wolf.'[113] He enriched his life by reading avidly, and he interested himself in arts and music, so much so that his parents scrimped and saved to buy him a piano. He also began writing poems and plays, and in 1918 Goebbels wrote a verse drama, *Judas Iscariot*, in which Judas is portrayed as a hero.

During his years at university and after, Goebbels steeped

himself in German culture. His doctoral dissertation in 1921 was on a nineteenth-century writer, Wilhelm von Schütz, and in later years Goebbels would insist on being addressed as 'Dr Goebbels'. He developed an intense nationalism as a young man, and came to believe in the idea of *Volksgemeinschaft*, or 'people's community', uniting different social classes in a common national purpose.

His anti-Semitic views were enhanced through the works of Houston Stewart Chamberlain, whose writings about the superior Aryan race, specifically over the Jewish race, had also impressed Hitler. Goebbels believed he saw evidence of this in the arts, in the economy and in international relations. Having set his sights on becoming a writer, he completed three plays and an autobiographical novel, *Michael Voorman's Youth*, and succeeded in getting articles published in local newspapers.

His views of religion, art and philosophy were compounded by periods of depression, loneliness and poverty. All over Germany there were strikes, riots and social disorder in the wake of the war. Goebbels had no interest in any political party but developed an anti-capitalist position.

Goebbels did not have access to public radio, and he rarely went to the cinema.[114] He believed that Russia represented the future, and he came to believe in the mystical folk communities he read about in Dostoyevsky, his favourite author; he also liked Goethe, Tolstoy and Gogol. Outside of Russian writers, he most admired Shakespeare, and knew several of the Bard's plays. He found little within German culture to inspire him apart from Gerhard Hauptmann and Thomas Mann.

He began seeing a young schoolteacher in Rheydt, Else Janke, who was considerably kind and patient to him, but to his horror, he discovered in 1923 that her mother was Jewish, tainting his feelings for her. And yet, he was unable to break up with her. His love for someone with Jewish blood tormented him endlessly.

Else gave him a notebook, which he began to use as a diary

and to reminiscence about his childhood and youth. He made his first entry on 17 October 1923, beginning the habit of a lifetime, revealing that he was totally enamoured of Else despite her Jewish ancestry: 'You Beloved, you Goodness! You pick me up and always give me new courage, when I doubt myself. I cannot express what gratitude I owe you.'[115] His feelings for her collided with his anti-Semitism, causing within him a tremendous conflict between his emotional and philosophical senses.

Biographers, such as Toby Thacker, have observed that his diaries were written in a literary and somewhat grandiose style, and that he wrote of himself as if he were a romantic hero at the centre of some titanic struggle. This image he had of himself is remarkably similar to that which Hitler also had, and although they had not yet met, they were destined to be soul mates when they eventually did. They shared a vision of nationalism, of anti-Semitism, and of themselves as artists – rather than politicians – engaged in some kind of romantic epic battle. They also reflected often on how they had had to overcome all kinds of adversity and economic deprivation, which in Goebbels's case had some justification, whereas with Hitler it was all a part of his image-building process.

Still believing his future was as a literary giant, he wrote a play in a fortnight, *Prometheus*. He then quickly wrote another, *The Wanderer*, in which Christ returns to the earth to visit suffering mankind. Although he saw few films, he must have seen the 1916 film *Civilisation* in which that very thing happens; if cinema was not yet an inspiration for him, it was something to plagiarise.

On 12 December 1923, he sent *Prometheus* to the City Theatre in Düsseldorf and *The Wanderer* to a theatre in Cologne. Just a few days into 1924 he received rejection letters from the theatres in Cologne and Düsseldorf, and quickly sent the manuscripts on to theatres in Frankfurt and Duisburg. He went to work on a new novel, *Michael Voorman: The Destiny of a Man in Pages from His Diary* – not a sequel to his earlier novel, which was never published, but a reworking of it in which the central character was a combination of both himself and his one and only schoolboy friend,

Richard Flisges, who had fought in the war and returned wounded. In the book Voorman is a wounded war veteran who leaves student life to work as a miner, and finds a sense of belonging and faith among the common folk before dying a hero in a mining accident. Goebbels had consciously modelled Voorman on Christ,[116] and was writing along the same lines as Wagner, even before knowing of Hitler and of his obsession with Wagnerian heroes destined to save others before meeting their own *Götterdämmerung*.

In February 1924 the name of Adolf Hitler reached him. Goebbels avidly read the newspaper reports of Hitler's trial for his part in the failed putsch of 1923 and his defiant speech in court. He wrote that in reading Hitler's speeches 'I am allowing myself to be inspired by him and carried to the stars.'[117] Goebbels began considering the National Socialist movement and what it believed on the matters of Christianity, the future of Germany, Communism and the Jewish question. In a sense, Goebbels seemed to have found his saviour outside of Catholicism. He had left his religious traditions behind, but had not lost faith in God altogether. He needed to find it again, and he had done so in Hitler.

'Socialism and God,' wrote Goebbels. 'Back to dedication and God!'[118] He marvelled at 'the Christ-like nature of this man'.[119] With Goebbels as a future disciple, and perhaps the most faithful and loyal of all the disciples, it is no wonder or surprise that Hitler would promote himself from being the forerunner of Germany's saviour to becoming the actual saviour – to go from being John the Baptist to becoming Jesus Christ.

Hitler compared himself to the Biblical Jesus:

When I came to Berlin a few weeks ago and looked at the traffic in the Kurfuerstendamm, the luxury, the perversion, the iniquity, the wanton display, and the Jewish materialism disgusted me so thoroughly, that I was almost beside myself. I nearly imagined myself to be Jesus Christ when he came to His Father's temple and found it taken by the money-changers. I can well imagine how He felt when He seized the whip and scoured them out.[120]

He identified not with Jesus Christ the Crucified but with Jesus the Furious who took a lash to the Jews who had defiled the temple in Jerusalem, as he saw the Jews now did to Berlin.

He succeeded in persuading his followers that he was a Christian, but added a new slant on the personality of Jesus:

> My feeling as a Christian points me to my Lord and Saviour as a father. It points me to the man who once in loneliness, surrounded by only a few followers, recognised those Jews for what they were and summoned men to fight against them and who, God's truth! was greatest not as a sufferer but as a fighter. In boundless love, as a Christian and as a man, I read through the passage which tells us how the Lord rose at last in His might and seized the scourge to drive out of the Temple the brood of vipers and adders. How terrific was the fight for the world against Jewish poison.[121]

His people spontaneously adopted a religious attitude towards him, and he accepted this Godlike role without hesitation or embarrassment. Whenever he was addressed with the salutation, 'Heil Hitler, our Saviour', he bowed slightly at the compliment, and believed it.[122] Over time he became more certain than ever that he really was the 'chosen one', and conceived himself as a second Christ sent to institute in the world a new system of values based on brutality and violence. He was so in love with his own image and celebrity that he had himself surrounded with his own portraits.[123]

This led him to the conclusion that he had to become immortal to the German people, and so everything had to be huge as befitting a monument in his honour. Anything built during his reign, especially designed from his own drawings, had to be able to stand for at least a thousand years. His highways had to be known as 'Hitler highways' and endure for longer periods of time than the Napoleonic roads. It became his obsession that he must stay alive in the minds of the German people for generations to come. To that end, he drew up extensive plans for his own mausoleum, which would become the Mecca of Germany after his death, rising some 700 feet high. He declared, 'My life shall not end in the mere form of death. It will, on the contrary, begin then.'[124]

To become the Germanic Messiah, Hitler needed a Joseph Goebbels, and Goebbels needed an Adolf Hitler to find his place in the world. He would become Hitler's own John the Baptist, and unlike Simon Peter or Judas Iscariot, Goebbels would remain faithful to the very last. He had become starstruck by Hitler: not by the personality, because he had not yet seen or heard Hitler, but by his words, and words were often enough for Goebbels, who had come to idolise Dostoyevsky almost as much as Hitler idolised Wagner. In time Goebbels would do whatever Hitler asked of him, even if it meant destroying the country to which they had both ostensibly dedicated themselves. But Hitler dedicated himself only to himself, and Goebbels dedicated himself only to Hitler. In a real sense, Hitler became Goebbels's religion. Hitler declared that Wagner was his God, and Goebbels declared that Hitler was 'Christ-like'. Goebbels would become Hitler's top publicist, and without a fanatical disciple like Goebbels to promote, publicise and market the *Führer*, perhaps there might never have been a Hitler in his most complete form, and therefore no Second World War or Holocaust.

Inspired by Hitler and the National Socialist ideals, Goebbels believed that he could now perceive all that was wrong with German culture: 'The Jewish spirit of decay is most terribly effective in German art and science, in theatre, music, literature, in schools, and in the press.' But he could not give up Else; 'I love her more than ever ... Else, I love you more than I had ever thought.'[125]

He was torn between his love for Else, who was of a race he despised, and his growing love for Hitler, and he tried to lose himself in reading and in revising *Michael Voorman: The Destiny of a Man in Pages from His Diary*, laboriously typing out several copies, four of which he sent to publishers.

With the *Reichstag* elections due in May 1924, Goebbels began attending meetings and getting into confrontations with Communists, having distanced himself from their philosophies. He had only a little experience of public speaking, giving lectures in schools, but he had his first chance to shine as an orator at small meetings of activists. He carefully wrote his speeches beforehand, highlighting the Jewish question.

Following the elections, Goebbels received rejections from all four publishers for his novel. He was short on money, but like Hitler, he had no intention of getting just any old job.

In mid-August he attended a meeting of the National Socialists in Weimar and for the first time experienced the excitement and grandeur of marching columns, flags, banners, swastikas and uniformed SA men singing. That weekend strengthened his resolve that 'one should think of nothing else today, that Germany must again be free'.[126] He decided his future lay in politics, and took every opportunity to speak at meetings, as well as writing articles for a publication called *Völkische Freiheit* (*Völkisch Freedom*). After speaking for an hour and a half at one meeting, he began to realise that he was able to command an audience.[127]

He landed the job of editing *Völkische Freiheit*, and Else volunteered to assist him with typing and secretarial duties. His reputation as a speaker grew, and by October he had built up an enthusiastic following of his own in nearby Elberfeld. He toured cities to deliver a series of speeches, and was soon considered the finest of all the National Socialist speakers with the exception of Hitler.[128]

Finally, in July, he met Hitler, and was overjoyed when Hitler sent a circular to all regional branches of the party praising Goebbels for a booklet he had written called *Das kleine ABC des Nationalsozialisten* (*The Little ABC of the National Socialists*).

In November, Goebbels was assigned to speak at a rally in Braunschweig where Hitler was the star attraction. There he met Hitler formally; the *Führer* shook Goebbels's hand 'like an old friend'. Then Goebbels left to give his speech, which was followed in due course by Hitler's star turn as 'the born people's tribune'. Wanting to see Hitler again, Goebbels did what many fans of celebrities do: he waited outside Hitler's house, and for his endeavours he received another handshake.[129]

Knowing of Hitler's obsession with Wagner, Goebbels shrewdly chose to visit Winifred Wagner at her Villa Wahnfried in Bayreuth. In 1926 Frau Wagner joined the National Socialist Party, and Goebbels noted in his diary, 'She is a fanatical supporter of ours.'[130] At Villa Wahnfried he met Houston Stewart Chamberlain, and he visited Wagner's grave before being taken to see the 'master's room', which had been preserved intact since Wagner's death. He later went backstage at the *Festspielhaus* and recalled the impact Wagner's *Tannhäuser* had made on him when he first heard it at the age of thirteen.[131]

Goebbels's obsession with the Nazi Party, his being constantly on the move in its service and his infatuation with Hitler and all it entailed, all seem to have finally overwhelmed Else to the point where she wrote him 'a brief, matter-of-fact, farewell letter' in June 1926.[132] He returned to Bayreuth in September to speak at Wagner's grave, and then met Else one last time in Cologne.

He had driven away the one woman in his life who adored him despite almost everything. What staggers the imagination is that here was a man who would become one of the most vile perpetrators of suffering upon mankind, someone who preached the gospel of ethnic cleansing, who claimed hatred for the Jews, and yet loved one of them so dearly that he never expunged his many loving entries about her from his diary. It was as if it were a doctrine he believed in because he believed in the cause, but found it a hard path to tread for personal reasons, or because of weakness in his faith. One could hypothesise that if fate had moved in a slightly different direction he might not have become an arbiter and harbinger of death. But he overcame his personal feelings because he had something more powerful than his love for Else. It was his love for Hitler.

At that time, not everything that spewed from Hitler's mouth appeared as gold to Goebbels. He did not agree with all of Hitler's policies, especially in regard to Russia, which Hitler saw as an inevitable enemy which had to be crushed. And yet he had no doubt that Hitler was Germany's anointed one. It was the classic struggle between a man of faith – with foibles and weakness which kept him from perfection – and his infallible God.

Hitler had perfected his act and was a master at playing Hitler. He was the brightest star in the National Socialist Party, and Goebbels idolised him, so much so that he was finally able to break down the barrier that had stopped him giving himself completely to the woman who loved him with such a deep and seemingly abiding passion – he stopped accepting her as a human being. And he did it for Hitler.

In the three years since becoming leader of the National Socialists, Hitler succeeded in organising the party into a tightly knit organisation with local branches springing up all over Germany. He also had a new paramilitary group to protect him, the *Schutzstaffel* – the storm squadron, better known as the SS, which was loyal to Hitler whereas the SA was loyal to Ernst Röhm.

In November 1926, Hitler appointed Goebbels as *Gauleiter* in Berlin, making Goebbels the head of the Nazi Party in the German capital and one of the most important men in Hitler's regime. The new *Gauleiter* published his own newspaper in Berlin, *Der Angriff* (*The Attack*), which he used to great effect in influencing thousands of people to join the National Socialists. From being released weekly, it went bi-weekly in 1929, then daily in 1930, becoming the most widely read Nazi newspaper in Germany. If Goebbels had failed to become the world-renowned author and playwright he had set his heart and hopes on being, he was, at least, writing and publishing for a living, and proving very successful at it too. He had in his hands one of the greatest tools to propagate Hitler's still increasing celebrity; he could write what he liked, and in advancing the Nazi cause he was advancing the personality and celebrity of Hitler, giving Hitler what he had desired more than anything.

Goebbels would, in his own way, come to write the Gospel of Adolf Hitler as they began to carefully craft the legend around the facts. And there even seemed to be a film deal in the offing.

CHAPTER SEVEN

THE HOLY FAMILY OF
THE THIRD REICH

Every year Hitler held a rally at Nuremburg. Supporters came from all over the country to take part and see their idol. The National Socialist Party was still only a minority party relatively, but it was exceptionally well organised and people became increasingly intrigued by a man who could attract such a large and devoted following. At the closing of the parade, thousands crowded into the Nuremberg marketplace hoping to see the party leader. Hitler was now a past master at staging a political rally as if it were a carnival, and it was a natural progression to put it all on film.

Goebbels had taken an interest in film as a valuable propaganda tool and got involved with a number of party pictures, beginning with a thirty-minute film of the party rally in 1927, then another in 1929. The films got longer; *Battle for Berlin* lasted almost an hour. Then in 1930, the party made the first of its *NS-Pictorial Report* films, featuring scenes from the funeral of one of the greatest Nazi heroes, Horst Wessel.

Wessel was almost a creation of Goebbels, who turned the life of an insignificant Nazi 'brownshirt' into a national hero celebrated in books and a major motion picture.

He was a talented musician, playing a *Schalmei* – a type of German oboe – and he wrote songs, including a Nazi fighting song, 'Kampflied', which Goebbels published in *Der Angriff*. The song later became a Nazi anthem and generally known as 'Horst-Wessel-Lied' – the Horst Wessel Song. But that would never have been his legacy if he hadn't been shot when answering a knock on his door on the evening of 14 January 1930. He died in hospital nine days later. Albrecht Höhler, a Communist, was arrested, tried and sentenced to six years in prison, and was later executed by the Gestapo. Doubts remain as to whether Höhler was guilty or a quick and easy solution to a Nazi problem that made a martyr of Wessel. Goebbels was instrumental in the virtual canonisation of Wessel, writing a detailed account of his death, 'Die Fahn Hoch!' (Raise High the Flag!), in *Der Angriff* on 17 February 1930.[133]

Wessel became one of the first to be elevated in the cult of celebrity, even if it was in death. His elaborate funeral on 1 March gave Goebbels and Hitler the chance to indulge in their cult of death at which they were become so adept. It became the perfect showcase for the art of the Nazi documentary film. By the time Goebbels had finished with the legend of Horst Wessel, it was said when a man died for the cause that he had joined 'Horst Wessel's combat group', or had been 'summoned to Horst Wessel's standard'.[134]

By 1929 the world was in the grip of an economic crisis. In Germany, unemployment figures topped three million and doubled within two years. Hardship and poverty were everywhere. The National Socialists' optimistic answer to the general depression was a programme of communal activities in which everyone, regardless of class, had a good time. They didn't offer a solution to the problem of poverty, but they did offer everyone fun and a sense of belonging. The Nazis set up self-help programmes and labour pools, declaring, 'Anyone who hasn't got a shirt on their back can always put on a brown shirt.'[135] The party handed out soup, all carefully staged and filmed, increasing its popularity. The image of Nazism was carefully promoted and presented like any film star, except that behind the image of the welcoming Nazi face lay something sinister and hidden. The economic crisis brought new members into the party by the thousand.

Goebbels had been such an effective and loyal *Gauleiter* that in April 1930 Hitler appointed him as Reich Propaganda Leader. One of Goebbels's first acts in his new role was to disrupt a screening of the American-made film about German soldiers in the First World War, *All Quiet on the Western Front*, based on the book *Im Westen nichts Neues* by Erich Maria Remarque, a German veteran of the war. The book describes the German soldiers' extreme physical and mental stress in the trenches. First published in the German newspaper *Vossiche Zeitung* in November and December 1928, it was released as a book in January 1929. The title is a reference to the official communiqué at the end of the novel and literally means 'Nothing New in the West'; it was named *All Quiet on the Western Front* by its English translator, Arthur Wesley Wheen, and under that title it was filmed by American studio Universal and directed by Lewis Milestone in 1930. Goebbels described the film as 'Jewish provocation' in his newspaper *Der Angriff*, and personally instigated several days of violent provocation, calling the protestors 'the bearers of our morality'. As a result, the film was withdrawn on 12 December 1930.

Goebbels oversaw a Nazi documentary that went by the title of *Der Angriff*, the same name as his newspaper. But most of the films he was behind were not entirely successful as propaganda because, for one thing, he was not a skilled filmmaker. Unable to shoot, cut and edit a film himself, he could only try to influence the content and final edit. Nazi films didn't reach a wide audience because there were few places they could actually be screened, such as at Nazi meetings.

Hitler had even become a regular feature of mainstream newsreels made by UFA which were shown in cinemas all over Germany. Goebbels studied their technical aspects, and he also studied himself whenever he appeared in them so he could learn how to better project on film. When he saw himself for the first time in 1932, he thought it 'quite alien ... otherwise fabulous.'[136]

When Hitler should have been at his busiest, he allowed men such as Goebbels to do the work while he spent time in leisure, often at Bayreuth with Winifred Wagner. He made surprise visits there, phoning her to say he was in Berneck, 12 miles from Bayreuth; she would pick him up in her car. She was the first woman in Bayreuth to get her driver's licence. She always drove Siegfried, even when they went by car to Italy. When the car broke down, she fixed it herself. 'She did the grease and oil changes herself, she did everything herself and didn't mind hard work,' said Wolfgang Wagner.[137]

Winifred Wagner recalled:

> [Hitler] usually came here alone. I often picked him up. I drove and he sat beside me, which he found very strange at first because whenever he saw a woman driver, he'd shout, 'Watch out! Woman driver!' to his chauffeur. But so he could come here anonymously and with no fuss, he really did get into my car and he even found words to praise my driving skills.[138]

He liked to be picked up at dusk. The children were rounded up and everyone got ready for Uncle Wolf's arrival. When he stayed, he was allowed into the nursery to bid the children goodnight. Siegfried tolerated the visits; Winifred told Goebbels that Siegfried displayed 'no jealousy, no interest. Siegfried is too soft.'[139]

Siegfried died in the summer of 1930, and his mother died a few months later. At thirty-three, Winifred became the guardian of the Wagner legacy, but despite appearances to the contrary, there was little money. She and Hitler became closer than ever, taking intimate boat trips on Lake Röhren, each of them rowing. 'She definitely found him sexually attractive,' said granddaughter Daphne Wagner.[140]

There were rumours in Bayreuth of a wedding. Wini, as he called her, visited his mother's grave. Before long, he proposed to her; a marriage to the Wagner heiress would serve his political aims. 'The idea of marrying Winifred came from Hitler,' said Gottfried Wagner. According to Philipp Hausser, the Wagner family doctor, he asked her twice between 1930 and 1933 to marry him, 'and she answered both times that she could only do so if he had an official position'.[141] She declined only because she felt she should wait until he achieved greater authority in Germany. She was the one woman in the whole of Germany Hitler was prepared to marry without hesitation, but it was she who hesitated.

Since 1926 Joseph Goebbels had been the Nazi Party's most

resourceful rabble rouser, and in Berlin as *Gauleiter* he had been preparing the way, leading his assault force straight into areas dominated by the Communists. Before long an underground civil war broke out, and the republic teetered. Hitler was waiting in the wings, ready to step onto the stage and into the limelight – the great saviour of Germany. All he needed was a Holy Trinity.

As if by providence, into Goebbels's life stepped 'a beautiful woman by the name of Quandt'.[142] She was Magda Quandt, the recently divorced wife of rich industrialist Günther Quandt.

They had a son, Harald, but Magda became bored and frustrated because Quandt was away on business often, and, aged twenty-three, she became drawn to her eighteen-year-old stepson Helmut, from Quandt's first marriage to Antoine Ewald. After Helmut died from appendicitis in 1927, she and Quandt toured America for six months, during which time she became attracted to a nephew of President Herbert Hoover.[143]

Quandt distrusted Magda and hired private detectives to watch her. They divorced in 1929 on friendly terms, and he gave her a very generous settlement. Hoover's nephew came to Germany to be with her, but they were in a car crash which left her with serious injuries.[144] Recovering, and with no need to work, she attended a National Socialist meeting in Berlin and was impressed by one of the speakers, Joseph Goebbels. On 1 September 1930 she joined the party and undertook voluntary work as secretary to Goebbels's deputy Hans Meinshausen. He assigned her to take care of Goebbels's private archives[145] and it was in his office that Goebbels first saw her.

He was instantly attracted to her when she arrived at his home on 28 January 1931 to work on his archive. He lived in a handsome apartment in Steglitz, south of the city centre, and quickly became infatuated with her, writing, 'I really wish that she loved me,'[146] and, 'I will love you very much,' calling her 'my queen'.[147]

Although she was involved with another man at that time, on 21 February 1931 Goebbels took her with him to Weimar for the weekend for a party meeting, and their relationship progressed through March after she ended her relationship with the other man. She continued to live in her own expensive flat in the Reichskanzlerplatz in the centre of Berlin with her nine-year-old son Harald; Goebbels liked Harald the first time he met him, noting he was 'quite blond and somewhat cheeky'.[148]

Hitler was also attracted to Magda and had made advances to her.[149] While Goebbels was away for a meeting in the Ruhr in September, she told Hitler she wanted to marry Goebbels. Hitler was 'cast down', but declared his loyalty to Goebbels and was 'resigned' to the inevitable. Goebbels recognised that Hitler had 'no happiness with women. Because he is too soft-hearted to them. Women don't like that.'[150]

Hitler's approach to Magda was more likely to have been to become his mistress rather than his wife, but although she turned him down, she remained very close to Hitler and took on the role of a surrogate mother by preparing his meals and patiently listening to his endless monologues.

The bond strengthened between Hitler and Joseph Goebbels, his most loyal and devoted disciple, when Hitler gave his blessing to the union, and took Goebbels's hands and tears came to his eyes. Goebbels recorded, 'My brave comrade and *Führer*! Fortune has not smiled upon him.'[151]

Magda's romantic rejection had left Hitler in a highly emotional state. Just a few days later, members of his staff found his niece Geli Raubal dead in his flat in Munich; she been shot in the lung. The official cause of death was suicide, based on the fact that her door had been locked from the inside. There was no autopsy, but a doctor estimated that her death had occurred the previous day, 18 September.[152] It was Hitler's Walther that had been used, and rumours circulated that Hitler had shot her, possibly for infidelity; but it was an unlikely scenario, Hitler having been in Nuremberg when she died.

He released a statement to the *Münchener Post*: 'It is untrue that I and my niece had a quarrel on Friday 18 September; it is untrue that I was violently opposed to my niece going to Vienna; it is untrue that my niece was engaged to someone in Vienna and I forbade it.'[153] Hitler was hardly known for his honesty, but there was no solid evidence that there had been any arguments leading up to her death.

Geli left a note, addressed to a friend in Vienna, which read: 'When I come to Vienna – hopefully very soon – we'll drive to Semmering.' The note was unfinished, as if interrupted. Ernst Hanfstaengl insisted that Geli killed herself following a 'flaming row' with Hitler, claiming Hitler had discovered she was pregnant by a Jewish art teacher in Linz.[154] An autopsy would have revealed if that was true or not.

The most plausible cause of her death was suicide, and she was driven to it by whatever madness Hitler seemed to rouse in his young lovers; Geli was not the first, nor would she be the last of his 'girlfriends' to attempt and even succeed in committing suicide.

When Hitler heard the news of Geli's death he returned immediately to Munich, where he went into a deep depression which was said to have lasted for months. 'He locked himself in Geli's room,' recalled Hitler's caretaker Herbert Döhring. 'The loaded pistol lay on the table. My wife saw it. He said, "Anna, I'm going to kill myself. Don't cook for me." She said, "You mustn't, Mr Hitler. Life goes on."'[155] Otto Strasser remained with Hitler for three days following the funeral, to prevent him from committing suicide.[156] Hitler often threatened to commit suicide during moments of personal crisis or defeat: in 1932 he threatened to kill himself if Gregor Strasser split the party;[157] then again in 1933 if he was not appointed Chancellor; and in 1936, if the occupation of the Rhineland failed.[158] During the Munich Putsch he told the officials he was holding prisoner, 'There are still five bullets in my pistol – four for the traitors, and one, if things go wrong, for myself.'[159] He threatened suicide in front of Frau Hanfstaengl directly after failure of the putsch when he was hiding from police in her home.

He was truly devastated by Geli's death, and he kept a bust or portrait of her in each of his bedrooms. Heinrich Hoffmann said that Geli's death 'was when the seeds of inhumanity began to grow inside Hitler'.[160] If this is true, if Geli had not died, Hitler's world might have proven to be a very different place to the one history has recorded with such horror. And yet Hitler was already on a path that had begun the night he received his vision while watching *Rienzi*. Geli's death was probably little more in the course of history than a tragedy that diverted Hitler for a while.

It was said that Hitler's depression over Geli's death lasted months, even years; according to Friedelind Wagner, he went into a severe depression each Christmas for several years after Geli's death, and wandered alone around Germany for days.[161]

However deep his grief ran, in October he was able to pull himself out of his depression long enough to deal with a crisis when Magda learned from her mother that she had not been legally married to Oskar Rietschel. This was devastating news; Magda became inconsolable and unable to continue with the wedding to Goebbels. Bringing calm to this crisis was Hitler, who was 'tenderly kind to her', as Goebbels wrote. Hitler laughed and told the couple that an unmarried woman with a child is preferable to a married woman without a child.[162] Even in the throes of intense grief, Hitler could be surprisingly kind; but his kindness was reserved for only a few devoted disciples.

The wedding went ahead on 19 December 1931 at a small Protestant chapel with just a few family guests in attendance. Goebbels and Magda were to be something unique and almost divine within his kingdom, and with Hitler as the head, they completed his Holy Trinity.

Goebbels delighted in having such an elegant and articulate woman at his side. They exuded Nazi-style glamour – they were the 'ideal German husband and wife', although, of course, they had far greater wealth than the average German married couple. They mixed with luminaries of showbusiness, and hosted gatherings of musicians, actors and painters. But they did not invite businessmen and aristocrats to their parties; Goebbels despised them.[163] He now preferred the company of Germany's most famous stars, and even as he was courting their favour, he was no doubt looking ahead to when he would control their lives, their work, and sometimes their deaths.

He enjoyed his celebrity status, and because of his power and influence he had finally become a published author. His novel *Michael: A German Destiny in Pages from a Diary* – which had begun as *Michael Voorman: The Destiny of a Man in Pages from His Diary* and had been revised – was published in 1929. In 1932 his memoir about his leadership in Berlin, *Kampf um Berlin* (*The Struggle for Berlin*), was published and reprinted several times. He was not to be merely a politician, but an artist, a man of culture – someone others wanted to be around. He had come a long way since his childhood days spent mostly in solitude, shunned by his peers.

Goebbels and Magda were now Germany's most celebrated couple, commanding vast columns of space in newspapers and magazines. And with children, they became more than two-thirds of Hitler's Holy Trinity – they became the Holy Family of the Third Reich, representing Hitler's vision of the new Germany which was waiting only for its moment to rise.

CHAPTER EIGHT

MERCHANDISING ADOLF

A new slogan was born – 'Hitler over Germany' – when he made his first propaganda tour by air covering twenty cities in seven days in an aeroplane in the spring of 1932 as five election campaigns were fought in a single year. He came swooping down out of the clouds, appearing more like the Messiah he was trying to promote himself as rather than just a politician. Thousands gathered to hear him tell them that he knew of their problems because he was one of them, and he spoke of his early life of abject poverty, saying that he had turned to politics out of a sense of desperation. This was the lie behind the image he was building to create the personality and celebrity that lay behind his success. He promised them that things would get better under him, without being specific as to *how* he would accomplish the miracle. Thousands came to see and hear him because they wanted to hear something to give them hope, and to see a great show. Most were caught up in the carnival atmosphere of one of Hitler's stage appearances, and the party's numbers swelled.

He declared that he would unite all in a new community of the people, and social barriers would be torn down. It was an extremely appealing message to hear in those troubled times, and that made Hitler himself hugely appealing. He played his part as the caring Messiah of Germany to near perfection, a masterful creation of his and Goebbels's cult of personality. It was so carefully stage-managed that before anyone could discover if Hitler was anything other than what they saw and heard, he was off into the air again. He was probably never so busy in his entire life, travelling anywhere to persuade the working men and the unemployed that they could all safely put their trust in him.

Hitler never felt more alive than when he commanded a massive audience. He was going to win or lose on his carefully honed talent. It was a huge gamble because he would be either his own instrument of victory, or the instrument of his downfall. At the time, Germany was primed for a Hitler, and he was primed for a Germany which needed a Hitler.

Despite all the adulation and the exhilaration he experienced, which was his only reason for doing it, there were times when his spirits sank, and like an actor giving his greatest Lear or a rock star performing his biggest stadium concert, he was prone to experiencing the dreadful low that can occur when the euphoria has passed. Some use drugs to deal with it. Hitler used Wagner. Hermann Rauschning, who was with Hitler during his rise to power, especially during 1932–1934, recalled that Hitler hummed motifs from Wagner's operas, but when he seemed preoccupied and moody he 'fell suddenly into a dry silence'. National Socialism was approaching a crisis. Hitler exclaimed, 'We shall not capitulate – no, never. We may be destroyed, but if we are, we shall drag a world with us – a world in flames.' Rauschning recalled Hitler then 'hummed a characteristic motif from the *Götterdämmerung*'[164] – it was as though Hitler had already planned his Wagnerian ending, and like Nero in legend, he would fiddle as his Rome burned.

Distressed by Hitler's ongoing absence, Eva Braun attempted suicide on 1 November 1932 at the age of twenty. She shot herself in the chest with her father's pistol, while in her parents' flat. 'She aimed for the heart,' the doctor told Hitler. She survived, and Hitler, wishing to avoid a scandal, brought her to the Berghof and, for a short time, paid her more attention. But he really had little time for her or anything else as he now felt he was close to bringing about the downfall of the republican government, which was powerless to stop the increasing surge of discontent and chaos spreading through Germany.

Finally the conservatives, seeing their republic close to destruction, came to the conclusion they could keep Hitler contained if he were a part of the government, and a deal was struck between the German National People's Party (*Deutschnationale Volkspartei*, or DNVP) and the National Socialists to form a coalition which would become the new government of Germany. On the morning of 30 January 1933, Hitler went to the presidential palace where President Hindenburg appointed him chancellor. *Machtergreifung* – the seizure of power.

The DNVP thought it could keep a rein on Hitler by allowing his party only three seats in the new Cabinet. Hitler was Chancellor, Wilhelm Frick the Reich Minister of the Interior, and Hermann Göring was minister without portfolio, although in a little-noticed development, he was named Interior Minister of Prussia, which gave him command of the largest state police force in Germany and allowed him to organise the Gestapo. Eight seats went to conservatives who were supposed to keep Hitler in check.

Hitler and Braun never appeared as a couple in public and as Hitler became Chancellor, she sat on the stage in the area reserved for VIPs as a secretary.

Listening to events on the radio at home in Bayreuth, Winifred Wagner told her children, 'Wolf has just been elected Reich Chancellor.' Hitler finally had the official position she wanted her prospective husband to have. But she had mixed feelings about the historic moment, and she told Wolfgang that she couldn't imagine that he would be in that position for long, given the share of seats of the parties. She was wrong, and Hitler, having achieved his goal, no longer needed her as his wife.

On 23 March he strengthened his position by issuing an emergency decree, 'For the Protection of the German People', in vague terms permitting the government to ban political meetings as well as the newspapers of rival parties. He justified his actions by telling journalists that certain newspapers had criticised Richard Wagner and his purpose was 'to preserve the present-day press from similar errors'.[165] This was the Enabling Act of 1933, which granted the authority to enact laws without the participation of the *Reichstag* (the German parliament) for a period of four years, after which Hitler renewed the Act twice again, in 1937 and 1941. This allowed

him to gain total control without the need for support of a majority in the *Reichstag*. Hitler had complete power over Germany, and
nothing could be done about it.

He decided that he would never marry, and told Albert Speer,
'Very intelligent people should take stupid wives. I could never
get married.' Hanfstaengl reported that Hitler frequently made the
statement that he would never marry because Germany was his
only bride.[166] But he remained close to Winifred Wagner, and he
arranged for her opera company to receive state subsidies and tax
exemption because it was almost bankrupt. In return, she virtually handed over the annual festival to him for his self-promotion;
Wagner's operas now became his own showcase.

Hitler and Winifred Wagner were still Wolf and Winni to
each other, but they were not as close as they had been. Power
had put distance between them – or rather, it had given Hitler all
he wanted, which did not include a wife. In public they always
remained formal with each other: 'He kissed my hand and greeted
me at the *Festspielhaus*, calling me madam,' she recalled. 'We all had
a good laugh about the play-acting.'[167]

With Hitler's backing, the Wagner family business was soon
back on its feet, and some of Germany's most celebrated conductors, such as Wilhelm Furtwängler and Richard Strauss, performed
at the festival, winning Hitler's favour and coming closer to the
centre of the cult of celebrity.

Hitler proclaimed 1 May a national holiday with pay, which
generations of workers had long fought for. Hitler was creating a
Community of the People. The following day stormtroopers occupied trade union offices. There was no resistance; all those who
opposed Hitler were subdued. The problem with the Community
of the People was that there was no 'opt out' clause; everyone was
brought into it, and all had to keep in line with unification. It was
even compulsory to eat hotpot on Sundays.[168]

Whenever Hitler appeared in public, there were always scores
of movie cameramen strategically placed to capture his image. All
the film was edited in a way that presented him as a monumental

figure, a hero from a Germanic epic. Close-ups of him standing with an outstretched arm as thousands of soldiers marched past were carefully composed and juxtaposed against long shots of formations of men in unified movement. It was the symbol of this new unified Germany, with everyone marching to the same drumbeat, magnifying the insignificance of the individual against the significance of only one individual who stood alone in granite solitude – *der Führer*.

All the time he was carefully honing his performance, studying his impact on his audience and continually improving his technique. He pored over pictures of himself taken by Heinrich Hoffmann so he could judge how best to improve his poses and gestures. He also took lessons from a celebrated magician, hypnotist and clairvoyant, Erik Jan Hanussen, who had built up a considerable business enterprise from a curious hunger Germany had for the paranormal.

Hanussen had predicted in March 1932, in his own weekly newspaper, *Berliner Wochenschau*, that within one year Hitler would become Reich Chancellor. In January 1933 that prediction came true. Shortly before Hitler's appointment was announced, Hanussen had gone to the Hotel Kaiserhof to meet secretly with him, and after examining his hands and counting the bumps on his head, declared, 'I see victory for you. It cannot be stopped.'[169]

Hanussen began coaching Hitler, according to psychologist Dr David Lewis (author of *The Man Who Invented Hitler*): 'He started to teach Hitler some of the tricks of oratory and theatrical presentation which he'd learned through his years in the theatre himself. The whole thing was stage-managed.' According to vocal expert Dr Epping Jaeger, 'The speeches were a great stage production. It's the emotions that dominate in the speeches. The emotions rise and fall. The technical control of his voice is extraordinary.'[170]

The extraordinary effect he had on his audience was not lost on foreign visitors, as noted by Michael Fry, who wrote in 1934, 'At times it seems as if [his words] are torn from the very heart of the man, causing him indescribable anguish.'[171] *Newsweek* reported, 'Women faint, when, with face purpled and contorted with effort, he blows forth his magic oratory.'[172] American writer Janet Flanner observed, 'His oratory used to wilt his collar, unglue his forelock, glaze his eyes; he was like a man hypnotised, repeating himself into a frenzy.'[173]

A correspondent for *Literary Digest* commented in 1933 upon Hitler's ability to hypnotise his audience. 'When, at the climax, he sways from one side to the other his listeners sway with him; when he leans forward and when he concludes they are either awed and silent or on their feet in a frenzy.'[174]

Otto Strasser commented that by the time Hitler finished one of his speeches, he had completely numbed the critical faculties of his listeners to the point where they were willing to believe anything he said. He was affected when the audience responded to him, and this reciprocal relationship was intoxicating for both him and them.[175]

Film of him speaking at the Berlin Sports Palace, just a few days after being appointed Chancellor, reveals much about his technique. After being introduced, Hitler did not immediately begin speaking even as the euphoric applause faded, but stood submissive and reflective, almost nervous, giving the illusion he was unsure of himself. It was all an act to create tension among the expectant crowd. His opening words were 'German comrades', then he fell silent again for around nine seconds before continuing in a quiet and expressionless tone. For much of the time his arms were folded. Gradually, the voice rose, the arms were released and his gestures became more vivid. From time to time he folded his arms again until they were needed to punctuate the words and whole sentences.

It was a masterful performance. He spoke of how the time would come 'when the millions who curse us today will stand behind us and together we will greet the new German Reich that we have created and fought a bitter and painstaking fight for – a Reich of greatness, of honour, of strength, and of the splendour of righteousness' and, without allowing a moment's pause, finished, 'Amen!' It was the climax of a speech that moved, roused and conquered his audience. Perhaps incapable of forming satisfactory personal relationships, he had discovered, in the moments when he and the audience were almost mystically and even erotically consummated, a substitute for sexual fulfilment. His speeches always left him physically drained and dripping with sweat in what has been described as 'blissful exhaustion bred of satisfaction'.[176]

His skill with his voice was no accident. He had received voice coaching from Germany's most celebrated actor of stage and screen, Emil Jannings, who told fellow actor Curd Jürgens, 'Adolf wants to be a great actor. I can't make him that. I can teach him how to speak.'[177] Jannings was the Laurence Olivier of Germany – a great actor with star presence. He had starred in the 1922 German silent film version of *Othello*, and as Nero in the 1925 *Quo Vadis?* Hitler loved Jannings's portrayal of Nero, who, like Hitler, was an emperor with an obsession with fire; Hitler's Reich was an image of the Roman Empire, with its flags and giant eagles. Jannings also worked in Hollywood, winning Oscars in 1929 for two films, *The Way of All Flesh* and *The Last Command*, and co-starred with Marlene Dietrich in the German- and English-language versions of *The Blue Angel* in 1930. During the Third Reich he made a number of films that promoted Nazism and for his contribution to German cinema, or just for teaching Hitler to speak, Goebbels named him *Staatsschauspieler* – 'Artist of the State' – in 1941. Through his efforts at voice-coaching, Hitler learned better how to convert people to whatever he wanted them to believe.

While Hitler spoke, Erik Hanussen needed to be silenced. He was a Jew, and no one could ever know that a Jew had anything to do with Hitler's success. Hanussen had also lent thousands of marks to Nazi leaders, including Hermann Göring, and none of them intended to repay their debts.

He was killed on 25 March 1933,[178] probably by the SA. His body, hastily buried in a field on the outskirts of Berlin, was discovered in late April. Hitler's image was preserved at all costs; Fascist dictatorships depend upon a cult of personality, and Hitler's personality was masterminded by Goebbels and protected by the stormtroopers.

Much like today's lucrative merchandising of celebrities, Hitler became highly marketable. Buttonhole souvenirs of his portraits sold in their thousands, as did albums into which were stuck postcard-sized photos of Hitler and other important members of the National Socialists. His pictures appeared on handkerchiefs, hand mirrors and ties. There was a brand of canned herring called 'Good Adolf'. Ashtrays and beer mugs were decorated with the swastika, and money boxes were made in the shape of SA caps. 'The masses need an idol,' said Hitler,[179] and he gave them one – himself.

There were still five million unemployed. Hitler launched the 'battle of work', touring the country to spread confidence among an uncertain populace. It was a tour that was more about image than actual productivity. He was filmed with a shovel, beginning work on the autobahn, a project prepared long before he came to power, and he laid the foundation stone for the new House of German Art in Munich. His popularity soared as the feeling spread that, at long last, life was improving for everyone under Hitler.

But there were those whose lives were to be blighted. In the spring of 1933 the first concentration camps were set up. At first, concentration camps were for the internment of political prisoners – that is, anyone who opposed Nazi policy in thought or deed. In time they became camps for torture, slave labour and ultimately extermination. While political prisoners suffered terror behind barbed wire, the ordinary folk joined in communal singing and family fun. Being German was like being in one big happy family, only nobody talked about the black sheep in the camps.

In March 1933 Joseph Goebbels was named Minister of Information and Propaganda, becoming 'the agent for the *Führer* and chancellor for everything that is concerned with the cultural and artistic side of life'. He declared that there had been a crisis in the country that had been intellectual as well as material and economic. 'This will continue', he said, 'until we have the courage to reform the German cinema right to its roots.'[180] In a number of speeches, Goebbels pronounced that the role of the German cinema was to serve as the 'vanguard of the Nazi military' as they set forth to conquer the world.[181]

Culture, and the cult of celebrity, was to be at the heart of conquest. It was also at the centre of Hitler's and Goebbels's political views; instead of policies, they gave the *Volk* art which, they claimed, would serve their needs – but only after they had been rescued from the clutches of the Jews. The Nazification of culture, and of all institutions, was under way. It was decreed that only those with German citizenship could practise a profession, and all Jews and foreigners were excluded from the film and cinema industry. Jewish music was banned, and Jewish musicians and entertainers were not allowed to perform except to Jewish audiences, and then only if they were members of the *Jüdischer Kulturbund* (the Jewish Cultural Union), set up in 1933. Its membership was made up of over 1,300 male and 700 female artists, musicians and actors fired from German institutions. It eventually grew to about 70,000 members,[182] but of course, in time, the *Jüdischer Kulturbund* would be curbed.

Not all Germans agreed with the regime's ban on Jews. Wilhelm Furtwängler, the distinguished conductor of the Berlin Philharmonic Orchestra, wrote in an open letter in the *Vossische Zeitung* on 11 April 1933 that Jews were 'genuine artists', such as Bruno Walter, Otto Klemperer and Rolf Reinhardt. Both Walter and Klemperer had already left Germany after threats that their concerts would be disrupted and the halls burned down, and because both musicians had international reputations they were able to pursue careers abroad, unlike other lesser-known musicians.[183]

Furtwängler argued in his open letter to Goebbels that the only distinction was the difference between 'good and bad' artists. Goebbels was an admirer of Furtwängler and had often praised him publicly and privately; in response to the conductor's open letter he thanked Furtwängler for the 'many hours of genuinely formative, great, and often overwhelming art' which he had given to 'his political friends and hundreds of thousands of good Germans'. But he declared, 'There can be no art in the absolute sense, as it is understood by liberal democracy,' and without directly referring to Jews he justified the exclusion of 'rootless' and 'destructive' artists from performing in Germany.[184]

Perhaps in part because of his admiration for Furtwängler, but also to a large degree his intention to mollify the famous conductor, Goebbels allowed Jewish musicians in the Berlin Philharmonic to continue performing with the orchestra, and personally assigned Furtwängler the privilege of conducting the orchestra at prominent state occasions. Nonetheless, in 1935 the Jewish musicians in the Berlin Philharmonic were finally excluded, and in that year Furtwängler's Jewish secretary Berta Geissmar escaped to Britain.[185]

Most Germans preferred to turn a blind eye to what was really going on. On 1 April 1933, while Winifred Wagner and daughter Friedelind lunched at the Reich Chancellery with Hitler, out on the street organised violence raged against the Jews for the first time as shops and business owned by Jews were boycotted.[186] Jewish lawyers and judges were physically prevented from reaching the courts, and some prominent Jews were rounded up by the SA and disappeared into concentration camps.

Hitler declared, 'So this state and this Reich may exist in future millennia, we can be happy in the knowledge that this future belongs entirely to us.' In actuality, he believed the future belonged entirely to himself.

CHAPTER NINE

SEVEN CHAMBERS OF CULTURE

Like Hitler, Joseph Goebbels was starstruck by movie stars, but what struck him even harder was the potential of films for the cause. Although music was his greatest love among the arts, he favoured cinema, not just because of its artistic and technical achievements but because it had become the universal medium of the age – and it could be controlled. A film, unlike a concert, or even a stage play, can be edited, scored and ready for screening in one complete form – total control – and Goebbels always had the final say on what finished form all films could be seen in, or not seen at all. His object was to ensure the world saw German films that portrayed the German people in a positive light, and that the German people saw only films that were of a wholesome nature in keeping with National Socialist policies. Films of the Reich did not need to be political to be effective propaganda. Both Goebbels and Hitler loved films that were larger than life, such as romantic sagas and historical epics. They both also saw cinema as being something much more than a form of entertainment. They intended to turn it into a powerful tool for social engineering.

Goebbels needed UFA, which was owned by publishing tycoon Alfred Hugenberg. Before Hugenberg owned it, UFA had long faced financial disaster due to various factors including the readjustment of the Reichsmark after a period of hyperinflation, and the failure to invest profits in infrastructure, as well as high production costs on films such as *Metropolis*. In 1925 the company was saved by a four-million-dollar loan from Metro-Goldwyn-Mayer and Paramount in Hollywood and an American distribution deal giving UFA 50 per cent of income from their own films shown in America. But America blocked most German films and brought UFA to the brink of closure. In the minds of Hitler and Goebbels, this was a Jewish conspiracy.

The company was rescued in 1927 when Alfred Hugenberg, the leader of the German National Party, bought it and immediately instituted reforms. His trusted deputy Ludwig Klitzsch, who effectively ran the company, paid off the loan to Hollywood, and established a system of production with producers under contract. Hitler struck a deal with Alfred Hugenberg, appointing him as his Minister of Agriculture and Economics in his Cabinet in exchange for his studio; within weeks of the *Machtergreifung* Hugenberg had turned UFA over to Hitler, who gave it to Goebbels to control. Some 3,000 Jews were immediately banned from working at UFA.

One of the most high-profile casualties was producer Erich Pommer, who, with director Erik Charell, also a victim of the cull, had produced *Der Kongreß tanzt* (*The Congress Dances*), which was Germany's most successful film of 1931. Fortunately, Pommer had foreseen the possible consequences of the Nazis' takeover and had taken steps to protect his professional and personal future. Although he had received assurance from Ludwig Klitzsch in 1932 that UFA would not discriminate against Jews, Pommer, unconvinced, negotiated with the Fox Film Corporation (later to become 20th Century-Fox) the foundation of a European production subsidiary in Germany or France.

Recognising that Pommer could prove invaluable to the new UFA regime, Goebbels had the Foreign Office suggest to Pommer that he could be awarded honorary Aryan status if he remained active in the national cinema industry. When Pommer's son, John, was banned along with all Jewish students from the forthcoming May Day parade, Pommer asked the Foreign Office negotiators how they could expect him to work in a country where his son was not good enough to march with his peers. He requested – and received – an exit permit and the necessary endorsements on his passport that would enable him to leave the country. He left that evening on the Berlin–Paris Express but fearing Goebbels might attempt to block his departure, he told his driver to travel to Hanover to meet his train, from where Pommer drove unchallenged into France to work for the Fox Film Corporation, which eventually led to him going to New York.

Another cinematic art form that offered tremendous propaganda possibilities was the documentary. Hitler had long been aware of the value of capturing major events on film, partly to elevate his own public persona, which he was still in the process of evolving, and also to record his rise to power using the most modern techniques available. By the summer of 1933 he had almost achieved his goal of seizing complete power. To bring Hitler's greatest gift – the spectacle of a Nazi rally – to the masses, he decided that the fifth Nazi Party rally, to be held at Nuremberg in September 1933, should be made into a film, and he personally asked actress-turned-director Leni Riefenstahl to make it.

Leni Riefenstahl, just thirty-one years old, had been a dancer from the age of sixteen, but after injuring her knee in 1924, she became fascinated with a film called *Die Weiße Hölle vom Piz Palü* (*The White Hell of Pitz Palu*). It was set in the mountains, a curious genre of movie which was big business in the 1920s, featuring daring men conquering the peaks and with pretty heroines thrown in for good measure. She travelled to the Alps in search of the film's director, Arnold Fanck, and found the mountain-climbing, skiing stars of the film up in the Dolomites.

Fanck quickly took to her and cast her in a number of his famous mountain films, always as an athletic and adventurous young woman. In the process she became an accomplished mountaineer as well as a popular star with the German public in a number of silent movies. One of her biggest fans was Hitler.[187]

She did her own stunts, and nothing was faked when they filmed on location high in the ice. Even the avalanches were real. 'Leni Riefenstahl had to work hard for her success. It took courage,' said Guzzi Lantschner, the cameraman on those pictures. 'But she accepted it and enjoyed doing it. She never grumbled that it was too difficult.'[188] After losing the lead role in *The Blue Angel* to Marlene Dietrich in

1930[189] she starred in Fanck's *SOS Eisberg* (*SOS Iceberg*), and repeated the role in English for the American version, directed by Tay Garnett.

While accompanying Fanck to the 1928 Winter Olympic Games in St Moritz, she became interested in the art of filming and photographing athletes.[190] She learned camera and filter techniques, and how to expose, develop and edit film. She was mostly self-taught, and when offered the chance to co-direct, with Béla Balázs, the romantic and mystical *Das Blaue Licht* (*The Blue Light*) in 1932, she jumped at the opportunity. She also starred in the film, which won a Silver Medal at the Venice Film Festival; her performance as a peasant girl who protects a glowing mountain grotto appealed to Hitler, who believed she epitomised the perfect German female.

Men were drawn to her, for her good looks and playful personality, but she was fiercely independent in a man's world. Said actor Bobby Freitag, 'She was capable, if need be, of running rings around men.'[191] Men competed for her affections. She seemed to favour cameramen and fell in love with cinematographer Hans Schneeberger (who also acted in a few films), but when he left her, her world collapsed, and she made up her mind that from then on she wanted no romantic ties.

During the making of *Das Blaue Licht* she read *Mein Kampf* and said she was so immediately impressed that she 'became a confirmed National Socialist after reading the first page'. Although hugely successful, *Das Blaue Licht* was not well received overseas, and Riefenstahl blamed Jewish critics for its failure.[192] When the film was released in 1938, the names of Béla Balázs and Harry Sokal, who wrote the screenplay with Balázs, were removed from the credits because both were Jews.

In 1932 she heard Hitler speak at a rally and was mesmerised, recalling in her memoir 'an almost apocalyptic vision' which 'touched the sky and shook the earth'. She wrote to Hitler, who responded by inviting her to meet with him; he was delighted that a star of her magnitude, and one he was clearly a fan of, should be an admirer of his. What may have struck a chord with Hitler was that having been rejected by the world of art and culture, here was an artist who not only didn't reject him but sought him out. This moment, when celebrity met celebrity, was to have lasting repercussions.

Although it had been Hitler's goal to take control of German cinema, he knew that of greater cultural significance was German theatre, which, like the film industry, had suffered.

The end of the monarchies in 1918 altered the theatrical scene, and court theatres became state institutions.[193] Without the royal support, funding now relied on box office takings and subsidies from regional bodies. Theatres in large states like Prussia adapted successfully, but provincial theatres struggled against the rising popularity of cinema as well as the financial instability of the Weimar Republic. By the end of the republic, many theatres were threatened with closure or were being forcibly merged with companies from neighbouring cities. Talk of the imminent disappearance of theatre as an art form was widespread.

German theatre was, ironically, saved by the *Machtergreifung*, but it was barely a peaceful salvation, nor a welcome rescue, but an aggressive takeover. Theatres were among the first Nazi targets during the *Machtergreifung*, and several municipal or state playhouses were stormed by SA detachments, while others were taken over by Nazi activists who had been operating for some time inside individual theatre companies. Within a few weeks, the swastika flag was flying over German theatres.

Because the theatre had possessed high political significance in the Weimar Republic with productions that explored controversial issues, it was the first part of German culture to undergo Nazification. The free-spirited artists and their Modernist approach were driven out by use of brutality and threats. Hitler would broach no controversy and he hated everything that was Modernist. Theatre, films and music were all to Hitler's taste – often staid and old-fashioned. Culture was snuffed out. As the Third Reich expanded, people were forced out of their positions in the theatre, and some literally had to flee. Some were driven to suicide. Some died in the camps. Within the party there were a substantial number of dedicated theatregoers who hailed a bright new dawn, but there were also some cultured Germans outside of the party who rejoiced at the purge of the theatres in 1933.[194]

Goebbels appointed Rainer Schlösser *Reichsdramaturg* (Reich playwright), head of the new theatre administration and chief censor of plays and opera. Schlösser was the son of a professor of literature and had been director of the prestigious Goethe and Schiller Archive. Born in Weimar, which was considered the official headquarters of the country's Shakespeareans – his brother became a noted Shakespeare scholar – he had been a literary critic and cultural-political editor of the *National Observer*, and, as a National Socialist, his work and talents had been noted by Goebbels.

He took part in the reconstruction of German cultural life under Hitler as *Reichsdramaturg* and also as Undersecretary at the Reich Ministry for Public Entertainment and Propaganda, and became the first Vice President of the National Writers Union in 1934. After he complained of the high proportion of Jewish composers and librettists in Germany, he carried out Goebbels's instruction for a 'cleansing'.

By 1942 he had graduated to Secretary of the Department of Culture and was engaged in implementing measures to transform German cultural life until, during the Battle of Berlin in 1945, he joined the remnants of an SS Panzer unit which was attacked and destroyed. Schlösser was lost, presumed killed. Few in the world of theatre mourned for him.

After the Nazification of theatre, it was the turn of the literary world to be consumed. On 10 May 1933, a fire was lit in every university town. Students hurled the works of banned authors into the flames. Some 20,000 books, judged by Goebbels to be poisonous to the German mind, were destroyed, throwing 'the demons of the past to the flames' as Goebbels put it. Just to read one of the books burned that night would result in immediate arrest. *Im Westen nichts Neues* (*All Quiet on the Western Front*) was among the thousands of books burned, Goebbels having declared that its author, Erich Maria Remarque, was descended from French Jews, although there was no evidence that was true. Goebbels also claimed, falsely, that Remarque had not done active service during the Great War. Also burned were books by Albert Einstein, who developed the theory of relativity and is widely regarded as the father of modern physics. In 1921 he received the Nobel Prize in Physics 'for his services to theoretical physics, and especially for his discovery of the law of the photoelectric effect'. He was visiting the United States when Hitler became Chancellor in 1933, and chose not to return home. Goebbels proclaimed, 'Jewish intellectualism is dead.'[195]

Leni Riefenstahl later claimed not to have known about the book burnings because she was away for six months making *SOS Eisberg*.[196] Some historians doubt this because her memories are often at odds with documented facts; she often made mistakes with dates in her memoir, for instance claiming not to have known about the 1938 pogrom that would become known as *Kristallnacht* because she was filming *SOS Eisberg*, when in fact she had been in America promoting *Triumph of the Will*. Perhaps she was abroad making *SOS Eisberg* at the time of the book burnings, in England, Switzerland or Greenland, but she was certainly back in Berlin on the afternoon of 16 May when Goebbels revealed to her his idea to make a 'Hitler film', which he believed she was enthusiastic about. That evening she accompanied Goebbels and Magda to see *Madame Butterfly*.[197] The 'Hitler film' was something Goebbels was clearly passionate about, and it was a project that simmered for many years.

Goebbels presided over the newly created *Reichskulturkammer* (Chamber of Culture). Its goals were: 'The promotion of German culture in the spirit of the people and of the Reich, to settle economic and social affairs of the cultural sector, and to balance the efforts of groups it controls.'[198] Within the *Reichskulturkammer* were seven chambers: Music, Press, Theatre, Radio, the Visual Arts, Literature and Film (called the *Reichsfilmkammer* – Chamber of the Cinema of the Reich).

Leading artists in the seven cultural fields were named 'Presidents' and 'Vice Presidents'. Richard Strauss became President of the

Music Chamber, and Wilhelm Furtwängler, capitulating to Goebbels's flattery, was made Vice President. Such people were chosen by Goebbels not just for their talent but also because – perhaps more importantly – they were among Germany's biggest celebrities; Furtwängler was one of the very few who dared suggest that the banning of Jews was wrong and got away with it. These were household names, which were popular choices for such lofty callings.

The *Reichsfilmkammer* controlled every aspect of film production and distribution, right down to admission prices and advertising, although Goebbels did not nationalise the German cinemas, which, for the most part, were privately owned and operated. However, Goebbels set down strict rules and regulations for all cinemas which included mandatory showings of documentaries and newsreels at every film showing; even if the main features were not political, which few of them were, audiences were still force-fed Nazi propaganda.

Film propaganda had the highest priority in Germany even under the severe conditions of the last years of World War II. In order to boost the propaganda effect, the Nazis supported films being shown in large cinemas to large audiences where the feeling of being part of the crowd was all the more overwhelming for the individual spectator. Film shows were arranged in military barracks and factories, and the Hitler Youth arranged special film programmes – *Jugendfilmstunden* – in which only newsreels and propaganda films were shown. To supply rural and remote areas with films, the Party Propaganda Department – *Reichspropagandaleitung* – operated 300 trucks and two trains that carried all the equipment, including projectors and screens, for screenings held in places like village inns.

Because there were no government subsidies for the film industry, Goebbels founded the *Filmkreditbank GmbH* in order to fund the industry; the money came from private investors, forcing the industry to remain profitable. A state-run professional school for politically reliable filmmakers, the *Deutsche Filmakademie Babelsberg*, was also founded, and membership to the *Reichsfilmkammer* was made mandatory for all actors, filmmakers and distributors. All films were pre-censored by the *Reichsfilmdramaturg*, which approved screenplays before filming commenced. A national film award was implemented to encourage self-censorship, and was given to films that demonstrated 'cultural value' or 'value to the people'.

The *Reichsfilmkammer* was personally directed by Joseph Goebbels, although the officially named President of the *Reichsfilmkammer* was film director Carl Froelich. He had become a member of the National Socialists in 1933 and had presided over the *Gesamtverband der Filmherstellung und Filmverwertung* (Union of Film Manufacture and Film Evaluation).

Froelich was much admired by Hitler because he had directed *Richard Wagner*, the first film about the Master of Bayreuth, in 1913. Like many important silent movies it had a music score composed especially to be played by a live orchestra. Because the royalties on Wagner's music proved too expensive, Giuseppe Becce, who played the title role, wrote a new musical score, so ironically nothing of Wagner's music was heard. Becce was an Italian composer who wrote many scores for German films, from silents to talkies, and in 1932 composed the score for Leni Riefenstahl's *Das Blaue Licht*. Since the end of the Great War, Becce had been director of the music department of Germany's major film studio *Decla-Bioscop AG*, which in 1921 became *Universum Film AG* (UFA), where he continued to direct the music department.

Goebbels's position as President of the *Reichskulturkammer* fulfilled all his dreams beyond his expectations. He once yearned to be a playwright, maybe even a producer of plays; now he had unparalleled power over every aspect of art and culture in Germany. The *Reichskulturkammer* had over 2,000 employees and hundreds of thousands of members from every area of the arts. The ideology of the chamber of culture was to eliminate the individual role of the creative artist, replacing it with a totalitarian role of the artist in a world where the state and culture were one and the artist a part of the *Volk*, which was the 'source' of the artist's 'fertility' according to Goebbels.[199] He declared with undisguised delight:

> We have a German theatre, a German cinema, a German press, German literature, German art, German songs and German radio. The objection which often used to be made that Jews could not be removed from artistic and cultural life because there were too many and we could not replace them has been brilliantly refuted.

Goebbels abolished film criticism in 1936 and replaced it with *Filmbeobachtung* (film observation). Journalists, who were also organised as a division of the Propaganda Ministry, were permitted only to report on the content of a film, not offer judgement on its artistic merit or any other worth. Goebbels was the only judge on what was good and what was suitable for public consumption.

Goebbels, the failed playwright and novelist, had essentially become not just the head of all things cultural in Germany but Germany's premier movie mogul, a position that thrilled him. 'Joseph Goebbels was in complete control of UFA,' noted Wolfgang Preiss. 'Nothing could be done without the approval of Joseph Goebbels who was the propaganda minister for the Third Reich. And if you made films, you made them for the Third Reich.' This effectively put every man and woman who worked in any section of German culture in a position of supporting the party, regardless of what their true politics were. 'I am sure there were some who were [Nazis] but most I worked with just wanted to do good work, and you couldn't work at all without working for UFA and that meant working for the Third Reich,' said Preiss.[200]

But Goebbels's plans went far beyond that of being the supreme head of the German film industry and all things cultural. His ambitions were limited only by the circumference of the Earth: he would be the supreme head of film and culture throughout the *world*. He said in 1941, 'It is my ultimate goal to establish the German film as the dominant cultural world power.'[201]

Leni Riefenstahl filmed the Nuremberg rally in September 1933, but she was unable to use the number of cameras she had wanted, so made do as best she could. While she was learning her craft as a documentary filmmaker, Hitler was still learning his craft – how to move, how to behave in front of the camera – and the same was true for other party leaders. As a result, her first documentary for the Nazis was a modest affair compared to what was to come.

Of the ritualistic closing ceremonies, Goebbels wrote, 'That is a church service,' adding, 'We don't need the priests for that any more.'[202] He described the film as a 'picture-symphony' when it was premiered in December 1933.[203] The relationship between Riefenstahl and the Third Reich would reach greater heights.

Her personal relationship with Goebbels, however, was fraught. She claimed that he often made attempts to seduce her, and generally wrote disapprovingly of him in her autobiography *The Sieve of Time*. However, Goebbels's diaries reveal no such animosity on his part, or any episodes of his attempted seductions.

A number of considerations should be made. Goebbels was precise with dates because he wrote in his diary every day. Riefenstahl kept no diary and wrote her memoir some forty years later. As a filmmaker, she was a storyteller, and like many filmmakers – and actors – she was prone to elaboration, sometimes combining different events into one, and relating conversations verbatim, as if she were writing a screenplay; this is familiar from almost any of the myriad of celebrity autobiographies available today. But biographers and historians have pointed to the many inaccurate dates in Riefenstahl's version of events and her verbatim dialogue as indication that her accounts may be false. She denied her own Nazism, and must have written of Goebbels with disdain to distance herself ever further from the Nazis.

However, considering Goebbels's reputation for pursuing attractive female film stars and engaging in affairs with some of them, it seems inconceivable that he would not have attempted the same with Leni Riefenstahl, and he would not have mentioned her rejection of him in his diary. While he was known for recording his life in considerable detail, it was more usually in regard to his emotions rather than documenting every single moment and aspect of every single day; there is barely a mention of the 'Hitler' film in his diaries, though it remained in his mind. His diary entries regarding his Jewish girlfriend Else Janke display a hugely romantic persona and one generally submissive to the object of his love, such as his subjugation to her numerous attempts to break up with him. To write of himself as a Lothario was not in his nature.

Riefenstahl recollects how shortly before Christmas 1932, while Magda Goebbels was in hospital, Goebbels telephoned her several times a day. One afternoon he turned up at her flat unannounced and asked her to admit that she loved Hitler. She denied it. He told her he wanted her as his mistress: 'I've been in love with you for such a long time.' He fell to his knees, sobbing and holding her ankles. She ordered him to leave, and so he did, head hung low. He returned to her flat on Christmas Eve with a present and a further attempt to declare his love. She told him his place was with his wife.[204]

One summer's evening in 1933 Goebbels called again on Riefenstahl while she was entertaining friends. Unable to invite him in, they got into her Mercedes to escape the rain, and she drove off to avoid them being seen together. As they were passing through the woods of Grunewald, he put his arm around her; he swerved, the car hit a mound of earth and ended up at a precarious angle. Goebbels told her to catch a taxi home as he couldn't be seen with her, and walked off into the darkness.[205]

On 14 July 1933, new legislation declared that 'the National Socialist Party of German Workers constitutes the only political party in Germany', and followed with threats of arrest and imprisonment for those who did not obey. That month, while visiting the Wagner family, Hitler talked at length about getting old and complained bitterly that ten years of valuable time had been lost between the Beer Hall Putsch in 1923 and his accession to power. He found this all very regrettable because he predicted that it would take twenty-two years to get things in adequate shape so that he could turn them over to a successor. He even talked about retiring when his work was done, when he would then take up residence in Berchtesgaden and, one supposes, sit as God guiding the destinies of the Reich until his death.[206]

Sometimes the seamless blend of politics, romance and history that Goebbels sought in his feature films broke down, in Hitler's opinion – and his opinion was about the only one that mattered. By and large Hitler did not interfere with Goebbels's work, as indeed he rarely interfered with any of his ministers' duties – once assigned a role in his ministry, he expected them to do their jobs and leave him alone. One of Goebbels's most cherished cinema projects was a film about the Nazi saint Horst Wessel, based on the book *Einer von vielen* by Hanns Heinz Ewer, a novelised account of the SA hero's life and death personally commissioned by Hitler. The book and film attempted to depict his life and his death at the hands of Communists. Goebbels had much admired the book when he read it in 1932,[207] and it seemed to him the basis for the perfect National Socialist film with Communist and Jewish villains and a German hero inspiring a nation. Ernst Hanfstaengl unofficially co-produced the film, which was directed by Franz Wenzler. It was a film commissioned by and made for the National Socialist Party.

The premiere of *Horst Wessel* was to be on 9 October 1933, what would have been Wessel's birthday; the day had come to be known as 'the anniversary', as a result of the cult that had built up around Wessel, carefully crafted by Goebbels. But before the picture could be seen publicly, Goebbels withdrew it, forbidding it to be shown anywhere. He gave a lengthy explanation in what was supposedly an interview in *Der Angriff* – he probably wrote the whole article himself – saying that any film made about National Socialist ideals had to be of 'absolutely first-class artistic quality'. He said the film was more important than others made about the SA, and the martyrdom of Wessel must not be sentimentalised; the film, however, contradicted the 'historical truth', and the character of Wessel in the film did not portray the real man. Goebbels did, at least, praise the music score. Asked by the 'interviewer' if the ban was an attack on artistic freedom, Goebbels replied that it was the opposite, and would be welcomed by true artists because it demanded the highest standards.[208]

Goebbels only allowed the film to be released after significant changes were made. The main character was renamed Hans Westmar and direct references to events in Wessel's life were removed. Some suggest that the name was changed so as not to demystify Wessel,[209] and that some scenes were reshot so that rather than alienating his family, Westmar instead preaches class reconciliation.[210] It has also been suggested that the depiction of stormtroopers goading the Communists into violent fights was not in keeping with the image the National Socialists were trying to project. Under the title *Hans Westmar*, the film was released in December 1933.

Goebbels certainly disliked the film in its original form for what he saw as its inaccuracies, and condemned it in his diary: 'Most bloody stupid dilettantism.'[211] He saw himself as the appointed defender of the cult of Horst Wessel, the ideologies of which embodied all that was fundamental within Goebbels's propaganda, which emphasised and glorified the pervading sense of divinity and the cults of sacrifice and death. Moreover, Goebbels felt he had the right to monopolise the cult of Wessel and resented Wessel's mother's attempt to share in it. These cults all combined into one: the cult of celebrity. Famous names would help create world Nazism, and Nazism would create famous names – and destroy those who opposed it. Few epitomised this Nazi cult of celebrity more than Leni Riefenstahl: as a film director, her name was as famous as any actor; and she rose with the Third Reich, a celebrity created by Nazism, while at the same time helping to create the image of the Third Reich on film and in the mind. She was, simultaneously, both its creation and co-creator with the Great Creator, Hitler.

'Prohibition of the film [*Horst Wessel*] is arousing great interest,' noted Goebbels. 'But I stand firm.'[212] He was supported by many, including Riefenstahl, who sat with him at his home the day before the anniversary and abandoned premiere, and 'rummaged through *Der Angriff* from Horst Wessel's time', he wrote. 'Blessed memories.' They were later joined by actor Willi Fritsch, another member of the Nazi Party.

The next day Goebbels met with Hitler and *Horst Wessel*'s co-director Ernest Hanfstaengl, who disapproved of Goebbels's actions over the film and was 'agitating' by refusing to offer Goebbels his hand. Goebbels noted Hitler's displeasure at Hanfstaengl's attitude – 'Chief is furious with him' – and refused to change his position on the film, claiming he was 'responsible for the remembrance of Wessel'. Hitler agreed with him. Following the meeting, Goebbels went to the Friedrichshain hospital where Wessel had been treated, to dedicate the room where Wessel died as a memorial chamber. He described Wessel's mother as 'insufferable'.[213] Then he went alone to Wessel's grave.

Hanfstaengl disliked the final cut of the film because 'it was too bourgeois in approach, emphasised Horst Wessel's Christian background too much, was not full of the National-Socialist revolutionary spirit, was trite – everything was wrong.'[214]

Goebbels may have had another reason to ban the film in its original form. Both the book and the screenplay had been written by poet, philosopher and adventurer Hanns Heinz Ewers, renowned as a writer of short stories and novels, and particularly famous for his works of horror. He recognised cinema as a legitimate art form and began writing scripts for films as early as 1913.

He was a world traveller and was in South America when the First World War broke out, at which time he relocated to New York where he continued to write. There he spoke as a representative of Germany in an attempt to dissuade America from entering the war as Britain's ally; this led to his arrest in 1918 as an 'active propagandist' and agent who had travelled to Spain during 1915 and 1916 using an alias and a false passport. He was also accused of travelling to Mexico to meet with revolutionary Pancho Villa in an attempt to persuade him to attack America.[215]

He was interned at Fort Oglethorpe, Georgia, without a trial, released in 1921 and sent back to Germany. Continuing his successful career as a writer, he became involved with the National Socialist

Party during the last years of the Weimar Republic, although he never officially became a member and disagreed with the party's anti-Semitism. In his trilogy of novels about fictional adventurer Frank Braun – based on himself – the hero's mistress Lotte Levi is Jewish, and a patriotic German. This would not have pleased Goebbels, who would have been ever more outraged to discover that Ewers had homosexual tendencies. Goebbels detested homosexuality and often tried to persuade Hitler to bring down the SA, within which it was rife.

Goebbels had liked the book *Einer von vielen* when he read it in 1932, and would have been aware of Ewers's past as a patriotic German agent during the war, but clearly he had no knowledge at that time of some of Ewer's sexual practices or he would never have approved of Ewers writing the screenplay for such a sacred project. It is possible that Goebbels, having become aware that Ewers had not joined the party and disagreed with the party's anti-Semitic approach, had the author investigated, and towards the end of 1933, prior to the film being premiered, was informed of Ewers's sexual practises. As the one 'responsible for the remembrance of Wessel', he had to prevent the memory of the Nazi saint from being tainted by such a corrupt soul as Ewers; consequently in 1934, just months after the film version of the Wessel story was banned, all of Ewers's works, including *Einer von vielen*, were banned in Germany and all his assets and property seized. His screen version of the life of Horst Wessel would never be seen. He died from tuberculosis in poverty in Berlin on 12 June 1943.

Homosexuals and Jews were not to be tolerated in Goebbels's new order of German culture. As well as being Germany's moral defender and arbiter of taste who decided what films could be made, which ones would ultimately be shown, and what music the people could listen to, he became obsessed with removing anyone even remotely suspected of having Jewish ancestry from whichever area of the arts they worked in. It took time to set up the necessary bureaucracy, so expulsions didn't begin until early in 1934. It would be another year before anti-Semitism would become a legality – to be ratified at the 1935 Nuremberg rally – and therefore obligatory for all Germans.

According to Riefenstahl, she was summoned to the Propaganda Ministry and asked by Goebbels to make a film about the Nazi press; she rejected the idea. He told her that he liked her because she had a mind of her own and said, 'I will never stop fighting for you'; then he grabbed her breast and tried to force himself on her. She attempted to escape, but he held her against the wall and tried to kiss her. She managed to press a buzzer, and he let her go just before his servant arrived. Following this event, she was summoned again; Goebbels accused her of criticising him and his staff and told her to get out of his sight.[216]

While Leni Riefenstahl was evading Goebbels's advances, an exodus was taking place.

CHAPTER TEN

EXODUS

German, Austrian and Hungarian writers, actors, directors and other celebrated artists, who were working in Germany and also happened to be Jewish, were getting out before it was too late. Among them was Max Reinhardt, a director of many acclaimed plays in Germany since 1902. Because of his Jewish ancestry, he left Germany for Austria in 1933; then in 1934 he went to America, where he had previously directed his own play *The Miracle* in 1924, to direct a stage production of *A Midsummer Night's Dream*, following it with the famous film version. Both productions featured James Cagney as Bottom and Olivia de Havilland as Hermia; the play was staged at the Hollywood Bowl, and the film was produced at Warner Brothers. The latter was subsequently banned by Joseph Goebbels in Germany because of Reinhardt's Jewish ancestry, and because the soundtrack featured music by Felix Mendelssohn, who was also Jewish.

Reinhardt returned to Austria in 1938, but fled Europe for good when Austria came under Nazi rule. *A Midsummer Night's Dream* was his only film with sound; he was more interested in continuing his outstanding work as a director and producer of plays on both coasts of America, and he also founded a Hollywood-based theatre workshop and an acting school in New York. His was a considerable talent for Germany to lose. He died in New York in 1943.

Samuel Wilder was born to a Jewish family in Sucha Beskidzka in Austria-Hungary, and became a screenwriter in Berlin, working with Fred Zinnemann and Robert Siodmak on the 1929 movie *Menschen am Sonntag* (*People on Sunday*). In 1933 he chose to leave Germany and settle in Paris where he directed his first film, *Mauvaise Graine*, and then moved to America to pursue his film career in Hollywood, where he became known as Billy Wilder and went on to write and direct such classics as *Some Like it Hot*, *Sunset Boulevard* and *The Apartment*. His mother, grandmother and step-father all died in Auschwitz.

Fred Zinnemann, from Vienna, had already left Germany in 1930 to study film in America and went on to direct *High Noon*, *The Nun's Story* and *A Man for all Seasons*. His friend Robert Siodmak was born in Dresden to Polish-Jewish parents, and became a screen-writer and director in Germany until the rise of the Nazis forced him to flee to Paris. At the outbreak of war he arrived in America and became established as a director of thrillers and *film noir*. He returned to Europe in peacetime and worked in both France and Germany.

Fritz Lang also fled. He was born in Vienna to a mother of Jewish extraction who had converted to Catholicism. He became one of Germany's leading filmmakers with such early masterpieces as *Dr Mabuse: The Gambler*, *Metropolis* and *M*. In 1932 his wife, the actress and screenwriter Thea von Harbou, joined the National Socialist Party, but Lang fretted over the new regime, partly because of his Jewish heritage, and before long their marriage broke down irretrievably and they divorced. His 1933 film *The Testament of Dr Mabuse*, a remake of his earlier *Dr Mabuse* picture about a mad doctor who is also a master criminal, had its premiere delayed by Goebbels for 'technical reasons'.[217]

At a meeting held at Goebbels's home, where Lang and several other German filmmakers discussed censorship, Goebbels declared that Lang's films displayed the style that Hitler wanted for German films.[218] Yet not long after, on 30 March 1933, Goebbels banned the film on the grounds that it would incite public disorder, as it 'showed that an extremely dedicated group of people are perfectly capable of overthrowing any state with violence'.[219]

Lang later claimed that Goebbels wanted him to make films for the Third Reich, so after the meeting Lang left for France that very night. Some dispute Lang's account because he didn't leave Germany until June, and even after that he made return trips to

Germany throughout 1934[220] but, as with many storytellers, he likely embellished his account to add to the drama. Goebbels wrote in 1938 that on looking at *The Testament of Dr Mabuse* he was 'struck by the dullness of its portrayal, the coarseness of its construction, and the inadequacy of its acting', and yet he must have admired it because he kept a private print of it, uncensored, which he took delight in screening for close friends.[221]

Lang moved to America in 1936, where he became acclaimed as a master of *film noir*, much to Goebbels's annoyance. Although Lang was a Catholic, his fears that he would have faced persecution as a Jew were realised when Nazi eugenics laws identified him as a Jew, by which time he was permanently absent from Germany.

Meanwhile, Lang's former wife Thea von Harbou did well for herself working for the Third Reich, writing and directing an adaptation of Gerhart Hauptmann's play *The Assumption of Hannele* in 1934, and writing the screenplay for *Der Herrscher* (1937), which celebrated unconditional submission under absolute authority. It was directed by one of Hitler's and Goebbels's favourite filmmakers, Veit Harlan.

The exodus of considerable talent continued, and it was not just Jews fleeing from the Nazis. Novelist Thomas Mann was not Jewish, but had spoken out against National Socialism; he fled to Switzerland to escape the concentration camps. Erich Maria Remarque fled Germany because Goebbels asserted he was of Jewish decent. In 1943 his sister Elfriede Scholz was arrested by the Gestapo and tried in the *Volksgerichtshof* – Hitler's 'People's Court' – where she was found guilty of 'undermining of military strength' because she had considered the war lost. The court President, Roland Friesler, told her, 'Unfortunately your brother has escaped us – you, however, will not escape us.' She was guillotined on 16 December 1943.[222]

Those who remained to write, to make films, to ensure that German culture didn't disappear altogether, had to toe the party line. With fear and paranoia spreading, neighbours began spying on neighbours, reporting anything that seemed in any way suspicious to the Gestapo. Film stars were no exceptions to the rule. While anti-Semitism was rife in Germany during Hitler's rule, many actors did not share such hatred, for instance Wolfgang Preiss, who began working in films during the war years: 'I can only speak personally. I am an actor, I have worked with many nationalities. Italian, English, American, French, Jew. I do not care about nationality or religion. But hate for Jews was among many Germans who believed Hitler.'[223]

In 1933, just after Hitler took power, Marlene Dietrich was in America, where she was under contract to Paramount. Her husband Rudolf Sieber, with whom she had one child, Maria, sent her a telegram warning: 'Situation Berlin terrible' and 'Jews in our business gone'.[224]

Dietrich had made several films in Hollywood, most of them directed by Josef von Sternberg, but had not intended to remain there, planning to return to Germany to make German films. Germany was her home, where her heart was. She had been born Marie Magdalene Dietrich on 27 December 1901 in Schöneberg, a district of Berlin. Her mother was from an affluent Berlin family who owned a clock-making firm, and her father was a police lieutenant. He died in 1911, and her stepfather, an aristocrat first lieutenant, died in 1916 from injuries sustained in the First World War. She was nicknamed 'Lene' (pronounced Lay-neh) within the family, and around the age of eleven she joined her two first names to form the then novel name of 'Marlene'. She wanted to be a violinist, but after injuring her wrist she became a chorus girl on tour with Guido Thielscher's *Girl-Kabarett*, in vaudeville-style entertainments and in Rudolf Nelson revues in Berlin.

In 1922 she failed an audition for theatrical Max Reinhardt's drama academy but landed small roles in plays. That same year she made her film debut in a minor role in *So sind die Männer* (*The Little Napoleon*). After marrying Rudolf Sieber in Berlin on 17 May 1923, her career progressed through a succession of plays and musicals and leading roles in films until she shot to stardom as Lola-Lola in *The Blue Angel*, directed by Josef von Sternberg; this brought her, and him, to Hollywood.

She wasn't Jewish, and was not at risk, but she was so alarmed by Sieber's warning telegram that she decided not to return immediately to Germany, and attended a reception in France for German immigrants, including acclaimed Austrian tenor Richard Tauber, who had co-starred with Dietrich in the 1929 film *Ich küsse Ihre Hand, Madame* (*I Kiss Your Hand, Madam*). He had been assaulted in the street by a gang of Nazi brownshirts because of his Jewish ancestry, so decided to leave Germany and return to Austria. He, and others like him, told her what was happening in Germany, and she became more determined not to return there while Hitler was in power,[225] even though her mother, sister Elisabeth and daughter Maria were still there. She returned to Hollywood.

Hitler and Goebbels called her a traitor for abandoning her country, but not all Germans felt that way. Actress Evelyn Künneke recalled, 'She didn't approve of what the Nazis were doing and had the chance to get away from it. It would be nonsense to think ill of her, or see it as treason.'[226]

The exodus continued. Fritz Kortner, the Austrian-born actor who made over eighty films from 1917 and famously portrayed Beethoven in *Das Leben des Beethoven* (*The Life of Beethoven*) in 1927, fled Germany in 1933. He worked in America as a character actor in many films, including two anti-Hitler films, *The Strange Death of Adolf Hitler* in 1943 and *The Hitler Gang*, playing Gregor Strasser, in 1944. He also directed plays and, after returning to Germany in 1949, directed several films.

The persecutions affected many who were not Jewish. Hans Albers, a legend of German cinema with over a hundred silent films to his credit, starred in the first German 'talkie' in 1929, *Die Nacht gehört uns* (*The Night Belongs to Us*). He had a Jewish girlfriend, actress Hansi Burg, daughter of the established actor Eugen Burg. She and Albers met and fell in love in 1925 and, knowing they needed to avoid a scandal, she moved into her own apartment. The couple were seen together only as friends and colleagues, while in private they continued their love affair. After Hitler came to power, Albers was one of many film stars and other

artists invited to the inauguration of Joseph Goebbels as President
of the *Reichskulturkammer,* but he didn't attend. He refused to join
the Reich Film Chamber, which was mandatory for actors, nor
would he attend government-sponsored events. He became one of
the very few actors who remained in Germany to work under the
Third Reich but didn't receive an autographed photo of Hitler,[227]
an indication his resistance had come to the *Führer's* notice. The
Gestapo began keeping a watchful eye on Albers.

Threatened with a ban, he finally agreed to join the Reich Film
Chamber, but was expelled from it in June 1934, his passport
withheld and payments due to him suspended. The Gestapo had
discovered his clandestine involvement with Hansi Burg. In Nazi
Germany, there were few such secrets, and it was well known in
the film business that the two were lovers; somebody had talked.
Neither Hans nor Hansi were arrested, possibly because Goebbels
had some unspoken sympathy for Albers's case, having loved a
Jewish girl himself. At the time, Goebbels needed stars of the cali-
bre of Hans Albers.

In October 1935 Albers wrote to Goebbels that 'in fulfilling my
duty towards the [government ... I have] solved my personal relations' with Hansi Burg, asking that he therefore be accorded 'the
protection [the state] gives its artists' and signing off with 'Heil
Hitler!' Goebbels was reported as being very happy with this
outcome.[228] In fact, Albers had arranged with a Norwegian, Erich
Blydt, to marry Hansi and live safely in Norway. Albers provided
them with money, and met with Hansi whenever he could.
Eventually Hansi left Norway for the safety of Switzerland, but
her father Eugen Burg remained in Germany and was murdered in
Theresienstadt concentration camp in 1944.

Hans Albers continued to work and proved especially popular
teamed with Heinz Rühmann in a number of successful films,
among them *Der Mann, der Sherlock Holmes war* (*The Man Who
Was Sherlock Holmes*) in 1937, with Albers as Holmes and Rühmann
as Watson. But without Hansi he was often lonely, as well as
depressed over losing friends to the Nazis, such as the actors Kurt

Gerron and Otto Wallburg, both Jewish. They were arrested in the Netherlands, deported and murdered. One of Albers's favourite directors, Herbert Selpin, with whom he made several films from 1938 to 1941, was denounced after declaring 'Fuck the Knight's Cross'; he was arrested and later found hanged in his cell.[229] Albers retreated to an estate on Lake Starnberg, while Hansi Burg fled to England in 1938; they would not see each other again until the end of the war. He tried to console himself with alcohol, and was known often to speak recklessly, especially under the influence.

There were others in a similar position to Hans Albers and Hansi Burg. Joachim Gottschalk was a romantic lead in the style of Britain's Leslie Howard, starring in a series of German films opposite the popular actress Brigitte Horney. He married a Jewish woman, Meta Wolff, shortly before Hitler came to power, and they had a half-Jewish son, Michael, a secret they managed to keep for a while. Gottschalk took Meta to a social function at the Arts Centre and introduced her to some prominent Nazis who were charmed by her, including Goebbels. But when he learned that she was Jewish, he decreed that Gottschalk would be required to separate from her. Gottschalk refused. Actor Will Quadflieg recalled, 'He was such a resolute and great person. If only there had been more like him who wouldn't go along with it.'[230]

But there was a price to be paid: Goebbels ordered that Meta and son Michael be transported to the Theresienstadt concentration camp. Gottschalk insisted on accompanying Meta and Michael to Theresienstadt, but Goebbels ordered that he be inducted into the *Wehrmacht*. With little time to spare before they were separated, in November 1941 Gottschalk and Meta sedated their son, then they turned on the gas, and all three died. Goebbels ordered no mention be made of Gottschalk's suicide in the German newspapers, but word got out and millions of German women mourned his death. Goebbels forbade any stars to attend the funeral at the Stahnsdorf Friedhof on the south-western edge of Berlin. But Brigitte Horney attended, as did Gustav Knuth and Werner Hinz in defiance of Goebbels, and regardless of political and career implications.

Goebbels was by then aware of considerable tension between him and the film community, although it's doubtful that he knew he was often referred to as Mickey Mouse 'because of his mousey face'.[231]

A long and distinguished career was no guarantee of survival for actors with Jewish blood. Ernst Arndt had appeared in silent films, but his first love was the stage, and in 1931 he was made an honorary citizen of Vienna for his stage work in Austria. But on 10 July 1942, at the age of eighty-one, he was deported to Theresienstadt, and from there, on 23 September, to Treblinka where he is presumed to have been murdered shortly afterwards.

The cult of celebrity only protected celebrities if they conformed to Nazi ideology and racial purity. In 1932 Max Ehrlich was one of Germany's most beloved comics, a master of ceremony and a top cabaret star in the *Haller-Revue* and others. He made forty-two films – ten of which he directed – recorded eight gramophone records, and wrote several books including the bestseller *From Adelbert to Zilzer*, a humorous collection of stories and anecdotes about his well-known friends in showbusiness. It was a true celebrity memoir long before memoirs were being written by everyone with the merest claim to celebrity. He also happened to be Jewish.

He went to Vienna to appear with the popular Rudolf Nelson Revue, but the show was interrupted by an organised group of Nazis with cries of 'Jews, get out of Vienna!' The troupe consequently left Austria to tour the show in Switzerland and the Netherlands. Homesick, and oblivious to the horrors that were yet to come, Ehrlich returned to Germany in 1935 where Jewish entertainers were permitted to perform only within the framework of the *Jüdischer Kulturbund*.[232] He even became director of the *Kulturbund*'s light theatre departments, but following the 1938 pogrom that would become known as *Kristallnacht*, he decided to leave Germany for good. Both of his farewell performances immediately sold out, so a third was added on 2 April 1939. Before a full house which cried out and applauded with tremendous affection, Ehrlich made his final appearance in Germany.

He returned to the Netherlands and joined Willy Rosen's *Theater der Prominenten* (Theatre of Celebrities). But in 1943 the war and the Nazis caught up with him, and he and his Jewish colleagues, along with thousands of Dutch Jews, were imprisoned in the Westerbork concentration camp. There he created and became director of the Camp Westerbork Theatre Group, a cabaret troupe that staged six theatre productions, all within the confines of the concentration camp. The majority of the actors were famous Jewish stars from Berlin and Vienna, such as Willy Rosen, Erich Ziegler, Camilla Spira and Kurt Gerron. There were also Dutch celebrities like Esther Philipse, Jetty Cantor and Johnny & Jones. The company included a full team of musicians, dancers, choreographers, tailors, make-up artists, lighting and other technicians, and stagehands. This was accomplished under the persistent threat of deportation to an unknown but deeply feared fate.

Most of the shows combined elements of revue and cabaret, on one occasion including a revue-operetta, *Ludmilla, or Corpses Everywhere* – a precursor of what was to come. Ehrlich ensured his theatre group never produced a show that was openly political or directly attacked the Nazi regime; to do so would have called for the entire company's immediate deportation. The Westerbork Theatre Group could only distract its audience momentarily from the surrounding horrors, but it gave people renewed hope and the courage to face an otherwise unbearable existence.

Inevitably, increasing numbers of Westerbork's prisoners were transported to the extermination camps to the east. Of 104,000 camp inmates, fewer than 5,000 survived. Max Ehrlich was number 151 on the list of prisoners to leave Westerbork on 4 September 1944. Upon reaching Auschwitz, he was recognised by a *Hauptsturmführer* and immediately taken before a group of SS officers who aimed their guns at him and ordered him to tell them jokes. On 1 October 1944 he was sent to the gas chambers. When British troops liberated Westerbork on 12 April 1945, there were only several hundred survivors, and of them only two were Theatre Group members.[233]

There were many others among Germany's celebrities who

either fled or were exterminated, and many more who were lesser known but might have become major stars had Hitler not had them removed or murdered. They were just a tiny minority of the millions who perished in the Holocaust, but they left gaping holes in the entertainment world, which did what it could to fill the breach.

The actors and filmmakers who remained seized the opportunity to demand higher salaries, which increased production budgets. Consequently, it became increasingly difficult to recover production costs especially as international boycotts cut the export of German films dramatically. (In revenge, Goebbels began banning some Hollywood films until 1941, when Hitler banned *all* American films.) In 1933, exports covered 44 per cent of film production costs, but by 1937, this figure had dropped to a mere 7 per cent. Many production companies went bankrupt, and the number of companies dropped from 114 (during the period 1933 to 1935) to 79 (1936 to 1938) to just 38 (1939 to 1941). Film production was maintained, however, because the surviving companies produced many more films than usual. This suited Goebbels, who had easier control over fewer film production companies, especially after UFA merged in 1942 with all the remaining companies – *Terra Film, Tobis, Bavaria Film, Wien-Film* and *Berlin-Film* – into the *UFA-Group*.

From outside Germany, actors and singers seeking fame and fortune realised that Germany was ripe for new stars, and they took advantage of the opportunity to become embroiled in the Nazi cult of celebrity.

CHAPTER ELEVEN

SLEEPER STAR

Four days after Hitler came to power, a film called *Der Choral von Leuthen* (*The Hymn of Leuthen*) was premiered. It was one of a score of German movies about the great Prussian king Frederick II, played by Otto Gebühr, who appeared in 102 films between 1917 and his death in 1962. In twelve of them he played Frederick II, and would appear as Frederick four more times after *Der Choral von Leuthen*, the last being in 1942 in *Der Große König* (*The Great King*).

Der Choral von Leuthen, commissioned by Goebbels, received the rare 'Film of the Nation' distinction. As a trailer for the movie, and as political propaganda, Otto Gebühr appeared in a short film, in his Frederick the Great costume, to tell the German people: 'This play is from a time when duty and sacrifice made a nation great. In our time too, duty and sacrifice are required. Give what you can for the Winter Aid for the German People.'

The *Winterhilfswerk* (Winter Help Work) was launched by Hitler in September 1933 to help the poor through the winter months. He explained, 'This great campaign against hunger and cold is governed by this principle: we have broken the international solidarity of the proletariat. We want to build the living national solidarity of the German people!' To raise funds there were monthly street collections, usually by the Hitler Youth, who began going door to door. Buttons were sold, some of which were hand sewn, and hand-crafted celluloid flowers. The Nazis claimed that in 1933–1934 *Winterhilfswerk* beneficiaries exceeded 16.6 million people, meaning that one out of every four Germans received assistance.[234]

Adding some glamour to the premiere of *Der Choral von Leuthen* was its leading lady Olga Tschechowa, one of Germany's brightest stars. Yet she was not a German. She was born in Aleksandropol in

Tsarist Russia on 14 April 1897 to Lulu and Konstantin Knipper, a railway engineer. Konstantin's sister Olga was a celebrated actress and married the great Russian playwright Anton Chekhov; she had the stage name Olga Knipper-Chekhova, but was usually referred to within the family as Olya. Her niece and future star of German cinema, Olga Tschechowa, was named after her.

The Knipper family had originated from Saarbrücken in Germany, but migrated to Tsarist Russia where Konstantin's father Leonard Knipper had done well enough in the building trade – he ran a factory in a small town called Glazov, in north-east European Russia – to send his children, Konstantin, Olya and Vladimir, to private schools. Konstantin was to become an engineer, Olya an actress, and Vladimir a celebrated singer and director at the Bolshoi under the stage name Vladimir Nardov.

Leonard Knipper died in bankruptcy, forcing his widow Anna to make ends meet by giving singing lessons. But it was a family bursting with talent, and Konstantin and Lulu sent their daughter Olga to study art in Moscow where she met and fell in love with Mikhail Chekhov, the great actor of the Moscow Art Theatre and nephew of playwright Anton Chekhov. They married in 1915 and their daughter was born the following year; true to the tradition of naming children after parents and grandparents and other relatives, they named her Olga, although she was always called Ada – Olga's sister's name – adding to the confusion within the family where there were many Olgas and now at least two Adas.

In later years Olga Tschechowa would claim she had been an actress at the Moscow Art Theatre, but that is one example of the way she exaggerated her life and career. She was considered by her aunt Olga Knipper-Chekhova to be something of an 'adventuress' – it would seem her sense of adventure was what prompted her to marry Mikhail Chekhov in haste. She took on her husband's surname but, as in the Russian tradition, added an 'a' at the end, becoming Olga Chekhova (before the Germans would rename her Olga Tschechowa).

Her marriage that ended in 1917 when, unable to cope any longer with Mikhail's drunkenness and infidelity, she left him, taking their daughter with her to live with her Aunt Olya in Moscow. Olga Chekhova's sister Ada also moved in, as did Konstantin and Lulu, to escape the danger Russia was facing as the First World War was coming to an end and the Bolsheviks were causing unrest. Konstantin and Lulu stayed only a while before moving to Siberia to escape starvation, which the citizens of Moscow were facing; they took with them Olga's daughter, while Olga remained behind with her sister Ada and their aunt.

Olga did her best to earn money selling pictures she painted, and she also managed to get a little work as an actress in the films *Anya Kraeva*, *Cagliostro* and *The Last Adventure of Arsène*, which were made without interference from the new Bolshevik authorities.[235] Determined to escape the troubled new Soviet Union, Olga chose to try her luck in Berlin; why she chose Berlin is unclear, but she arrived there sometime in 1920, probably in August. She expected to be back in Moscow within six weeks, but she didn't return for another twenty-five years.

In Berlin she found that her name Chekhova carried some weight among the Russian community, which led to her being able to meet important people such as a Russian grand duke for whom she did some sculpting. He introduced her to film producer Erich Pommer of the UFA studios and also to director Wilhelm Murnau. She told them she had worked at the Moscow Art Theatre and in a few small Russian films, and Pommer gave her a screen test. She was given a leading role in Murnau's *Schloß Vogelöd* (*The Haunted Castle*), which was a success when premiered on 7 April 1921. She was not an overnight star but she had a new name, Olga Tschechowa, though it was still pronounced Chekhova.

UFA was still an expanding studio, having been founded in 1917 under military sponsorship to make propaganda films. Erich Pommer was turning it into the largest studio in Europe, producing films by such great directors as Ernst Lubitsch, Fritz Lang and Wilhelm Murnau. (Lubitsch emigrated to America in 1922 to further his career, not to escape the Nazis, and Murnau did the same in 1926.) Olga had arrived at just the right time and played in more than forty silent films during the 1920s.[236] She learned to speak German well and shook off her Russian accent, enabling her to work in the *Berliner Renaissance-Theater*. Germans affectionately referred to her as *Die Tschechowa*, or even *La Tschechowa*. She never commented on politics, either those of the German Weimar Republic or any of the more extreme parties, or even about the Communist Soviet Union. She saw herself as a 'fellow traveller', but secretly she had agreed to assist Soviet intelligence, having been recruited by her brother Lev.

Lev Knipper had become a composer of operas with a considerable reputation. He had been a White Guard during the civil war and escaped Russia for a time, returning in 1922 when he was recruited by the OGPU (forerunner of the NKVD and later the KGB); his reputation as a composer and conductor allowed him to get in and out of many countries relatively easily. He recruited Olga in Berlin as a 'sleeper' whose contacts in 'high places' might be useful. Her incentive was the provision of exit visas for her mother and daughter – her father had died in January 1924 – and so Lulu, little Olga/ Ada and a niece, Marina, came to live with Olga in Berlin.[237]

Olga Tschechowa made four or five films a year to keep earning reasonable money at a time when inflation was rife. She moved from her apartment at Berchtesgadener Strasse 21 into a much larger one, with fifteen rooms, at Klopstock Strasse 20 in the Tiergarten district of Berlin. After her disastrous marriage to Mikhail Chekhov, she was determined never to have to rely on a man again, and worked so hard she had no time for personal relationships. She worked by day on films at the studio in Babelsberg, then often in the evenings in plays at the *Berliner Renaissance-Theater*, but all the hard work allowed her to commission a very expensive stained glass panel with the Knipper coat of arms on it, and she bought a new Talbot convertible and hired a chauffeur, although she preferred to drive herself. She was in control of her own life.[238]

Her film star status ensured that her plays were well attended by her fans; on 16 March 1924 she wrote to her aunt Olya that 'the theatre is full all of the time', and she found it 'funny that I have become famous here', noting that 'people go to the theatre just to see me and that they believe in me'.[239] In 1927 she had a new fan. Adolf Hitler saw her in *Brennende Grenze* and admired her greatly;[240] he also saw her in the first of the films about Frederick the Great, *Die Mühle von Sanssouci* (*The Mill of Sanssouci*), in which Otto Gebühr made one of his many appearances as Frederick II – later she would make *Der Choral von Leuthen* with him.

She also directed one film, *Der Narr seiner Liebe* (*The Fool of Love*), casting her ex-husband Mikhail Chekhov in a leading role. By this time Mikhail – known as Michael Chekhov to English-speaking audiences – had established his place in stage history, having studied under Russian theatre practitioner Konstantin Stanislavksy and thereafter developing and teaching his own variation of the 'method'. In 1928 he arrived in Berlin to run his own actors' studio aided by Olga, who found him and his second wife Xenia a small apartment near to her own so Ada, then eleven, could visit her father. She also helped him find work in films, leading to their collaboration on *Der Narr seiner Liebe*. In 1930 Olga and Mikhail were cast together in *Troika*, his last film for more than a decade – in 1931 he moved to Paris to found the Chekhov Theatre Company, and established himself as a star of the stage as Hamlet, Malvolio in *As You Like It* and in Strindberg's *Erik XIV*. He took the Chekhov Theatre on tour to New York and in 1938 moved to the United States to start his own school, and to direct and act. He was nominated for an Oscar for his performance as the psychiatrist in Hitchcock's 1945 thriller *Spellbound*, which starred one of Mikhail's students, Gregory Peck. Other famous students of his included Marilyn Monroe, Gary Cooper, Ingrid Bergman, Anthony Quinn, Jack Palance, Yul Brynner and Elia Kazan.

Mikhail was a featured player in MGM's 1944 pro-Russian film *Song of Russia*, which starred Robert Taylor as an American conductor who falls for a Soviet pianist, played by Susan Peters, during a tour of Russia in which happy, healthy Soviet citizens live in bliss until the Nazi invasion. This film would later come under scrutiny from the anti-Communist House Un-American Activities

Committee, which cited *Song of Russia* as one of three noted examples of 'pro-Soviet propaganda films' made in Hollywood, the other two being Warner Brothers' *Mission to Moscow* and RKO's *The North Star*. The blame was laid on the film's two screenwriters, Paul Jarrico and Richard J. Collins, who were subsequently blacklisted.

In 1930 Olga went to America to make the romantic comedy *Love on Command* for Universal; the studio hoped she would become its own Marlene Dietrich or Greta Garbo. Olga quickly learned to enjoy the Hollywood lifestyle, such as the big parties where she met Douglas Fairbanks, Harold Lloyd, Charlie Chaplin and Garbo, but Universal criticised Olga for looking too heavy and critics complained about her Russo-German accent, so she returned to Germany where she was already an undisputed star.

Her daughter Ada also became an actress: aged eighteen she was cast in *Pompadour*, released in 1935, then co-starred with her mother in *Der Favorit der Kaiserin* (*The Favourite of the Empress*) under the name Ada Tschechowa. (Ada's daughter would also become an actress, known as Vera Tschechowa.)

To celebrate Hitler's appointment as Reich Chancellor in January 1933, Goebbels gave a reception at the Propaganda Ministry. A number of Germany's greatest celebrities were invited to add glamour to the proceedings; it was Hitler's desire to be surrounded by famous people. In Hitler's Germany, a curious relationship between culture and politics had evolved, not necessarily out of a true political design but out of Hitler's obsession with his own celebrity cult which, once it had taken root, was carefully cultivated for no real purpose other than to feed his vanity. In his Germany, celebrities, whether they were actors, writers or musicians, could be only one of two things: tremendous status symbols for the regime – that is, those who were compliant – or traitors, if they resisted or were Jewish. Therefore, those who were compliant, regardless of their true motivations – either because they were true Nazis or just eager to maintain a career – were seen as Nazi sympathisers. In time, they would all pay a price, but not as heavy as those who were sent to the extermination camps.

The presence of Hitler's favourite actress Olga Tschechowa was required by order. She attended accompanied by the 69-year-old *grande dame* of German theatre Adele Sandrock, who called Olga 'Mouse' for reasons that were unclear even to Olga. Sandrock had become one of Germany's first film stars with her screen debut in 1911, and by 1933 was one of Germany's most beloved celebrities. Hitler approached Olga and Adele and went into one of his monologues, in which he talked about the *Burgtheater* – where Adele was currently playing – and about how much he admired the plays there except for one in which Jewish actors had been enthusiastically applauded. At this point, Adele cut him off: '*Herr Reichskanzler*, please drop this subject. I don't want to talk about it. But between you and me, I must admit that my best lovers were Jewish.' Hitler was stunned into silence as Adele rose from her chair and said to Olga, 'Mouse, can you take me home, please?'

'Of course, dear Adele,' Olga replied, and bade Hitler and Goebbels, '*Alles Gute, meine Herren*.'[241]

This may or may not be an embellishment, but Olga did certainly meet Hitler for the first time at this event, as she recounted to Colonel Shkurin of SMERSH, the Soviet counter-intelligence organisation: 'When Hitler came to power in 1933 I was invited to a reception given by Propaganda Minister Goebbels where Hitler was also present. I and other actors were introduced to Hitler. He expressed his pleasure at meeting me. Also he expressed his interest in Russian art and in my aunt, Olga Leonardovna Chekhova [Olga 'Olya' Knipper-Chekhova].'[242]

The OGPU, and later the NKVD, hoped Olga's celebrity status would bring her into contact with people in 'high places', and it did. None were higher than Hitler, who now had what he had wanted for so long: to shine brighter than any other star in Germany and leave the hard work to others. His ministers ran the country while he travelled to deliver speeches, receive adulation and generally escape his responsibilities in Berlin.

Hitler's life had become one of indolence, as recalled by Fritz Wiedemann, his personal adjutant:

Hitler normally appeared shortly before lunch, quickly read through the newspaper cuttings of Reich Press Chief Otto Dietrich, and then went into lunch. When Hitler stayed at the Obersalzberg [where the Berghof was built] it was even worse. There he never left his room before two in the afternoon. Then he went into lunch. He spent most afternoons taking a walk. In the evenings, straight after dinner, there were films.'[243]

Otto Dietrich recalled how Hitler's indolence caused governmental chaos:

In the twelve years of his rule in Germany, Hitler produced the biggest confusion in government that has ever existed in a civilised state. I've sometimes secured decisions from him – even ones about important matters – without his ever asking to see the relevant files. He took the view that many things sorted themselves out on their own if one did not interfere.[244]

Hitler saw his responsibility as little more than presenting an image of himself to the public as a confident and strong leader whose orations, when he appeared at the Nuremberg rallies in the 1930s, promised a new and powerful Germany. He told a massed crowd of Hitler Youth:

We want to become one people. And you, my young people, are to become this people. You cannot help but be joined with us. Today, the extended ranks of our movement are marching victoriously through Germany, and I know that you will join these ranks. And we know, before us lies Germany, within us marches Germany, and behind us comes Germany.

That was all he had to do. There were no policies, just powerful speeches given with tremendous Wagnerian gusto that had his audience spellbound, so that they could do nothing else but be joined with him and his Germany.

The image he projected was of an omnipotent leader who prevailed over a system of total order, but in truth the structure of command in Hitler's government was 'very disorganised and rather chaotic', as Ian Kershaw put it: 'a remarkable system, if you can call it a system at all of one where there is no collective government but yet where the head of state himself actually doesn't spend all his time dictating'.[245]

He had finally found the life he had sought – that of an artist who spent much of his time in leisure, doing the least amount of work and enjoying the perks of the job. On the afternoon of 26 July 1933 he arrived in Bayreuth for a concert and stayed for several days. On 29 July he was the guest of honour at a reception given to him by Winifred Wagner. The next morning he laid a wreath at the Master's grave, and in the afternoon left Bayreuth for further undemanding duties he had set himself.

On 12 August he took part in a Richard Wagner festival in Neuschwanstein where, during his speech, he referred to himself as completing the plans of King Ludwig II, who had ruled Bavaria from 1864 until his death in 1886. Ludwig was an eccentric who commissioned the construction of several extravagant castles and palaces; he was also a devoted patron of Richard Wagner, sponsoring the premieres of *Tristan und Isolde*, *Die Meistersinger von Nürnberg* and, through his financial support for the Bayreuth Festival, *Der Ring des Nibelungen*. Without the king's support Wagner would almost certainly not have been able to complete his opera cycle or his final opera, *Parsifal*. It was as if Hitler was claiming credit for the success of the Bayreuth Festival, which in a sense was true, because without continuing financial support from the Nazis the festival might well have closed.

Ludwig told the actress Marie Dahn-Hausmann, 'I wish to remain an eternal enigma to myself and to others.'[246] Hitler was taking his cue from the king, who was revered by Bavarians, although there remains the suspicion that the eccentric Ludwig may have been clinically insane, while some believe he may have suffered from the effects of chloroform used to control his chronic toothache. Hitler disputed any suggestion Ludwig was insane, and yet Hitler himself was hardly the epitome of sanity.

He continued shirking his formal responsibilities, preferring to spend his time going to the opera and seeing movies. Alfred Rosenberg, leader of the party's foreign political office responsible for encouraging links between the new regime and Great Britain, was indignant that Hitler shunned a demonstration he had organised in favour of an ice revue.[247] It was left to Joseph Goebbels to defend his *Führer*'s inexplicable actions: 'What we are constantly endeavouring to bring to bear has become for him a system in world-wide dimensions. His creativity is that of the genuine artist, no matter in what field he may be working.'

CHAPTER TWELVE

THE WILL TO TRIUMPH

In late 1933 Hitler indulged his creative impulses to instigate and design what would become an annual celebration of the anniversary of the failed 1923 putsch in Munich, turning the disaster into a legendary triumph: '9 November 1923 was the most fortunate day of my life.' The annual celebration began with a march of victory through Munich, during which Hitler laid a wreath in memory of the sixteen stormtroopers who were martyred during the failed coup. The procession continued on to two shrines erected on Hitler's order in memory of the martyrs, whose names were read out in a roll of honour. Hitler proclaimed that in that hallowed place the fallen heroes had begun their eternal vigil. The solemn spectacle was captured on film, shot from every angle, the whole event carefully planned with Hitler himself virtually directing it as well as starring. Cinema, Hitler had learned, was the greatest form of communication of the twentieth century, and he had by then learned to control and use it to his best advantage. He had himself filmed solemnly paying his respects alone, in long shot, a solitary figure in magisterial isolation.

Hitler was free to be an artist with the whole of Germany as his canvas, putting little effort into governing Germany. Goebbels too had become free to indulge his creative interests by producing films and, more importantly to him, writing books published without fear of rejection. *Vom Kaiserhof zum Reichskanzlei* (1934) was his account of the seizure of power, lifted straight from his diaries. It was published in English in 1935 as *My Part in Germany's Fight* and sold even better than it had in Germany.[248] Goebbels also published a collection of his speeches in a pamphlet entitled *Revolution of the Germans*, which sold over 10,000 copies in 1934, and a photo-journalism book, *Das Erwachende Berlin* (*Berlin Awakening*), all adding to his now-considerable income as a minister, making him a wealthy man. He rented a lakeside house in Kladow on the Wannsee for himself and Magda, where they often entertained celebrities of film and music. He bought several new cars, and a motorboat in which he travelled the many waterways around Berlin and Potsdam.

The image Joseph and Magda presented of the ideal German marriage was a sham. He was opinionated, she strong willed, and they quarrelled frequently. Nevertheless, on 13 April 1934 Magda gave birth to a girl, Hilde; Goebbels was disappointed that the baby wasn't a boy[249] and complained that family life was making him 'unbearably unfree'.[250] The freedom he desired was to seduce glamorous actresses, but he was stuck in a marriage that was becoming increasingly miserable, and it was a problem he was becoming desperate to solve.

Hitler had a major problem of his own in 1934. The cause of it was Ernst Röhm, who had long wanted his SA, consisting of four million stormtroopers, to destroy the *Reichswehr* – Germany's regular full-time army, which was later renamed the *Wehrmacht* – and stage an armed revolution to seize complete power by force.

‡

On 29 June 1934, Hitler struck the fatal blow to the SA: accompanied by the SS, led by Heinrich Himmler, he arrived at Bad Wiessee, a holiday spa town on Lake Tegern in Bavaria, where he personally arrested Ernst Röhm and other SA leaders.

That night became known as 'the Night of the Long Knives', during which senior SA officers were arrested and shot, including Röhm. The exact number of men killed remains unknown but it is estimated at between 150 and 200. Goebbels's propaganda revealed that Röhm and other SA leaders were homosexual, even though Hitler had known for many years of the sexuality of Röhm and many of his SA officers.

A month after the Night of the Long Knives, President

Hindenburg died. The nation mourned the man who had been little more than a figurehead for some time, and was the last obstacle in Hitler's path. Two days later the *Reichstag* was dissolved, and Hitler became the *Führer* of all Germany. He was where he wanted to be – top of the bill.

At the Nuremberg rally in September 1934, Hitler announced to his party officials that the transfer of power was complete. 'For the next thousand years,' he declared, 'there will be no revolutions in Germany.' Banners and marching columns moved in endless combinations and patterns through the masses. Hitler understood the power of imagery. 'A mass rally is designed to switch off the thinking process,' he declared. 'Only then would the people be ready to accept the magical simplifications before which all resistance crumbles.' Instead of policies he gave the people pageantry and spectacle.

Leni Riefenstahl filmed the rally, and this time he gave her all the cameras she needed – no less than forty. The climax of the rally was the homage to the dead. Huge blocks of people formed the long, straight so-called 'Road of the *Führer*' down which Hitler walked to the memorial, with Himmler and the new SA chief, Viktor Lutze, behind him. Hitler never commemorated life, but he had learned to how celebrate death. He believed in three basic themes which all such ceremonies needed to project: power, order and solemnity. He had learned this from theatre, opera and most especially Wagner. His inspiration for his cult of death was *Götterdämmerung*, and he harboured morbid thoughts of his own *Twilight of the Gods*.

Leni Riefenstahl had all the imagery she needed to create cinematic magic, and the film she created, *Triumph of the Will*, is still considered the twentieth century's most effective propaganda movie. She filmed using high cranes, and shot close-ups of individuals otherwise lost among the thousands of 'extras'. The camera tracked along a line of blond Hitler youth, and adopted unusual camera angles to show the people looking up adoringly to Hitler while he looked down at them with what appeared to be love; in so doing Riefenstahl succeeded in conveying the 'love' between Hitler and the people.

From the opening shots of the clouds above the city, moving to float above the assembling masses below, portraying beauty and majesty and capturing the crucifixion-shaped shadow of Hitler's plane as it passes over the tiny figures marching below – accompanied by Wagner's *Die Meistersinger von Nürnberg* – through to the climax with the giant swastika banner fading into a line of silhouetted men in Nazi Party uniforms marching in formation, *Triumph of the Will* is a visual masterclass in screen imagery, and it captivated and seduced the population who hadn't seen the event in person.

Her images of Hitler turned him into the idol he wanted to be. 'When Hitler was seen in a film, he was always seen as the public wanted to see him,' said Wilhelm Schneider, Hitler's bodyguard. 'He was really quite different. He himself said, "I'm actually the greatest film actor in Germany."'[251] He was also the film's unofficial executive producer, and the overriding theme of the film is the return of Germany as a great power, with Hitler as the German Messiah bringing glory to the nation.

With Riefenstahl's help, Hitler was fulfilling many of his dreams at once: performing, creating an illusion, if not with paint brushes then with the camera, and all the time enjoying the limelight and surrounded by thousands of extras. It was the making of the public Adolf Hitler; it was him as he wished he really was. Nobody was more famous than he. But more than that, he had become the figure of his fantasy, created by Wagner, to be the knight who would save the world, and enhanced all the more by Leni Riefenstahl's brilliant cinematography, editing and sound. He was literally playing out the role he had created for himself, in a production of his own making, and Germany was his stage; music drove him forward as if life had become transformed into an opera in which he was the star, his cohorts his supporting cast and the nation his cast of unlimited extras.

Riefenstahl denied for the rest of her life that *Triumph of the Will* was a propaganda film. Even as late as 1976 she was on television arguing that the film was 'purely a documentary with no influence from the Party'. She later said she hadn't wanted to do it. 'I had only ten days to prepare *Triumph of the Will*. I had given it to another director, Walter Ruttmann. I didn't want to make it. Not because I was against it but I really wanted to act, not direct.'[252]

The German army was unhappy about *Triumph of the Will* because they had played no part in it, so they commissioned Riefenstahl to make *Day of Freedom*. Filmed during manoeuvres, she turned sabre-rattling into an epic, capturing magnificent celluloid images of men, weapons and machinery, using close-ups to look down the barrels of big guns, and filming horsemen against the sun to create mystical silhouettes which John Ford would emulate in his cavalry Westerns.

Leni Riefenstahl was now a Nazi celebrity. She later denied having had anything to do with politics. Actor Bobby Freitag argued:

> How can you be apolitical when you're shaking all the leaders' hands and looking into their eyes? You had to be a believer and act like a believer if you wanted to be involved. Whether she pretended or whether it suited her. It probably did suit her. Once you're in there and have the power, which she did, and are involved, then it's very hard to resist it.[253]

Riefenstahl's friends maintained she was not anti-Semitic and had helped Jews under threat from the SS, such as the family of actress Evelyn Künnecke, whose father had Jewish in-laws. Riefenstahl intervened, asking Hitler to give the Künnecke family special dispensation. He ordered the SS to leave them alone,[254] demonstrating that she had influence with Hitler.

But she was anti-Semitic; either that, or curiously naive. When in 1933 Béla Balázs asked her for what he considered to be his share of the profits from *Das Blaue Licht*, she asked her friend Julius Streicher, the Nuremberg *Gauleiter*, to represent her in the claim against her by 'the Jew Béla Balázs'.

Her influence with leading Nazis, especially with Hitler, began to wear on Goebbels. Their working relationship had begun well, and he had written in his diary, 'She is the only one of all the stars who understands us'; but he saw her as a rival for Hitler's affections.[255] Wilfred von Oven, an advisor to Goebbels, recalled, 'Leni Riefenstahl had a very good relationship with Hitler and she got what she wanted from him.' For instance, she demanded scores of camera operators for the party congress films, but because there were never enough cameramen, production of other films, for which Goebbels was responsible, virtually came to a standstill. 'After that he really hated her,' said von Oven. 'In response, she published the story that he'd put his hand up her skirt.'[256]

Not wanting or needing any conflict in his entourage, Hitler invited them to his villa for a reconciliation meeting. He also invited the press. Goebbels and Riefenstahl had no choice but to set aside their hostilities while they were photographed chatting with Hitler on the veranda and strolling with him through the garden. Watching the footage, it is hard to tell if the smiles are sincere or faked for the camera; Riefenstahl had long been an actress, and Goebbels had learned to perform as well.

With the endless conflicts of the German Republic now history, the German people settled into believing they were happy and at peace, but there was still widespread injustice and persecution of minorities, as well as unemployment and lasting humiliation by foreign powers. Despite what was going on behind the barbed wire of the concentration camps, Goebbels worked hard to promote a popular image. Christmas celebrations in the totalitarian welfare state were stage-managed, and Goebbels was filmed handing out presents to children. At a big Christmas party, Santa announced, 'Now dear Uncle Göring will say a few words,' and dear Uncle Göring did: 'I am very pleased that you've all come along so that we can celebrate Christmas here together. And now my dear children, we should at this time give our *Führer* a thought.' Uncle Göring was the cuddly human face of the Nazi Party, filmed handing out sweets and biscuits to children in public.[257]

The unemployed enjoyed totalitarian welfare, and some were taken on holidays on steamers to Madeira and the Norwegian fjords; or rather, a select chosen few were taken and filmed, while all the rest hoped in vain their turn would come next.

Hitler encouraged large families, despite his obsession with *Lebensraum* – the 'living space' he sought for his ethnic Germans in the territories he intended to seize in eastern Europe. Babies were bred to grow into soldiers; boys and girls were prepared for their roles in the National Socialist state in militarised camps.

Goebbels and his wife Magda played their part by having six children in all: Helga Susanne (born 1 September 1932), Hildegard Traudel (13 April 1934), Helmut Christian (2 October 1935), Holdine Kathrin (19 February 1937), Hedwig Johanna (5 May 1938), and Heidrun Elisabeth (29 October 1940).

It is curious that all the children's names began with 'H'. Some believe this was in tribute to Hitler but Magda's mother, August Behrend, insisted that Magda merely continued a tradition begun by her first husband, Günther Quandt, of naming his children – he had two with his first marriage, Helmut and Herbert, and one with Magda, Harald – after his first wife,[258] but *her* name was Antoine, so Magda's mother's explanation cannot be true. It seems unlikely that the jealous Joseph Goebbels would have allowed his children to be named with an 'H' because Magda's previous husband had decided it should be a tradition. Naming them in honour of Hitler seems the more likely explanation.

Magda and the children became popular features in magazines and newsreels, and letters arrived from all over Germany seeking her advice and often intervention in matters of housing and child custody. Goebbels had little interest in his first son, although he had become exceptionally fond of his eldest daughter, Helga.

There was another Nazi couple whom the people could celebrate. Hermann Göring married Emma Sonnemann, who had been an actress at the National Theatre in Weimar. She became Emmy (changing her name from Emma) Köstlin when she married actor Karl Köstlin in late 1916; they later divorced. She made her film debut relatively late, aged thirty-eight, in *Goethe lebt!* (*Goethe Lived!*) in 1932, and starred in *Guillaume Tell* (*William Tell*) in 1934 with Conrad Veidt. Veidt was a major star of German cinema, and one of the casualties of the anti-Semitic laws governing the arts. He was not Jewish, but his first wife Ilona was, and when he had to fill in the form to ensure he was racially pure in order to continue working in German films, he put his ethnic background down as 'Juden'. He quickly fled Germany in 1933, another refugee in the mass exodus from the German film industry, with his second wife, Felicitas. They settled in England where Veidt starred in the 1934 British film *Jew Suss*. He became a British citizen in 1939 and is best known for his role of Major Strasser in *Casablanca*.

Emmy's marriage to Göring on 10 April 1935 in Berlin Cathedral was a major state affair – a movie star marrying royalty, with the best man being the greatest of all men, Hitler, who, along with Goebbels, could only dream of marrying a major celebrity like Emmy. Göring actually did it. It clearly irritated Goebbels, who, judging the sumptuous event beforehand, noted, 'I must keep myself simple and not allow this pomp-hysteria to disturb me.'[259] Goebbels liked to think himself above all that.

Emmy promptly gave up acting, instead serving as Hitler's hostess at many state functions and assuming the role of First Lady of the Third Reich; this created animosity between herself and Eva Braun, who felt that position belonged to her.

Being married to one of the richest and most powerful men in Europe, Emmy became a bigger celebrity than she ever was as an actress, and received constant public and media attention.[260] Because her husband owned mansions, estates and castles in Austria, Germany and Poland, as well as confiscated art and a share of the wealth stolen from Jews, she enjoyed a lavish lifestyle.

Hitler's own love life was still far from perfect or in any way stable. Eva was a green-eyed lover who became sick with jealousy even when Hitler experienced the mass hysteria that always greeted him. But she was unable to give him up, and when she learned that Hitler had become close with an English girl, 21-year old Unity Valkyrie Mitford, a member of the aristocratic Mitford family (her sister Diana was married to Oswald Mosley, leader of the British Union of Fascists, and Unity herself was a public supporter of Fascism and had come to Germany with the express purpose of meeting Hitler), she was again driven to suicide. On 28 May 1935, she took an overdose of sleeping pills. 'I've decided to take thirty-five of them. This time it must really be a certainty,' she wrote. She was found in time, and Hitler began to pay her more attention again. 'Through her suicide attempts she procured his company,' said Herbert Döhring. 'She was the driving force in their relationship.'[261]

Hitler arranged for the substantial royalties from widely published and popular photographs of him taken by Hoffmann's photo studio to pay for a villa for her in Munich. This income also provided her with a Mercedes, a chauffeur and a maid.

Not all the top Nazis enjoyed the company of glamorous females – Heinrich Himmler shuffled his feet and was gauche and uneasy in female company whether famous or not[262] – but having beautiful film actresses around the leaders of the Reich had become almost a lifestyle. 'All those men – Hitler, Goebbels, Göring, they liked beautiful actresses,' said Wolfgang Preiss. 'They liked to be with movie stars. But only Herman Göring married an actress.' Goebbels didn't stop trying to bed the actresses he helped in their careers. Preiss, like many who worked in films during the Third Reich, was aware that Goebbels had his own 'casting couch' – 'Goebbels, you know, much enjoyed the company of film actresses.' Some certainly slept with Goebbels;[263] Jenny Jugo was one of them.

Jugo was a very beautiful actress who had been starring in films since 1924. Her popularity was considerable, and she had made thirty films by the time Goebbels began running the film industry. She went on to make many more, possibly in part due to her affair with Goebbels, although her popularity had shown no sign of waning. Curd Jürgens thought it wasn't 'a classic case of the star sleeping with the studio head to get the best parts', but that Jugo was a victim of 'sexual coercion'.[264]

Another actress who may have been one of his casting couch conquests was Irene von Meyendorff, who with her parents had fled to Germany from her home town of Tallinn in Estonia follow-ing the October Revolution. As a teenager she became a volunteer film editor at UFA where, as a beautiful nineteen-year-old, she was suddenly given a role in a film in 1935, and began a flourishing career in films and plays. Her sudden film stardom may have had something to do with Joseph Goebbels, of whom she said, '*Ach, der mit seinen Regenwurm!*' ('Oh, him with his little worm!'), suggesting she had experienced his casting couch technique.

Goebbels tried hard to promote himself as the arbiter of culture while at the same time using his position to acquire the sexual favours of glamorous women. He made most of the important decisions about what could and could not be enjoyed by the German people in all areas of the arts, but not all his efforts succeeded. In 1933 he commissioned the *Thingspiel* – a form of outdoor theatre which combined music, speech and movement, performed in Greek-style amphitheatres – intended to be reminiscent of the *Thing*, a meet-ing place of ancient Germanic tribes where the *Volk* gathered. The *Thing* sites were built in natural settings among rocks, trees, lakes, ruins and hills, often in locations of historical or mythical signifi-cance. Some were built in cities, in areas surrounded by trees.

Goebbels was trying to set in motion a range of films and plays about Hitler, and from this quest came Richard Euringer's *Thingspiel Deutsche Passion* (*The German Passion*), which performed to consid-erable success in the summer of 1933 and was hailed as the model of National Socialist drama. In this German passion play, Hitler appears as a resurrected unknown soldier with a crown of thorns on his head, coming into a world ruled by profiteers, stockholders, intellectuals and proletarians because he 'had mercy on the people'. As he faces crucifixion, he gives them the miracle of '*zu Gewehr und Gewerk*' ('Warfare and Workfare') and reconciles the living with the war dead in the great people's community. He ascends into heaven saying, 'It is finished!'[265]

Hundreds of *Thing* sites were planned but only around forty were completed because *Thingspiel* proved only to be a short-lived cult, faltering as early as 1935 and giving Goebbels cause to reflect on the

Nazi penchant for expressing its many ideas and beliefs as 'cults'. Speaking in September to propaganda officials at Nuremberg, he said that he would 'only hope that we will keep words like "cult" or "*Thing*" or "mysticism" out of our linguistic usage for at least ten years.'[266] Some of the sites that survived the Second World War came to be used as venues for classical and rock concerts.

By 1935 Goebbels, having become Hitler's favoured advisor on all major issues, had become a rather isolated figure, feared even by officials of the party.[267] He and Hitler were also very close friends, attending concerts and watching films together. Hitler went on boat trips with Goebbels, and often visited the various homes of Goebbels and Magda; he particularly enjoyed her company, and that of their daughter Helga. However, although Goebbels was constantly astounded by what he considered to be Hitler's mastery of foreign policy, he was personally mortified by the prospect of war, which he saw as an increasing probability.

Outside of enjoying friendships, art and leisure, and whatever sexual gratification he could achieve, Hitler occasionally set his mind to the work of turning Germany into the land he envisaged, and in September 1935, the Nuremberg Laws – *Nürnberger Gesetze* – were ratified at the annual Nazi rally. There was now a clear legal method of defining who was Jewish and who was not. Those with four German grandparents were 'German or kindred blood', while those descended from three or four Jewish grandparents were Jews. A person with one or two Jewish grandparents was a *Mischling*, a crossbreed who was deprived of German citizenship – although legally a *Mischling* was a revocable preliminary Reich citizen who had virtually no rights and was forbidden to marry Germans. Sexual relations were made illegal between Jews and Germans, Jews were prevented from participating in civic life, and Jews could not convert to Christianity.

Actor Gustav Friedrich had initiated a self-help organisation in 1933, called the *Reichsbund christlich-deutscher Staatsbürger nichtar- ischer oder nicht rein arischer Abstammung e. V.* (Reich Federation of Christian German Citizens of Non-Aryan or Not Purely Aryan

Descent). Initially it attracted only 4,000 members,[268] but in October 1934 the name was shortened to the more manageable *Reichsverband der nichtarischen Christen* (Reich Association of Non-Aryan Christians) and in 1935 it elected literary historian Heinrich Spiero, a 'state citizen', as President; as a consequence the federation's journal was improved and the membership rose to 80,000 by 1936 – unsurprisingly, given the precarious legal position all *Mischlinge* were in.[269] The organisation would undergo a further name change, but to no avail as it was soon outlawed by Hitler. A new organisation sprang up in 1937, *Vereinigung 1937 vorläufiger Reichsbürger nicht rein deutschblütiger Abstammung* (1937 Association of Provisional Reich Citizens of Not Purely German-blooded Descent), but Hitler quickly prohibited any 'state citizen' from being a member, which meant Spiero could no longer lead; without him, the organisation faded and dissolved in 1939.

Not long before the Nuremberg Laws were passed in September 1935, Olga Tschechowa somehow came to learn of the details and grew concerned for her daughter Ada, who was at risk of being a *Mischling* – her paternal grandmother, Natalya Golden, had been Jewish. This was a time when she could expect no assistance from Goebbels, so in August, a month before the law was ratified, her sister wrote to Mikhail Chekhov's Aunt Misha to send a 'certain document' which Misha and Mikhail both signed, testifying that the entire Chekhov family was of Russian Orthodox descent. In the document, Mikhail's mother became 'Natalya Galdina',[270] and in this way, Olga Tschechowa's daughter Ada was saved.

At all other times Olga appears to have been at liberty to call upon Goebbels to discuss her 'worries and joys' and 'professional concerns', as he noted in his diary.[271] To him she was always 'a charming Fraulein'.[272] Although she did not frequent the Reich Chancellery or the Berghof, she was at many of the major Nazi receptions, which always aroused a great deal of publicity. The Soviets perceived her to be the 'prima donna of the Nazi film industry'.[273]

CHAPTER THIRTEEN

LEADING LADIES OF
THE THIRD REICH

Now that he had achieved his goal – to be undisputed leader of all Germany – Hitler's thoughts turned to what he perceived to be his destiny as prophesied by Wagner. His euphoria at his triumph put him in the mood for Wagner, and as he listened to the prelude of *Parsifal*, he entered a state of meditation, uttering, 'One can serve God only in the garb of the hero.'[274]

Inspired by Wagner, foreign politics was next on his to-do list – and then war. In violation of the Versailles Treaty, Hitler introduced conscription and began to rearm Germany. On 7 March 1936, he sent his troops into the demilitarised Rhineland.

In the summer of 1936 the Olympic Games were held in Berlin, giving Hitler the chance to play host to the whole world, which suspected him of governing by terror. He presented a pleasing portrait of a peaceful nation in busy contentment, which was so convincing that during the opening ceremony most of the nations, including the French but not the British, joined in the Hitler salute. The whole event was captured on celluloid by Leni Riefenstahl, recording Hitler's arrival into the stadium as if he were entering a giant arena like a Roman emperor, as the masses stood and gave the Nazi salute to the sound of trumpets. Riefenstahl always filmed Hitler's best side – his left – and, as often as possible, in an aura.

She maintained she had no interest in politics, just art – 'I am only interested in what is beautiful,' she said. But Hitler and Goebbels were governing through art and culture, so she was perpetuating that government even if she didn't realise it. In filming the Olympics, she wanted to portray heroes and heroines, regardless of their nationality or colour. It was such a mammoth task that she spent two years editing *Olympia* into a four-hour-long film.

Not all the footage could be used. Hans Ertle, a leading camera operator who became Riefenstahl's lover for a period of time, captured a moment when a woman from the crowd managed to reach Hitler and threw her arms around him and kissed him while he struggled to break free. The SS converged on Ertle in an attempt to confiscate his camera and the offending film, but Riefenstahl stepped in and assured them that they would have the film after she had cut the scene out. The forbidden footage was not seen publicly for many years. Nor was disturbing film Ertle shot of Hitler as he sat watching the swimming, constantly swaying back and forth in his seat, rocking to and fro – an image of a deranged man. Ertle kept the footage and what the audiences of 1936 never saw was eventually revealed in the 'Leni Riefenstahl' episode of the documentary series *Hitler's Women*.[275]

Riefenstahl loved filming athletes in motion – strength and beauty, she called it – and after the games were over she spent weeks filming tiny scenes of athletes to insert into the Olympic footage. Her tracking camera captured a near-naked man running and throwing a javelin; she filmed him to look just like a classical Greek Olympian, a perfect example of strength and beauty, and the perfect Aryan shape. Even if unwitting, she produced a film that served its propaganda purpose. Watching the film upon its release Klaus Bölling, who was a member of the Hitler Youth, and some like-minded friends left the cinema thinking, 'If a nation has heroes like these who won so many gold medals in Berlin in 1936, then we Germans really can't lose the war.'[276]

When Riefenstahl had finally completed the first part of *Olympia* in 1938, it was premiered on Hitler's forty-ninth birthday, her birthday gift to him; he was overwhelmed by it. Goebbels, who had never recovered from Riefenstahl's rejection and their subsequent feud, had to swallow his pride and announce her as a winner at the German film prize ceremony that year for *Olympia*.

It was during the Berlin Olympics that Goebbels met the

woman who would cause the biggest scandal of his life and almost bring down his career. He had made the most of his fame and wealth, and in March 1936 had bought a villa at Inselstrasse 8 in Schwanenwerder, on the outskirts of Berlin. He already had a summer house at Kladow, and before long he would also have a secluded log cabin on the Bogens Lake, near Lanke, where he then built another house in the woodlands there especially for guests; his lake house would become his retreat, where he could entertain artists and people from the world of cinema, theatre and music. It just so happened that film star Lída Baarová was living close to his house in Schwanenwerder.

Lída Baarová, born in Czechoslovakia on 7 September 1914, had studied acting at Prague Conservatory and made her film debut at the age of seventeen in a Czech film, *Obrácení Ferdyše Pištory*. After becoming engaged to German actor Gustav Fröhlich, star of Fritz Lang's *Metropolis* in 1927, she starred with him in several films. She turned down an offer from Hollywood in 1935 and moved in with Fröhlich at Schwanenwerder.

In June 1936 Goebbels met Baarová for the first time[277] and was instantly attracted to her, which isn't surprising as she was a very beautiful young woman. Ironically Goebbels preferred dark-haired, more exotic-looking women, than the blonde Aryan types he promoted in films and propaganda. He pursued Baarová for many months. She wrote in her autobiography *The Sweet Bitterness of My Life*, 'His voice seemed to go straight into me. I felt a light tingling in my back, as if his words were trying to stroke my body.' They met often, and even though it was at the start a platonic relationship, she kept her liaisons with Goebbels a secret from Fröhlich. Most importantly, they were kept secret from the public; Goebbels was the patriarch of the ideal German family, and his image could not risk being sullied.

Hitler too had to maintain his public image – that of a single man dedicated only to the Third Reich in order to make him appealing to women. His female fans were never to know that he had a young mistress. His private life was as stage-managed as his speeches, and he felt it was vital that he maintain his image in the same way Hollywood studios did for their younger stars, whose appeal was bolstered by their carefully crafted unmarried and romantically unattached images. They were forbidden to go on dates that their studios hadn't arranged, and under no circumstances were they to marry without consent from the studios; it was thought their appeal to the fans would only last if they remained 'available'. Hitler believed this was true of himself. His godson Egon Hanfstaengl confirmed, 'He was at pains to conceal his relationship with Eva Braun for the simple reason that German women were not supposed to know that he had formed an attachment. They should all be able to fantasise that one of them could still win him.'[278] Goebbels was behind the propaganda machine that created the illusion of the *Führer* who was married only to his people – and they to him.

The German people had no idea about Braun's relationship with Hitler until after the war, yet in 1939 a story was published in America, in *Time* magazine, that Eva Braun and Hitler were an item; they even predicted that Hitler intended to marry her. It reported, 'Mr Adolf Hitler has at least partly supported Miss Eva Braun for several years, and last spring she hopefully confided to intimates she expected him to marry her within a year.'

In November 1939, pictures of Hitler and Braun sunning themselves on the terrace at Berchtesgaden were published in *Life* magazine, and an article appeared, written by a 'Richard Norburt', who was a source 'inside Germany which we have always found dependable' – he was someone who didn't want his true identity known to Hitler. It read:

> In the closing days of last August the object of his affections – a blond Bavarian girl named Eva Helen Braun – moved into Hitler's official residence in Berlin, the great Chancellery on Wilhelmstrasse. There she occupies the honoured position of typical German Hausfrau in the Hitler ménage, and there she conducts herself as if she were the wife of the Nazi dictator.

Calling Eva 'Evi', the report noted with the flair of a Hollywood gossip columnist, 'Hitler also favours Evi's special Thuringian potato dumplings.'[279] 'Richard Norburt' added:

> When the Nazis finally achieved undisputed power over Germany, one of the first things Hitler did was obtain a house for Evi in a fashionable district in Munich. It was listed in the directory under her own name: 'Wasserburgerstrasse 12; telephone 480844'. The Nazis considered it natural that Evi's years of faithful service should thus be rewarded, and her relationship to Hitler remained undefined.

By 1936, Eva Braun was at Hitler's household at the Berghof near Berchtesgaden whenever he was in residence there. She was never allowed to attend when business or political conversations took place, though Albert Speer recalled that Braun was allowed to be present during visits from old party associates. But when other dignitaries of the Reich, such as Cabinet ministers, appeared at the table, she was 'banished'. Speer recorded that 'Hitler obviously regarded her as socially acceptable only within strict limits.' Speer sometimes kept her company 'in her exile'; he felt sympathy for 'her predicament [and] soon began to feel a liking for this unhappy woman, who was so deeply attached to Hitler'.[280]

Officially she was known as 'Miss Braun', one of several secretaries. She was most unhappy when beautiful actresses were invited to the Berghof, and while he showered attention on them, she was pushed into the shadows.

Cameraman Walter Frentz, who shot much of the film of Hitler we see today, once told Eva as they took a stroll, 'You're the most envied woman in Germany,' to which she replied, 'Mr Frentz, I'm just a prisoner in a golden cage.' She could have set herself free – if she had really wanted to – but she stayed. She wrote, 'Me, the beloved of the greatest man in Germany and on earth.'[281] Speer said, 'Eva Braun will prove a great disappointment to historians.'[282]

She was a keen photographer, and for her birthday in 1936 Hitler gave her a cine camera. She was already an accomplished stills photographer, thanks to Hoffmann, and became enthusiastic about making films. Home movie cameras were new and expensive, but Hitler was keen on the technology, and he knew the potential of mass communication through film.

The public face of Hitler was all that Germany, and indeed the rest of the world, was allowed to know about him. Every private moment, even the occasional off-guard event, was carefully concealed. The *Führer*'s image had become more important to him than his duties, and he disliked appearing in Eva's films because the many masks he wore in public were off. He might have been flattered by the attention of a young woman, but he occasionally admitted that he considered himself too old for her, and in one shot of colour film she took of him, he said to her in a kindly manner, 'What are you filming an old man for? I should be filming you.'[283] Braun's private 16mm home footage revealed a Hitler the world didn't know.

He had a private cinema installed in the basement of the Berghof where he would treat his intimates with the latest films, both from home and abroad. Goebbels had given him a number of Mickey Mouse cartoons as a birthday present.[284] Hitler would watch movies deep into the night; one of his favourites was the 1935 Hollywood movie *The Lives of a Bengal Lancer*, set at the height of the British Empire in India. 'He liked this film', wrote Sir Ivone Kirkpatrick, 'because it depicted a handful of Britons holding a continent in thrall. That was how a superior race must behave and the film was compulsory viewing for the SS.'[285] Herbert Döhring, a member of Hitler's SS bodyguard from 1936 to 1943, watched the film several times along with other members of his SS guard, recalling:

It was certainly his favourite film. He couldn't wait to see it. He would sit down and rub his hands together. 'It's starting, it's starting,' he would say. And he would always talk about it – this huge English empire – how such a relatively small people could establish and manage something like that and keep it in order.[286]

The film reinforced Hitler's belief that the British rule in India was evidence of the superiority of the Aryan race. Wagner was not his sole inspiration; Hollywood also had its influence over him. His life had become increasingly separated from reality and was becoming almost like a film but in real time – had cameras always been present it would have been the first reality show – and he was billed above the title.

‡

Hitler loved films so much that as busy as he was – or pretended to be – he insisted on seeing almost every new film. Alfred Zeisler said that Hitler had a standing order to have every new film, German and foreign, delivered to the Chancellery. The ones he seemed to enjoy the most were the American musical comedy films and crime pictures, although he frequently enjoyed biographical films, especially those of persons involved in wars. *Viva Villa*, about Pancho Villa, gave him great pleasure and he had it shown a number of times. Any film he enjoyed would have to be shown repeatedly.[287] Albert Speer never forgot how Hitler kept all his guests up into the early hours of the morning as he lectured them on whatever film they had just seen.

His love of films was noted even in Hollywood where Cornelius Vanderbilt Jr wrote a tidbit of gossip for *Photoplay* magazine in 1937 called *Der Führer and the Brothers Marx*.

Hitler often goes into the censorship booth with Goering (sic), presumably to watch the latest antics of non-Aryan American actors. I'm told, though I have no proof of this statement, that the Marx Brothers are his favourites; however, his national policy allows him to pass upon only a very few, very dull American pictures. It might interest you to know that five years ago he expelled me from Germany for making a film which showed interiors of concentration camps.[288]

‡

In his private cinema his closest friends also watched Eva's home movies, which she edited herself. Hitler was fascinated with technology, and when he had the advanced technical aspects of the latest 16mm camera explained to him, he said, 'Every German must have one. Every aspect of the nation's growth would be captured.'[289] He may have been the first person ever to envisage a day when every household would have a camera that took moving pictures.

Braun was forbidden from attending the Nuremberg rally in 1936, but Lída Baarová was there, sitting just a short distance from Goebbels, who had been obsessed with her since they first met, inviting her onto his yacht and taking her on long chauffeur-driven trips. He asked her to come to hear him speak at Nuremberg and said that he would touch his face with a white handkerchief during his speech as a sign of his devotion.[290] She suddenly panicked and decided to leave Berlin, but Goebbels sent a messenger to catch up with her at the station, presenting her with roses and his picture. She recalled, 'He was a master of the hunt, whom nobody and nothing could escape.'[291]

By September 1936, Goebbels was deeply in love with Baarová and wrote in his diary, 'A miracle has happened.'[292] She later insisted, 'Yes, Goebbels fell in love with me but I didn't love him.'[293] He phoned her incessantly, and whenever Gustav Fröhlich answered, he gave his name as Herr Müller and left an innocuous message.

Finally, in front of a blazing fire inside his log cabin on the shores of Lake Lanke, he kissed her for the first time; 'I have never in my life been so inflamed with love for a woman,' he wrote.[294] They met whenever he could get away from Magda, usually at his log cabin where he would amuse her with impressions of Hitler. He also confided to her some of his doubts about Nazi ideology.

Towards the end of her life, Lída Baarová insisted that she finally gave in to him out of fear. 'I was afraid of him and what he would do because I kept turning down his offers, although he always behaved charmingly and was always very nice to me.'[295]

Goebbels clearly did not recognise that Baarová's love was not all it seemed. He wanted to be with her, but knew a break from Magda would reveal him to be a fraud in his depiction of being the ideal German husband, which in turn would bring to an end all the wealth and power he had worked so hard for. He might have been a romantic, but he was also a pragmatist. There were many problems in the marriage, and he and Magda came close to separating a number of times, but somehow they always managed to pull back from the brink.

When Goebbels summoned his favourite movie stars, they were expected to drop everything and attend. Personal proximity to the political leaders became a determining factor for the success of film actors, and Goebbels operated an informal system of listings which decided how frequently an actor would be cast. The five categories extended from 'to cast at all costs even without a vacancy' – for Zarah Leander, Lil Dagover and Heinz Rühmann, for instance – to 'casting under no circumstances'. Hitler considered film stars so vital to the image of the National Socialist government, and to him personally, that in 1938 he granted generous tax concessions for prominent film actors and directors; they were allowed to deduct 40 per cent of their income as professional expenses.

The price those in the top category paid was their presence whenever and wherever it was required. Olga Tschechowa, who was named *Staatsschauspielerin* (State Actress) in 1935, was more concerned with finishing the day's filming than being at a Nazi event. One morning she received an invitation to attend one of Goebbels's numerous receptions that very evening, and she decided to ignore it. But her director persuaded her that the studio and all who worked there could not afford for her to snub Goebbels, on whom they all depended for their careers.

She left the studio earlier than the usual 7 p.m. that day. A car from the propaganda ministry was waiting to take her straight to the reception in Wilhelmstrasse. En route she demanded that the driver stop to allow her to buy a rose to brighten her dress;

German film star Ferdinand Marian had a secret Jewish daughter from his first wife, and he hid a Jew in his home; to protect himself he agreed to play the immoral and untrustworthy Joseph Oppenheimer in *Jud Süß*.

LEFT Classical Shakespearean actor Werner Krauß, famous for playing grotesque stereotypical Jewish characters such as Rabbi Loew in the film *Jud Süß*, was a dedicated Nazi, personally appointed by Hitler to be his cultural ambassador.

RIGHT Joachim Gottschalk, the romantic leading star, had a Jewish wife and son; when Goebbels ordered his family be sent to a concentration camp, Gottschalk and his family killed themselves.

Actress and singer Renate Müller fell or was pushed from a third-storey window of a hotel in Berlin. Her death remains a Monroe-type mystery as the suspicion remains that she may have been silenced to protect one of Hitler's most perverted secrets.

Lída Baarová, seen here with Raoul Schránil in *Za tichych noci* (*In the Still of Night*), was Goebbels's mistress, causing a scandal that threatened to engulf Hitler's regime.

Hans Albers, seen here as the eccentric and colourful *Münchhausen*, sacrificed his own happiness to save his Jewish girlfriend by allowing her to marry a Norwegian and escape to Switzerland.

Lil Dagover was one of Hitler's favourite movie stars and among the few on an elite list Goebbels drew up which UFA studios was ordered to 'cast at all costs'.

RIENZI

5 ter Aufzug

Rienzi: Allmächt'ger Vater, blick' herab,
Hör' mich im Staube zu Dir fleh'n!

Text mit Genehmigung von Adolph Fürstner, Berlin.

ABOVE The Bayreuth *Festspielhaus*, designed specifically by Wagner for the performance of his own operas, was the temple where Hitler worshipped his 'god', and became Hitler's control centre for his aggressive policies.

LEFT Wagner's *Rienzi* told the story of the white knight who became the people's saviour. Hitler declared that it was 'in that hour', when he saw the opera for the first time, that he received his personal revelation to become the saviour of Germany.

ABOVE LEFT Swedish actress and singer Zarah Leander found fame and fortune as one of Germany's biggest movie stars and was a personal favourite of Hitler, who remained blissfully unaware that she was a Soviet sleeper agent.

ABOVE RIGHT Hungarian born Marika Rökk found fame in a series of filmed operettas at UFA while funnelling information to Soviet intelligence.

LEFT An embodiment of Aryan purity, Swedish actress Kristina Söderbaum became one of the highest paid stars of German cinema. She said that her part in *Jud Süß*, directed by her husband Veit Harlan, ruined her life.

The Führer stands isolated in glory, carefully framed by one of his bodyguards and the mystical Blood Banner.

Maintaining the illusion that Hitler worked harder than anyone else in Germany, the Führer is seen presiding over the Reich Chancellery. In reality he was hardly there, leaving his ministers to run the country while he pursued a life of leisure and art.

Hitler doing what he did best – delivering mesmerising speeches and standing in splendid isolation.

ABOVE Hitler on tour, about to be driven to meet his next audience and still wearing his flying hat, having just arrived by aeroplane; his tour carried the slogan 'Hitler Over Germany'.

LEFT A photo-op at Obersalzberg, one of Hitler's favourite retreats.

ABOVE Olga Tschechowa seated next to Hitler, her most ardent fan, at a lavish garden party given by Joachim von Ribbentrop for the diplomatic corps in May 1939.

BELOW From the left: Frau Emmy Göring, one-time actress; Frau Ley; Contessa Attolico, wife of the Italian ambassador; and head of the German Labour Front Robert Ley.

when she arrived at the reception, she received a curt greeting from Magda Goebbels: 'So late, Frau Tschechowa.'[296]

The purpose of the reception was for Hitler to talk about his expectations of the arts, and he harked back to his experiences as a young painter. When he spoke privately to Olga, talking about her film *Burning Frontiers*, 'Hitler flooded me with compliments,' she recalled, impressed that he made an effort to be charming. He displayed an 'Austrian courtesy' while Goebbels got by on his 'polished intellect' and a sunray lamp.[297]

Nothing was more important to Hitler than being in the company of famous women – Zarah Leander, Leni Riefenstahl, Olga Tschechowa were just a few – and yet he was always the centre of attention. He didn't speak of politics, but of art; not of conquest, but of the cinema; and while it all seemed innocent if egotistical, there was a darker and seamier side to Hitler's 'Austrian courtesy' that few would come to know about or, if they did, admit to.

On 19 December 1936 Olga Tschechowa surprised everyone, including her family, by getting married again. She had fallen for a Belgian businessman, 41-year-old Marcel Robyns. Perhaps at the age of thirty-nine, Olga had suddenly begun to feel a gap in her life now that she had all she could want from being a film star. It had been a whirlwind romance and she had been swept off her feet.

Fearing the marriage would strip her of her prized German nationality, a few weeks before the wedding she sought help from Joseph Goebbels, asking if he would to talk to Hitler about it. 'I will do it gladly,' Goebbels wrote in his diary. 'She is a charming woman.' Consequently, the day before the wedding, Hitler invited her to a small breakfast reception in the Reich Chancellery where he gave his permission for her to retain her German nationality.[298] There could be only two reasons why Olga wanted to retain her German citizenship: to maintain her position as a *Staatsschauspielerin*, which was now essential to her career, and to remain a 'sleeper' agent; her heart, after all, was still in Russia, not Germany, and so were many of her family.

After the wedding ceremony at the register office in Berlin-Charlottenburg, Olga and Robyns went to Brussels to settle into his apartment on the Avenue des Nations, where she took on the subsidiary role of hostess for her husband's boring business dinners. She quickly became despondent, and when her sister Ada came to visit in January 1937, she chose to return with her to Berlin for a couple of weeks' respite. She spent as long as she could there, even doing a play, *Der Blaufuchs* (*The Blue Fox*). Robyns came to see it and basked in her glory, but behind his back, her family had nicknamed him 'Herr Tschechowa'. His mother, daughter and a governess were brought with him to Berlin, and moved into the apartment that Olga had provided for her own mother, daughter and sister, at Kaiserdamm 74. Sister Ada wrote to Aunt Olya in Moscow, 'Our Belgians have turned the whole household upside down. It's a mystery to me why Olga married him, as she has to pay for everything with her own money.'[299] Before long, an exasperated Olga sent Robyns back to Brussels while she remained in Berlin. She divorced him in 1938, and when Goebbels heard the news, he wrote, 'Well, that's Life!'[300]

Almost immediately, she embarked on an affair with actor Carl Raddatz, with whom she was filming *Befreite Hände* (*Freed Hands*); he was fifteen years younger than she. He was amusing and a regular visitor to her new house at Gross Glienecke, where she found peace away from the family apartment. It was a simple, single-storey wooden house, and easy to drive to from Babelsberg.[301]

But for all her private bliss, she remained at the beck and call of Hitler and Goebbels. For Olga Tschechowa, and other leading women of the Third Reich, celebrity offered not just the usual trappings of fame but the additional burden of being part of an increasingly menacing political machine which would include murder in its cultural revolution.

CHAPTER FOURTEEN

THE SINGING SPY

Hitler was a big fan of Marlene Dietrich. Herbert Döhring, Hitler's caretaker, recalled, 'We saw a lot of American and English films which weren't shown publicly. He always praised Marlene Dietrich for her work as an actress. But he called her a hyena. He didn't like her because she left Germany.' Nevertheless, Hitler told those around him, 'No one's as good as her', and was convinced that she had been talked out of returning to Germany by Hollywood.[302]

To counteract what he saw as an American conspiracy, he tasked Joseph Goebbels with getting her back to Germany in what would be a huge propaganda coup. In November 1937 she returned to Europe, but got no closer to Germany than Austria. En route she stopped in Paris, where a Nazi envoy met her to persuade her to come to Germany to meet with Goebbels. 'That would be a big win for us,' Goebbels wrote in his diary. Concerned for her mother still in Berlin, Dietrich gave a diplomatic response, writing to Goebbels, 'Unfortunately meeting not possible at present because of long term contracts.' Receiving this missive, Goebbels wrote in his diary on 12 November, 'Marlene Dietrich can perform in Berlin only in a year's time but she is firmly committed to Germany.'[303]

Goebbels continued to make overtures to her, but she saw through his intentions to make propaganda out of her. She was not merely an opportunist taking advantage of what Hollywood could do for her; she wanted to work in Germany, but, unlike others who remained to become a part of the Third Reich's film industry, she remained in self-imposed exile. 'She hated the Hitler regime,' said actress Brigitte Mira. 'She was smarter than a lot of others.'[304]

Dietrich's continued presence in Hollywood and Hitler's

admiration for her aroused suspicions that she was a German spy, and the FBI questioned her. She told them that she thought Hitler was 'not a normal human being', describing his 'evident feeling' for her as 'a tick for me'. Convinced that she admired Hitler in return and was pretending to oppose the regime so she could spy for him, FBI boss J. Edgar Hoover had his agents compile a huge file on her; the file remained open until 1967 when it was finally concluded that she had not been a Nazi sympathiser. She took out American citizenship in 1937 or 1939 (sources differ on the year), sending a clear message to Hitler, 'so there are no misunderstandings'.[305]

UFA wanted a replacement for Marlene Dietrich, and Zarah Leander from Sweden was their choice. Born Sara Stina Hedberg on 15 March 1907 in Karlstad, she had studied both piano and violin as a small child, and sang on stage for the first time at the age of six. Despite her talents, she had no intention of becoming a professional musician: she wanted to be a star dancer.[306]

From 1922 to 1924 she lived and worked as a secretary in Riga in Latvia, where she learned German and met Nils Leander, whom she married in 1926; they had two children. In 1927 she became a showgirl, and in 1929 was engaged by the entertainer and producer Ernest Rolf to tour in cabaret; she sang 'Vill ni se en stjärna?' (Do You Want to See a Star?) which in time became her signature tune. In 1930 she starred in cabaret in Stockholm and made her first records, including a cover of Dietrich's 'Falling in Love Again'. She had a deep throaty voice but was arguably a much better singer than Dietrich. She appeared in two films in 1931, mainly just singing, and had her breakthrough on stage as Hanna Glavari in *The Merry Widow* in 1931, by which time she had divorced Nils Leander.

She continued to build her career, singing on stage, making films in Scandinavia, and performing with the Swedish revue artist-producer-songwriter Karl Gerhard, who was a prominent anti-Nazi, and also pro-Communist and a regular visitor to Moscow. Covert reports by Soviet agents went from Germany to Russia through neutral Sweden; behind the secret traffic were Zoya Rybkin and her husband Boris Rybkin, who both worked for the NKVD out of the Soviet embassy in Stockholm. Their Swedish contacts included Karl Gerhard, whose popularity in Moscow opened all kinds of doors for him.[307]

He introduced Leander to left-wing groups and in 1934 wrote her a song, 'I skuggan av en stövel' (In the Shadow of a Boot), which condemned the Nazi persecution of the Jews. She became the voice of opposition to Hitler, although this might not have been her actual intention according to Finnish journalist and historian Carl-Adam Nykop, who said, 'She sang, she always said, "because it's my job. They give me the text and I sing the text as best I could."'[308]

Whatever her motivations, 'I skuggan av en stövel' was immensely popular in Sweden, especially among the anti-Nazis to whom it appeared that she had taken sides against Hitler. She received offers from Hollywood, but as a mother of two school-age children she ruled out moving to America because, she said, she feared the consequences of bringing the children with her such a great distance and subsequently finding she was out of work. It was a most unusual attitude for someone so ambitious, suggesting she actually valued her family life above career. Despite the political situation, Austria and Germany were much closer geographically, and Leander was already well versed in German, so she went to Vienna where in 1936 she was a sensation in the world premiere of *Axel an der Himmelstür* (*Axel at Heaven's Door*), a parody on Hollywood in which she played a star not unlike Marlene Dietrich or Greta Garbo.

She starred in an Austrian film in 1937, *Premiere*, which was popular in Germany, and very quickly UFA offered her a contract. UFA was as good as most Hollywood studios, and she realised that this could be the way for her to achieve the stardom she had worked so hard for, but she turned down the offer because she didn't want to leave Sweden. There were also offers from Britain, and she was screen-tested singing in English. She decided to make the move to Germany after all, and signed with UFA. It was assumed by many in Sweden that she was only going to make one or two films, and then come home.

Leander quickly realised how badly UFA needed her, and

demanded and received a higher fee than was normal. 'She came from Sweden to make films in Germany. She wanted to be a star, and Germany had very few stars,' recalled actor Wolfgang Preiss.[309] She would earn 200,000 Reichsmarks over two years – a German worker earned barely 2,000 marks a year. Half her fee was paid in Swedish crowns. She was suddenly the highest-paid film star in Germany, earning more than Hans Albers, Germany's biggest male star. In the opinion of actor Will Quadflieg, 'She came [to Germany] from Sweden to earn money – she did it very cleverly and very well.'[310]

She insisted she had no interest in politics and went to Germany for one reason only – to work, make money and be a star. But Germany at that time asked much more of any artist than just turning up on time and getting the work done: their terms meant becoming a Nazi sympathiser, or in other words, to look away from what was really happening. To be a star in Hitler's Germany you had to fuel Goebbels's propaganda machine, which had only one aim – to promote Nazism, which in essence meant to promote Hitler.

Because of her song 'I skuggan av en stövel', Goebbels considered Leander an 'enemy of Germany', and he criticised her in his diary: 'I think this woman is very overrated. I wish there were no Swedes.' He seemed particularly suspicious of her, but the German people disagreed with him and took her to their hearts; her first German film, *Zu neuen Ufern* (*To New Shores*) was a huge success in 1937.

She was a new kind of star in Germany. 'She was quite different from the "ideal German woman",' observed Wolfgang Preiss:

Zarah had curves and dark brown hair, and for the men she was something fresh and different, and for the women she was someone who had curves which grew larger quite quickly. She was not a sexy woman, but she had great charm and a lovely face, and that appealed to many men. She was a good actress – not great. She had a wonderful presence on screen. She was herself on screen. That's why she was a star.[311]

Being different to the usual Aryan type of actress was in her favour; German women were expected to be faithful mothers-in-waiting, and Goebbels insisted that vamps be played only by foreigners. Zarah Leander fitted the bill of the German vamp. She also had a good singing voice, with a low, appealing husky tone to it. She quickly became Germany's biggest star, and Marlene Dietrich was forgotten. Actress Ilse Werner recalled of Leander, 'When she joined UFA she was groomed as a star. She had people around her who just looked after her.'[312]

UFA had the same kind of control over its stars as the big Hollywood studios had over theirs. When she was sent on a visit to Holland, she was given a list by the studio of what she was to wear – dresses, hats, shoes, jewellery, hairstyles – and they told her what to say. Zarah said to them, 'I say what I like, don't I?' They informed her she was to say only what *they* wanted her to say. It had nothing to do with Nazism; UFA was Hollywood on the Rhine. But she quickly discovered that becoming a UFA 'diva' had its advantages and she always had the best table, often in a separate room, in the best restaurants, and when she took her two children shopping at the *Kaufhaus des Westens* store in Berlin, the department store was closed to the public just so she could shop in privacy.[313]

She met Goebbels for the first time at a party, where he said to her, 'Isn't Zarah a Jewish name?'

She replied, 'Yes, but what about Joseph? Isn't that a Jewish name?'

He was stunned. Then he laughed and said, 'That was a good answer.'

He accepted that Germany now had a new star, and he courted her presence whenever the opportunity arose simply because she was an attractive and famous woman. But he was not an enthusiastic fan as Hitler was. 'She was one of Hitler's favourites,' said Preiss. 'He spoke of his admiration for her.'[314] Herbert Döhring, Hitler's caretaker, recalled, 'Hitler called her a world-class actress. He was a passionate admirer of her many films. I remember him praising her in front of the whole audience. He was enthusiastic.'[315]

Hitler coaxed his dog Blondi to impress and entertain his inner circle of friends, secretaries and officers with her 'singing', telling her, 'Sing lower, Blondi, sing like Zarah Leander!' Blondi howled like a wolf.[316] But despite his adoration of Leander, Hitler refused to grant her the honorary title of *Staatsschauspielerin* – State Actress. She said she was obliged to dine with him at least once, and because he was short and she tall, he didn't approach her until she was seated.[317] Neither spoke about politics; their main topic of conversation was his hairstyle, and she noted how he kept sweeping his fringe off his forehead.

The Soviet diplomat Valentin Berezhkov, who worked as an interpreter for Vyacheslav Molotov at negotiations with the Nazi leaders in 1940, said that at each diplomatic event he attended, Zarah Leander was always at the *Führer*'s side.[318] This would seem an exaggeration as Hitler would hardly have had Leander at his side at *every* important diplomatic meeting, but it does suggest that Leander met Hitler more often than she would later admit. She was adored and feted by a number of Nazi leaders. Rudolf Hess listened obsessively to her records, and Hermann Göring tried to seduce her in Swedish.[319]

She made one hit film after another, and she was also enormously popular in France where she dubbed her own films into French. 'They wrote films for her,' recalled Preiss. 'They were not pictures about real life.'[320] Her films were sentimental melodramas with emotional songs that sold on records all over Europe. She became such a huge star that whenever she was driven to public events such as a premiere, she was always flanked by policemen on motorcycles to protect her from adoring fans who packed the streets, clamouring for her. Every day after filming, she returned to her house to be greeted by newspaper photographers. She was in the limelight wherever she went, whatever she did, but she didn't allow success to go to her head. 'She was pleasant to her co-stars,' said Wolfgang Preiss. 'She liked to drink and smoke and could be a lot of fun. But she knew she was the star.'[321]

A huge star like her was an important propaganda tool. 'Goebbels knew that, and he had her do a lot of things for the Third Reich.'[322] She was happy to be filmed collecting for the winter relief fund.

In the opinion of Ingrid Segerstedt-Wiberg, who served in the Swedish resistance, 'She didn't hesitate to be used.'[323]

Leander gave the strong impression of being a supporter of Hitler and his regime. 'I would say she was a Nazi sympathiser,' said Preiss.

> She came to Germany knowing what she must do, and she did it very well and it was because the Third Reich allowed her to be what she wanted to be. She had so many opportunities in her work, in her style of life, and she did it with Goebbels's blessing and support.[324]

She became a regular guest of Goebbels, who was, after all, her boss, and she seemed fascinated by him, saying he 'was an extremely interesting man'.[325] She found him intelligent and cultured, and he also made her laugh. 'One of the reasons Zarah liked Goebbels was because he had a sense of humour,' said Preiss:

> He was amusing and witty and Zarah didn't object to that. He didn't care for her when she first came to Germany. But when he saw how popular she was, he changed his mind about her. She met Goebbels many times. She was invited to his soirees. Clearly he wanted more from her, but she called him the little man with the limp and wanted nothing to do with him personally, but she needed his power.[326]

She maintained, however, 'Whatever else [Goebbels] did is none of my business.'[327] She turned a blind eye to what Goebbels and Hitler and the whole Nazi regime were doing.

Many Swedes were appalled by her fraternising with Adolf Hitler and Joseph Goebbels, seeing her as 'going over to the other side'[328] and branding her a Nazi. They believed her only motivation for going to Germany was to become a star and make a lot of money, not knowing she had an ulterior motive. Probably from the time she met Karl Gerhard she had become a member of, or sympathised with, the Swedish Communist Party.[329] The Soviets believed Zarah would be an ideal person to put in the midst of the Nazi hierarchy; it was well known to the Russians that Hitler and Goebbels and their Nazi cult of celebrity welcomed the most famous, and especially the most beautiful, celebrities.

Leander was recruited by NKVD either before going to Germany or during her early years there. She was given the code-name Rose-Marie, becoming a courier for the Russians because she was free to travel between Berlin and Stockholm. This might well have been what finally prompted Leander to accept the UFA contract and settle in Germany. 'Leander helped us build a picture of the situation throughout northern Europe and of the various British, American and German interests in the region,' said Pavel Sudoplatov, a former head of the NKVD. Leander's party card is said to be in the KGB archives.[330]

She may have been a contact in Berlin for assassin Igor Miklashevsky, whose mission to kill Hitler never happened, but overall she was little more than a regular courier. During her frequent trips between Stockholm and Berlin she was often invited to the German embassy, where she socialised with the ambassador and his senior guests from Germany, who enjoyed hearing the news from Germany's film world while they carelessly told her of the latest gossip in political circles.

In private, she preferred the company of fellow actors and singers to politicians, and each Sunday she invited several of her colleagues to lunch, including Willy Birgel and Heinz Rühmann, whom she entertained with her imitation of Goebbels.[331]

Actors such as these may well have enjoyed a mutual disrespect for their Nazi leaders and literal employers, but they also enjoyed flourishing careers under the totalitarian state. Willy Birgel was one of Germany's biggest movie stars and one of Goebbels's favourite actors who, since his acting career began before the First World War, had made a number of high-profile films under the National Socialist regime that promoted Nazi ideology. Goebbels named him *Staatsschauspieler* in 1937.

Heinz Rühmann was a highly popular comedy actor and singer throughout the 1930s. He had a Jewish wife, Maria Bernheim, and refused to speak openly about politics. When he divorced his wife in 1938, critics of the state accused him of merely securing his career; Goebbels and Hitler welcomed him to the fold and named him *Staatsschauspieler*. But Rühmann had remained married to his first wife through the first six years of Nazi rule, and his marriage broke down for personal reasons, although after the war the couple admitted on German television that state-sponsored anti-Semitism caused the terminal blow to their marriage. Bernheim became involved with a Swedish actor during the final stage of her relationship with Rühmann, and married him soon after their divorce, leaving Germany to settle with him in Stockholm shortly before the outbreak of war.[332] However, it transpired that Rühmann had actually approved of his wife's extramarital affair and subsequent remarriage to a Swede, and had even instigated it so as to save her life. 'When Heinz Rühmann was married to a Jew, he saved her life by divorcing her so she could marry a Swedish husband and move to Sweden before the real hell broke out,' said Curd Jürgens.[333]

Rühmann remarried quickly, to a woman who had a Jewish grandfather, and although this caused him some difficulty with Nazi cultural leaders, he still refused to speak openly against the state. Perhaps because of Rühmann's important position in popular German culture, Goebbels overlooked the fact that his second wife had a Jewish background.

Hitler's strict laws governing anti-Semitism, and Goebbels's ways of persuading stars to cooperate fully with his own aims, formed a wave of terror that would sweep through the otherwise privileged world of celebrities.

CHAPTER FIFTEEN

THE DEPTHS OF HELL

Hitler felt his most important act as Chancellor was to show his Third Reich as a modern industrial state to its foreign visitors; indeed in many areas it led the world, such as its development of airships. Yet Hitler encouraged outdated and mythical elements to Germanic life that were rooted in lore and culture, such as the glorification of blood, soil and farm life, and the revival of the ancient Germanic drama played as open-air theatre. He also practised the Cult of the Blood Banner; Hitler passed along endless rows of flags carrying the sacred *Blutfahne* flag, which was said to have been carried by the fallen Nazis during the Munich Putsch, and from which mystic power flowed into all the banners and flags it touched.

His more essential duties as Chancellor were not his priority. He was lazy but gave the illusion of being busy. He was seldom in Berlin to conduct business but travelled to give speeches; he ensured he was always in demand. He moved from one theatrical stage to another, and the audience was always guaranteed. Workers were fed with the myth of their *Führer*'s years of toil and hardship. He was introduced onto each stage as 'The greatest worker of the party, Adolf Hitler', and he repeatedly told the people, as if it was one of his greatest hits, 'Germany is before us. Germany marches within us and Germany is behind us.' He never told them anything other than rhetoric; his whole act was built upon favourite sound bites, which were favourites like hit songs that the people expected to hear over and over. But he never gave a speech that had the eternal ring of a Gettysburg Address.

After each tour Hitler grew vague and apathetic, lost in the fantasy of his youth of living in style and having to do little to maintain it all. 'A single stroke of genius', he would say, 'is more valuable than a lifetime of uninspired drudgery.'

He rarely stayed in one place for any length of time but he frequently stayed at Bayreuth, which had become a Nazi stronghold. A Jewish resident, Pinchas Joeli, recalled, 'I stood in front of the house in Richard-Wagner-Strasse and a unit of SA men marched past. They sang a song. "When Jewish blood spurts from the knife, things are going well.""[334]

The citizens of Bayreuth were proud of their opera house, which Hitler elevated to a place of worship and where he held Nazi conferences which always began with music from *Rienzi*.[335] This was the model for the spectacle which he adapted to his political career but on a grander scale. The parade at the Day of German Art in Munich in 1938, celebrating 2,000 years of German culture, exemplified Hitler's penchant for the grand operatic spectacle combined with what was supposedly a glimpse into Germany's past: knights on horseback, massive flags, floats showcasing the *Hoheitsadler* – the state symbol of the eagle and swastika – all representing the chosen German people. This was Hitler's version of a German past that never existed, conjured from his own boundless delusions. He even planned to invent a new religion based on vegetarianism which he believed would supplant Christianity.[336]

For the Nazis, art and abuse merged into one, never more so than inside the concentration camps where the emaciated forced labourers worked to the sounds of Wagner arias. In Hitler's version of German culture, art lost its virtue.

Whenever he appeared at the Bayreuth Festival, the crowds came to cheer, salute and adore him, turning it into a Hitler Festival. '*Führer*, show us your good will,' they cried. 'Come now to the window sill.' He appeared at the window to tumultuous acclaim. The crowds had no idea that the *Festspielhaus* had become Hitler's control centre for his aggressive policy where, in 1936, he had made the decision to send German soldiers to the Spanish Civil War.[337]

A few watched anxiously. They were the Jews of Bayreuth. Brigitte Pöhner recalled her father watching 'that man with the raised hand' and 'the roaring crowd', then saying softly to his family, 'We'd better leave.'[338]

Winifred Wagner basked in the limelight as hostess of Hitler's patronage. She extended a building her husband had used and called it 'the *Führer's* annexe'. There Hitler received guests including Unity Mitford and her sister Diana Mosley. Winifred's family became his own substitute family. Betti Weiss, Winifred's foster daughter, recalled that when Hitler visited, 'children had to be quiet at the table. But for me it was like a rich uncle visiting from America.'[339]

After each performance in the *Festspielhaus*, Hitler had the family gather around the fireplace in his annexe for a ritual that never changed. 'No matter how hot it was, the fire had to be lit,' Winifred recalled, 'and he sat beside it, poking at the fire for hours. He enjoyed that immensely.'[340] Fire had a special significance for Hitler: it was how the Twilight of the Gods would happen, and as he gazed into the flames, he must have imagined how it would be if the whole world was engulfed in an inferno; the great fire was coming, and he knew it.

He delivered endless monologues on his favourite subjects: Wagner, vegetarian food, dogs and history. Winifred was always the first to go to bed while her sons remained with Uncle Wolf to stay up till after midnight to hear of his amazing plans that would follow the final victory. After the world was conquered, Wieland would run all the theatres in the West, and Wolfgang the theatres in the East. Hitler had become their substitute father, and he paid Wieland extra pocket money for taking exclusive photos of him.

Wolfgang was forced to join the *Jungvolk* – the Hitler Youth – but quickly left 'because of the way they behaved'. He told Hitler that their behaviour was 'terrible', and recalled, 'He said he'd have done the same thing.'[341] Hitler's reply to Wolfgang Wagner indicates a rare moment where Hitler did not wholly believe in his own doctrines, where reality fleetingly broke through his delusions. But aside from these scarce instances, he was bent on fulfilling his destiny, even to the point when he would envisage bringing in the

Twilight of the Gods, which he saw like a vision in the flames of the fireplace in the *Führer's* annexe.

The gods resided in Bayreuth, which had become such a sacred place to Hitler, and anyone of consequence in the Third Reich had to go to the Festival every year. It was forbidden not to adore Wagner.

Hitler preferred to hold ceremonies at night, with organised torchlight processions giving the proceedings a mystical glow. A state visit by Benito Mussolini, Italy's Fascist dictator, ended with a nocturnal rally in the stadium in Berlin. Mussolini was treated to a giant rotating swastika created by a mass of people holding aloft flaming torches. The Fascist cult of fire was a portent of the fire that would consume the world. Hitler was enthralled by the mystical spectacle he had created, and so completely seduced by the adulation surrounding him that he approved of having his face recreated by fireworks.

The cinematic quality of the nocturnal event was ideal for the movie cameras, which captured it all for the German people to marvel at. Standing in a sort of glorified glow created by powerful arc lights, and filmed in long shot by a camera slowly tracking past – a cinematic technique very common today – Hitler announced:

> To you it appears puzzling and mysterious what it is that has brought these hundreds of thousands of people together, what it is that can be endured in adversity, suffering and privation. The order did not come from an earthly power. God gave us the order – God, who created our nation.

Whenever he entertained foreign visitors, he had to pull himself out of his indolence and treat them to a wordy explanation of his pet projects. He was a master of the monologue and would not be interrupted by anyone. Among his most passionate of endeavours was the rebuilding of numerous cities, and able now to indulge himself in the design of anything he wanted regardless of the true opinions of anyone else, he worked with Albert Speer and other architects on these grandiose ideas, often producing his own sketches. 'If I hadn't become involved in politics, I would have been one of Germany's finest architects,' he declared.

Berlin was to be rebuilt, which meant the old Berlin would have to be razed. In his new planned capital, 30,000 square yards were set aside for the Riefenstahl Studios, Hitler's gift to Leni Riefenstahl. But that project, like most of the others, never got beyond the planning stage. One that was completed, however, was the new chancellery, designed by Albert Speer and built in nine months. It became a monumental folly. Hitler's study was seldom used, and no Cabinet meeting was ever held in the Cabinet room.

On 12 March 1938, Hitler and his forces crossed the border into his birthplace of Spital in Austria as his long-planned *Anschluss* was put into operation. Austria was now a part of Germany, the first act in a programme of expansion which was the fulfilment of an old dream of the German nation that now rejoiced at the news. He entered Vienna, the city that had seen his early failures and now gave him a hero's welcome. From the balcony of the Imperial Palace he announced, 'As *Führer* and Chancellor of the German nation and Reich, I hereby make the historic announcement that my native country is now a part of the German Reich.'

As the German army was marching into Vienna, the Austrian-Jewish cabaret and film star Fritz Grünbaum was appearing in the play *Simplicissimus* with his long-time collaborator Karl Farkas. For several years Grünbaum had commuted between Berlin, where he made films and wrote scripts as well as composing popular songs, and Vienna, where he starred in cabarets, which, after the Nazi takeover of Germany in 1933, had become more political.

With the arrival of the Nazis in Austria, both Grünbaum and Farkas were banned from continuing their play under Nazi anti-Semitic laws. The next day, Grünbaum tried to flee to Czechoslovakia, but he and his wife, Lilli Herzl, were turned back at the border. Karl Farkas was able to escape from Austria with his wife, Annie Hän, and they made their way to Paris and eventually New York.

Grünbaum and Lilli had to go into hiding in Vienna, but were eventually betrayed and transported to Dachau. They were later taken to Buchenwald, then returned to Dachau where Fritz put on a New Year's show for his fellow prisoners. He was killed on 14 January 1941. His wife Lilli was deported to Minsk in 1942 where she presumably died. A star was later dedicated to Fritz Grünbaum on the Walk of Fame of Cabaret in Vienna; he is buried at Vienna Central Cemetery, Old Israelite Part, Gate 1.

Grünbaum was a well-known art collector with a collection of more than 400 pieces, eighty of them by Egon Schiele. The Nazis took the whole lot. A small portion of the collection appeared on the art market in the early 1950s through a Swiss art dealer, but the fate of the rest remains unknown.

Events such as the *Anschluss* and visits to Italy maintained the illusion that Hitler was working endlessly, while in fact much of his time was spent doing as little as possible.

In May 1938 a Reich Music Festival was held in Düsseldorf. Goebbels felt it important enough to set aside the matter of foreign affairs for, and attended so he could deliver a speech to 'all of Germany's creative musicians':[342]

Jewry and German music are opposites, which following their nature, stand in the starkest contrast to one another. The fight against Jewry in German music, which Richard Wagner once took up completely on his own, is therefore today our great, never to be relinquished, historic task.[343]

Goebbels was confirming that Wagner's works were anti-Semitic, and Hitler was continuing the work that Wagner had begun. This was a clear statement of Nazi doctrine. It had nothing to do with politics and everything to do with culture and the cult of celebrity, as well as Hitler's assimilation of the church; God and celebrity were one and the same thing. This was the divine law that governed Germany and brought the world into catastrophic conflict.

Richard Strauss was a special star guest conductor at the festival. A conference on the subject of 'Music and Race' was held there, and an exhibition on 'Degenerate Music' where visitors listened to examples of 'Jewish music' and 'nigger jazz' on headphones. Lurid pictures of Jewish and black musicians were on display.

This ideological and cultural assault on Jews and all others considered 'alien' paralleled the actual physical intimidation happening all over Germany and now Austria, and matters were coming to a head, spurred on by Wagner; just before attending a performance of Wagner's *Tristan and Isolde* at Bayreuth on 25 July, Hitler and Goebbels felt it appropriate to discuss the 'Jewish question'. Goebbels's conclusion to their discussion was, 'The main thing is that the Jews are forced out. They must be out of Germany in ten years. But for the time being we want the rich ones as a security.'[344]

Music itself actually meant little to Hitler, who preferred that music go hand in hand with drama, hence his love of opera. If he had to content himself with a gramophone record, it was always a poor alternative to actually being at the opera. When he played records, it was usually to listen to the grander scenes from Wagner, and he had little interest in listening to symphonic works or chamber music. As he sat through countless performances of Wagner's operas, his interest often shifting to the stage techniques and character interpretations rather than the music. As music without drama meant little to him, so too did drama without music; he had stopped going to the theatre to see plays and went only to the opera for his live stage fix. The greatest experience of all was to be *at* the opera, and for him the supreme expression of opera was the finale of *Götterdämmerung*; whenever he saw it at Bayreuth, when the citadel of the gods collapsed in flames, he took the hand of Winifred Wagner, who always sat behind him in his box, and moved to tears he kissed it.[345]

Hitler's craving for opera gave him the feeling that, with the exception of when he was in his own private world, he was always on a stage, acting a part, and needing resounding alarums and startling special effects. His greatest fear was that he would bore his audience and while he could legitimately create a whole stage production around his public appearances, his need to project himself fed his own addiction to be much more than the failed artist from Linz, and it spilled over more and more into his off-stage life. The edges between fantasy and reality became increasingly blurred.

Goebbels, always working much harder than Hitler, had to squeeze in time to see more of Lída Baarová while seeing less of Magda, who enjoyed her own extramarital activities. He had become merely a visitor to the family home in Schwanenwerder, largely because of his demanding work in the Propaganda Ministry where he had a flat, which from April 1938 was virtually his permanent residence.

Goebbels and Baarová had managed to maintain their affair in relative secrecy. He sometimes attempted to provide himself with an alibi for the evenings when he wanted to be alone with Lída by inviting himself to Olga Tschechowa's apartment, stopping off to see her briefly before going to Lída's. Olga was expected to cover for him if anyone should ask.[346]

In 1938 rumours of his affair with Baarová spread when Goebbels ensured that financial support was given to a film she was making which had run into trouble. Lída's fiancé, Gustav Fröhlich, realised the gossip was true when he discovered them in the back of Goebbels's car parked on the road heading towards Goebbels's villa. He berated Goebbels – some sources say he actually punched him – and broke off his engagement to Baarová.

Goebbels phoned Lída and said he wanted her and Magda to meet. When the three were together, a distraught Magda suggested to Lída that they share Goebbels, who sealed the love triangle by giving each of them gifts of jewellery. Magda told Lída, 'I am the mother of his children; I am only interested in this house in which we live. What happens outside does not concern me. But you must promise me one thing: you must not have a child by him.'[347]

Goebbels moved Baarová into his villa, but Magda had a change of heart, and in August 1938 she asked Hitler to personally intercede to save her marriage. It is thought that Hitler had no idea what Goebbels had been up to, because those around him who had heard the rumours never had the courage to tell him. But Baarová later hinted that Hitler had known about the affair: 'I remember [Goebbels] once gave me a gold bracelet for Christmas. Hitler made a huge fuss about it.'[348]

Eager to prevent a public scandal surrounding his Propaganda Minister, and also disapproving of Goebbels's treatment of Magda – he was obviously unaware of her own infidelities – he took her side completely and summoned Goebbels to Berlin on 15 August. Goebbels was shocked by the summons and told Baarová, 'My wife is the devil.' At the meeting, Goebbels asked Hitler for permission to divorce Magda so he could marry Lída, but Hitler told him unequivocally to end his affair with the actress immediately. Goebbels may have courted Hitler's anger less for his infidelity than for conducting it with an 'inferior' Slav.

The very next morning Goebbels telephoned Baarová, and through tears told her that his request for a divorce had been denied and he was forbidden from seeing her again. 'I love you, Liduschka,' he said. 'I cannot live without you.'[349] He obeyed his *Führer* and never contacted her again, and sank into a deep depression.

Baarová was summoned to the police station and told she was banned from appearing in films or plays and from all social functions. The Gestapo hounded her and organised hecklers to shout 'Whore!' when she defiantly attended the premiere of her film *Der Spieler* (*The Player* – aka *Gambler's Story*). Her next film, already finished in 1938, was banned from being shown. She received a direct order from Hitler through his adjutant to remain in Germany. She later said of Goebbels, 'Thanks to him I fell into the depths of hell.'[350] Thanks to Goebbels and Hitler, millions fell into the depths of hell. Unable to work, and in fear for her life, Lída fled to Prague, having no idea that Czechoslovakia would within a short time come under Hitler's jackboot.

Goebbels's affair with Lída Baarová was almost his downfall. Hitler's displeasure showed no sign of abating any time soon, and with the prospect of having to face Magda's unforgiving presence each day and night, he devoted himself solely to his duty, which was his only consolation.[351] Rumours of Goebbels's disgrace circulated, and the British ambassador in Berlin, Nevile Henderson, reported to London on Goebbels's 'recent considerable loss of prestige'.[352]

His own propaganda machine swung into gear on his behalf, and newspapers published pictures of the Goebbels family looking happy to avoid the scandal that was threatening to engulf Hitler's regime. But he was now seeing little of Magda, and even less of Hitler. He lived for the most part in isolation and his interest in his work waned. He was unable to concentrate on reading or music, and was so overcome by grief that he resolved never to see Magda again, or even speak to her by telephone.[353] He was only able to sleep with the help of narcotics and was on the verge of a nervous breakdown, a victim of the Nazi cult of celebrity which he had helped Hitler to perpetuate.

Six months after marching into Austria, Hitler met with the Prime Ministers of Britain and France to demand that the Sudetenland be ceded to Germany. The Sudeten territory, an area in the northern, south-west and western regions of newly created Czechoslovakia, formed after the First World War when Austria-Hungary broke apart, was inhabited mostly by ethnic Germans, and Hitler wanted it. Both Prime Ministers signed the agreement, and the Czechoslovak government had no choice but to abide by it. German troops marched into the Sudetenland in October 1938 and were welcomed as liberators. It was called *Blumenkrieg*, the 'war of flowers', because women and children threw flowers to Hitler in his car and at the troops, demonstrating to the world that Hitler had remedied an injustice without resorting to open force. What the world didn't see was the violence practised behind the scenes as all opposition was soundly put down out of sight.

Hitler was greeted by scenes of near hysteria from the Sudeten German females of all ages. Overhead a Zeppelin flew like a giant phallus. Hitler was the supreme star and solo act, and he knew exactly how to manipulate the masses. Overjoyed and overwhelmed young women surged forward in the faint hope of touching their idol. He stood Christ-like, as if he were showing the wounds in his hands. The tension among the huge crowd reached breaking point, and then he reached down, allowing those at the front to touch the sacred hands. The tension was released, girls cried, swooned and fainted and had to be carried away in virtual ecstasy. It was comparable to the scenes of adulation, overwhelming emotion and sexual release in the 1960s which became known as Beatlemania.

But through it all Hitler maintained an image of a monumental figure standing unmoved amid the mass hysteria. The distance he put between himself and the hysterics transformed the belief they had in him – and which he had in himself – into a religious fervour. Underlining it all was an element of eroticism which he created and manipulated, knowing it was the very thing which bonded him and his people together, hence he declared: 'Where are the democracies of other countries? Where is it possible that the people and their leader, the nation and their government, merge into each other to such an extent and stand so close by one another's side?'[354]

His shows were the greatest on earth; he was the magnificent showman. There was a vital factor to these mass encounters which went beyond mere self-gratification: they recharged his energies, which lapsed during the long days of inactivity, and he was renewed for further acts of aggression.

Towards the end of October Goebbels, unable to bear his isolation any longer, asked Göring to intercede with Hitler on his behalf, and consequently Goebbels went to see Hitler at Berchtesgaden for a long and apparently friendly talk. Magda was also summoned, and Hitler helped them agree on a truce. Despite taking the world to the brink of disaster, and with every intention of waging war, Hitler was fond enough of both Goebbels and Magda, his Holy Family, to take the time to reconcile them. When this private peace had been agreed upon, the Goebbels children were brought in, and they all posed for photos to be published in the newspapers so that no one was in any doubt the Goebbelses epitomised the Nazi family unit.[355]

As fond as Hitler was of them both, he remained irritated with Goebbels, and on Goebbels's birthday in 1938 Hitler refrained from gracing the numerous ceremonial functions attended by colleagues, artists and party members. He sent only 'a short, frosty telegram' to wish him a happy birthday. 'Can a man endure and suffer all that?' Goebbels wondered at falling from the grace of the man he not only idolised but had helped set on his high throne. 'I am at the end of my strength.'[356]

In Munich Goebbels, still depressed, anxious and suffering from insomnia, attended the commemoration of its Putsch 'martyrs' on 8 November 1938, and there heard the news that a German diplomat in Paris, Ernst von Rath, had been shot by a Polish Jew. The next day, in a state of mind that was more merciless, Goebbels outlined his plan to Hitler for a violent demonstration against the Jews that very night. After the sun set on 9 November 1938, Hitler allowed Goebbels to burn down the synagogues. *Kristallnacht*! Over 1,000 synagogues were destroyed, 100 Jews killed, many more injured, and around 30,000 sent to concentration camps.

On *Kristallnacht* Leni Riefenstahl was in America as a goodwill ambassador of Germany, part way through a tour to promote *Olympia*. The film's value as propaganda for a country that had shown its hostility was evident to many. Wilhelm Schneider, Hitler's bodyguard, declared, 'Miss Riefenstahl and her artistic skills were an enormous boost to German propaganda. What she achieved is indescribable.'[357] While the world was introduced to her film, Jews were being attacked and killed in Germany.

To the American press she was a major celebrity, and they were more interested in knowing if she was romantically involved with Hitler than in Nazi politics. She denied it all with a smile. In Germany there were rumours that Riefenstahl and Hitler were involved. When later asked about *Kristallnacht*, she was able to say with complete honesty that she was in America at the time and knew nothing about it.

After the November pogroms the *Jüdischer Kulturbund*, the Jewish Cultural Union, was allowed to continue its activities, but the discrimination and persecution of Jews had driven many into impoverishment, and the number of members dwindled.

On 16 December Hans Hinkel, Goebbels's state commissioner for Prussian theatre affairs, including the *Kulturbund*, declared in front of Dr Werner Levie – who was a Dutchman and therefore one of the few available members of the *Kulturbund*'s executive board not in hiding or arrested – that the existing seventy-six Jewish German publishing companies were to be shut down or sold to 'Aryans'. The few publications which would be permitted to appear were to be directed by a publishing department within the *Kulturbund*.[358]

Goebbels missed the traditional Christmas celebrations that year when he was rushed to hospital after collapsing with severe kidney pains. The New Year brought him no better fortune as he sank into a deeper depression. On 23 January 1939 he signed a nuptial contract with Magda, a formal agreement that they would both maintain the marriage, although she was now involved with one of Goebbels's own officers, State Secretary Karl Hanke. Goebbels continued to live away from home for most of the time and saw little of his children. Hanke further betrayed Goebbels by presenting Hitler with a list of all the women from whom Goebbels demanded sexual favours.[359] Goebbels's 'casting couch' was no longer a secret, though it is doubtful that Hitler had been wholly unaware of it.

Goebbels had little time to devote himself to his favourite duty, managing the film industry, but his recovery from his illness was helped by working alongside Hitler on the preparation of a speech, a 'real masterpiece', given to the *Reichstag* on 30 January 1939 in which Hitler prophesied a European war that would bring with it 'the extermination of the Jewish race in Europe'. Goebbels stood with Hitler to watch the torchlight parade, but his spirits were low as he thought back 'to the time six years ago. It was good then. Everything now is awful and terrible.'[360]

In January 1939, the *Kulturbund*'s book-publishing department opened in the offices formerly used by the Zionist publication

Jüdische Rundschau, which had been one of the most popular German-Jewish weeklies from 1902 until banned in 1938. The former editor of *Jüdische Rundschau*, Erich Liepmann, managed the publishing department. The *Kulturbund* prevented a considerable amount of book stocks from other Jewish publishers from being pulped when Levie allowed Jewish publishers, now obliged to liquidate their companies, to export their book stocks until April 1939 if the respective purchasers would pay in foreign exchange to the *Reichsbank*. The *Kulturbund*'s publishing department bought the remaining book stocks from their old proprietors at a discount of 80 to 95 per cent of the original price.[361]

Goebbels permitted the *Kulturbund* to continue only if it changed its statutes to the effect that Goebbels could at any time interfere in the affairs of the executive board, and even dissolve the *Kulturbund* and dispose of its assets. The new statutes came into effect on 4 March 1939; clearly Goebbels had no intention of allowing the *Kulturbund* to exist indefinitely. On 11 September 1941 the Gestapo ordered the closure of the *Kulturbund*, except for its publishing department, which was to be taken over by the *Reichsvereinigung der Juden in Deutschland*,[362] an administrative branch subject to the *Reich*'s government established on 4 July 1939. All persons identified as Jews were compulsorily enlisted as members.

During 1939 Hitler made his annual visit to Bayreuth, where he recounted the night he and Kubizek went to see *Rienzi* and of the vision that had come upon Hitler.[363]

In March 1939 Hitler invaded the rest of Czechoslovakia, despite all his promises to the contrary. He entered Prague with his troops, and occupied the old royal castle overlooking the city. From its window he acknowledged the applause of the hastily assembled crowd; there were few who turned out to greet him like a hero, and no flowers either. Himmler and Heydrich accompanied him for the whole world to see, and it was their henchmen who occupied the country.

A wave of fear swept through Europe as people learned that Germany had mobilised. Nations hurriedly began to organise defences, but no one was properly prepared for the prospect of war.

Four weeks after conquering Prague, Hitler celebrated his fiftieth birthday. Winifred Wagner decorated the *Festspielhaus* and gave him a very special birthday present, Richard Wagner's original scores for *Das Rheingold* and *Die Walküre* (*The Valkyrie*), which were priceless and irreplaceable; they were lost during the last days of the Second World War.[364] Goebbels gave him a collection of 120 films for screening at the Berghof. Hitler often kept all his guests up into the early hours of the morning as he lectured them on whatever film they had just seen.

Marking the occasion was a huge military parade designed by Hitler himself to fire the enthusiasm of the hesitant German public, and to show the world what they faced if they opposed him.

Hitler didn't need policies when he had all this to give to the German people – an awe-inspiring spectacle to convince them that their country was strong at last. He had a talent for the art of deception, and he made them believe this strength would secure peace. But he had only war in mind. His aims were far more than the unification of German territories. It was the conquest of *Lebensraum* – his living space was to be found by seizing territories in eastern Europe, beginning with Poland. His hope was for a dominion that would stretch all the way from the North Sea to the Urals.

He kept up the deception, and visitors to Berlin met an amiable and relaxed *Führer*, happy to give them all his time. As soon as he had done his duty as Chancellor in Berlin, he retired back to his retreat at the Berghof, which had virtually become his official residence. From there, he could look across the Untersberg Mountain, the legendary resting place of Emperor Frederick Barbarossa. Hitler said that it was at the Berghof, gazing at the mountains, that he made all his most important decisions. He rarely came to a quick conclusion over any matter, and sometimes spent weeks mountain-gazing, allowing months of inactivity.

Few saw the private Hitler but his regular visitors to the Berghof, who were always the same close friends with their wives, aides and secretaries. Eva Braun filmed them on her colour 16mm camera which Hitler had given to her. The development of the 16mm camera, and the projectors that ran the film stock, long preceded the video and digital camcorders of today in allowing individuals to record and view moments from their personal lives. The film that Braun took of one of these functions at the Berghof can still surprise and fascinate the viewer. The cast included Joachim von Ribbentrop, Hitler's Foreign Minister, and Joseph Goebbels, who came from Berlin for this friendly get-together. Albert Speer, Hitler's favourite architect, had a house of his own on the Obersalzberg, so was there more often than most. Heinrich Himmler and Reinhard Heydrich, the dreaded SS chiefs, were dressed in middle-class suits rather than their uniforms of terror. They all laughed and joked on the terrace, full of bonhomie, while Hitler took little part in the fun and games. He emerged looking awkward and inhibited as Eva turned the camera on him, yet Eva caught one surprising moment when Hitler appeared to imitate someone he and his henchmen had been discussing.[365] There are some shots of Eva herself, and one can only speculate whether Hitler himself used the camera on her.

The film taken of this jocular gathering is misleading. Recalling the atmosphere at the Berghof, Albert Speer remembered 'only a sense of oppression and emptiness' which surrounded Hitler wherever he went. Whenever Hitler left the house, for meetings or mass rallies, which were becoming rarer, the gloominess went with him.

In May 1939 Goebbels went to see Olga Tschechowa performing in the play *Aimée* – 'The piece was not up to much, but *la Tschechowa* played wonderfully,' he wrote.[366] He visited her after the performance, talking and laughing with her and Carl Raddatz before finally retiring late to bed. Ten days later Olga invited Goebbels for Sunday lunch; Goebbels had been working that morning and noted what 'a beautiful, sunny Sunday' it was, and he 'laughed and chatted all afternoon. That does do much good after a day's work.'[367] Perhaps Olga Tschechowa felt some sympathy for him because of his broken heart – or perhaps she was in the role of 'Rose Marie', listening to anything he had to say with greater interest than he ever imagined.

Later that month, Tschechowa was seated next to Hitler at a

lavish garden party given for the diplomatic corps by Joachim von Ribbentrop. That evening she danced with Count Ciano, Mussolini's son-in-law and Foreign Minister, who broached the subject of her playing Anna Karenina in Italy. As Olga was leaving the party, she heard Goebbels say to Magda that she and Contessa Attolico, the wife of the Italian ambassador, should keep the Italians in the little salon as they are 'poking their noses everywhere'. Perhaps Goebbels disapproved of the Italians trying to poach *la Tschechowa*.[368]

Olga attended an increasing number of Nazi functions, including a huge candlelit reception given by Hermann Göring as part of eight days of celebrations in honour of the Yugoslav regent, Prince Paul, and his wife Princess Olga. Every guest was dressed in the period of Frederick the Great, using costumes from the numerous films that had been made about him. 'After supper I sat in the garden with the royal couple, and we spoke about my films and my guest appearances,' she said,[369] later maintaining that her presence had been specially requested by the prince because his half-Russian wife Princess Olga was a fan and had wanted to meet her; this may have been true, but may also have been and attempt to create a smoke screen for her more covert activities.

Olga's role as a 'sleeper' agent was to establish contact with German generals and officials who opposed a war with Russia, but it is thought that she had lost touch with Moscow from 1937 as a result of the purges Stalin had carried out on the Red Army. Her brother Lev Knipper was still active and had continued to travel extensively because of his growing reputation as a composer, earning plaudits in 1934 for his Third and Fourth Symphonies; this allowed him to carry out assignments for the OGPU, most of which were to provide intelligence on émigré intellectuals, and also to report on Russians of German origins within the Soviet Union.

In the summer of 1939 Goebbels and Magda attended the Salzburg Festival, where she confessed that she was having an affair with Propaganda State Secretary Karl Hanke, plunging Goebbels deeper into despair. At the Bayreuth Festival, Magda came close to a public breakdown. Goebbels took the position of the injured party, which had the effect of lightening his spirits. He also arranged for Hanke to serve in the *Wehrmacht*. Goebbels was now seeing more of Hitler, who, preparing for war, needed his Propaganda Minister and publicist at his side.

CHAPTER SIXTEEN

THE FÜHRER VERSUS THE PHOOEY

It was not just the Jews of Europe who had reason to fear Hitler's new laws. In Hollywood in 1938, movie legend Charlie Chaplin received a package sent from Germany. Inside it he found a book, *Juden sehen Dich an* (*The Jews are Watching You*), by Dr Johann von Leers, a vehement anti-Semite Nazi. The book included names and photographs of leading Jews worldwide – activists, bankers, economists, journalists, academics and entertainers – and warned the German people that these people were forming an international network aimed at world domination. In the section named 'Artistic Jews' Chaplin found his own name and photograph, branding him a 'pseudo-Jew'.

The book had been sent to him by a filmmaker called Ivan Montague, who was working in Berlin. Chaplin wrote back to Montague, thanking him for the book, a warning that he was on Hitler's hit list of Jews to be murdered; many of the people featured in the book had already been killed.[370]

Goebbels mistakenly thought Chaplin was Jewish; it was a common mistake, but Chaplin refused to deny it. He declared, 'Anyone who denies this in respect of himself plays into the hands of the anti-Semites.' In response to seeing himself on the book's hit list he made *The Great Dictator*, the first film made in Hollywood to satirise Hitler and the Nazis.

When Chaplin first started working on his script in 1938, the United States government was still anxious about stirring up trouble with Hitler, and nearly all the major Hollywood studio heads were cautious in presenting films that were disagreeable to Hitler, Mussolini or Spain's Francisco Franco, for fear of losing income in European film markets. Many of the studio heads warned Chaplin not to make his film, and Will Hays, the head of the film industry's Production Code Administration, stated anti-Nazi films were in violation of the nation's neutrality stance. The British government announced that it would prohibit its release in the United Kingdom in keeping with its appeasement policy concerning Nazi Germany.

Nonetheless, with more than one million of his own dollars behind the film, Chaplin prepared the story throughout 1938 and 1939, turning Adolf Hitler the *Führer* into Adenoid Hynkel the *Phooey* of Tomania. Filming began in September 1939, Chaplin directing the movie and playing two roles: a simple Jew living in the fictional nation of Tomania, and Fascist dictator Adenoid Hynkel.

‡

A week before filming began, Hitler launched his attack on Poland on the morning of 1 September 1939. On 3 September, England and France declared war on Germany. The world went to war against Germany for the second time.

‡

Unity Mitford was so distraught upon hearing of the declaration of war she went to the English Garden in Munich, took a pearl-handled pistol, given to her by Hitler for protection, and shot herself in the head.[371] Miraculously, she survived the suicide attempt and was hospitalised in Munich where she was visited by Hitler, who paid her bills and arranged for her return home. She died in 1948 from meningitis, caused by the cerebral swelling around the lodged bullet, which doctors had decided had was too dangerous to remove. She had succeeded in committing suicide after all, joining the list of women close to Hitler who took their own lives.

Hitler visited the front line in Poland, officially to congratulate the troops, but he had turned the war into a media opportunity and was congratulating only himself. He was followed by Leni Riefenstahl, who arrived in the small Polish town of Końskie five days after the first attack. She came with a film crew, hoping to film German victories, but all she saw was horror and devastation. She and her crew visited a military base where several *Wehrmacht* soldiers had been shot in an attack; their bodies lay covered in blood. Leaving the camp, Riefenstahl witnessed thirty-one Jews being rounded up to dig the graves for the dead soldiers. Then they were shot. Riefenstahl watched in horror and fainted. She had not imagined the German victory would look like this, and she and her crew left Poland. She nevertheless remained devoted to her *Führer*.

Eight days after the war began, German troops reached Warsaw and began their siege. The Soviet Union invaded Poland from the east: Hitler had struck a bargain with Stalin. The precise boundaries had been drawn up; the Soviet part of Poland was to be renamed the Western Ukraine.

After only two weeks of war, Warsaw fell. When Hitler saw the burning city, he was literally spellbound, always overwhelmed by the vision of fire and smoke and devastation, and probably seeing some vision of the world in this destructive state. He warned that this was the fate awaiting all who opposed him.[372]

At this time, Lev Knipper was called to active duty by the NKVD, which had superseded the OGPU, and sent into the so-called Western Ukraine. Issued with a Walther pistol, he travelled with a group of Red Army dancers as a cover, but his real purpose was to interrogate Germans picked up by the NKVD; Soviet intelligence was positive that the *Abwehr*, Germany's secret spy network, was infiltrating Soviet Poland, and Lev was said to be responsible for unmasking German espionage as well as identifying an *Abwehr* agent with the codename Alma.[373]

Fritz Hippler, who had a high position in the Propaganda Ministry's film office, and scores of film cameramen had been sent by Goebbels into Poland with the *Blitzkrieg* – lightning war – to film the invasion and occupation of Poland which became the documentary *Feldzug in Polen* (*The Campaign in Poland*), which featured breathtaking footage that had cinema attendances in Germany rising dramatically.[374] Hippler remained in Poland to film scenes in the Jewish ghettos that were set up for a film Goebbels personally commissioned, *Der ewige Jude* (*The Eternal Jew*). The title was the German term for the character of the 'Wandering Jew,' a figure from medieval Christian folklore who taunted Jesus on the way to Calvary and was cursed to wander the earth until the Second Coming.

There had been a 1934 British film called *The Eternal Jew* which had portrayed the Jews in a favourable light and as the victims of persecutions through the ages. Goebbels liked it so much he wanted it remade with the emphasis on portraying the Jews as wandering parasites; it was a violently anti-Semitic remake.[375] The film had been planned for around a year, and even before the invasion of Poland, Goebbels had called the film 'the most cutting anti-Semitic propaganda that could be imaged'.[376] The invasion of Poland provided Goebbels and Hippler with the opportunity of filming real Jews in squalid conditions.

Hippler filmed the most abject examples of poverty he could find in Warsaw and Łódź. An early shot in the film shows a pack of rats emerging from a sewer and is juxtaposed with a crowd of Jews in a bustling street in a city in Poland. Over close-ups of Jews with twisted facial features, the narrator – German theatre and voice actor Harry Giese – relates how Jews are the vermin of the human race which spread disease and corruption. Scenes depicted Jews preferring to live in filthy homes, unwilling to spend their riches on better and healthier surroundings. The film portrayed Jews as people who found pleasure only in money and a hedonist lifestyle while the Aryans found satisfaction in physical labour. The Jewish preference for the decadent and grotesque was contrasted to the Aryan's appreciation of culture.

With the assistance of the SS, Hippler forced Jews to slaughter animals and read from the Torah for scenes intended to condemn Jewish religious and kosher laws. 'The Torah scroll is rolled to the place to be read,' said the narrator. 'What sort of "truth" does it teach? …This is not a religion – it's a conspiracy against all non-Jews by a sick, deceitful poisoned race against the Aryan peoples and their moral laws.'

Hippler filmed a scene featuring the 24-member *Judenrat* (Jewish Council), which had been set up by the Nazis to be responsible for implementing Nazi orders in the new Jewish ghetto. On 4 October 1939 they appointed as its head Adam Czerniaków, a Polish-Jewish engineer who had been elected to the Polish senate. For his scenes in *Der ewige Jude* he was made to gesticulate wildly because, Hippler said, 'That is how Jews speak.'

(On 22 July 1942, the *Judenrat* received instructions from the SS that all Warsaw Jews were to be 'resettled' to the east. Czerniaków went to work immediately to secure exemptions for a number of individuals such as the wives of Jews who had already been exempted because of certain kinds of work – factory workers, hospital staff, sanitation workers, and Jewish ghetto police – but he was unable to secure exemptions for the children from the Janusz Korczak orphanage. The very next day, 23 July, Czerniaków committed suicide by swallowing a cyanide pill.)

Footage of many notable Jews was included in *Der ewige Jude*, breaking copyright laws which neither Goebbels nor Hippler cared about. Albert Einstein was shown adjacent to a series of images that suggested Jews controlled the pornography industry. Charlie Chaplin was also featured. So was Peter Lorre, featured in a scene from Fritz Lang's *M* in which he played a Jewish child murderer.

The final scene featured footage of Hitler giving a public speech in January 1939 which ended with him saying, 'If the international finance-Jewry inside and outside Europe should succeed in plunging the nations into a world war yet again, then the outcome will not be the victory of Jewry, but rather the annihilation of the Jewish race in Europe.'

The Nazi publication *Unser Wille und Weg* told the German people that the film revealed 'a full picture of Jewry' and provided 'the best treatment of this parasitic race'. The film was complimented for 'its portrayal of the Jews' vulgar methods and the brutality and all-devouring hatred they exhibit when they reach their goal and control finance.' The uncredited author of this piece urged, 'We are the initiators of the fight against world Jewry, which now directed its hate, its brutal greed and destructive will towards us. We must win this battle for ourselves, for Europe, for the world.'[377]

Goebbels credited Hippler 'for his excellent work in the newsreel department',[378] but after the war Hippler – an active Nazi for many years – tried to dissociate himself from the party's actions, particularly in relation to the Holocaust, insisting he knew nothing about the Jews in the death camps. He also disavowed his role in making of *Der ewige Jude*, maintaining until his death in 2002 that he merely shot some of the footage while Goebbels put the film together, and that Goebbels was the creator of the film under Hitler's close supervision – an unlikely scenario because Hitler did not involve himself in the work of his ministers. Hitler approved of films like *Der ewige Jude* but took no part in the making of them. However, Goebbels did work closely with Hippler on editing the film for a year.

Hippler regretted being named director on the film's credits because that resulted in him being interrogated by the Allies, which he thought unfair because he had nothing to do with the killing of the Jews.[379] In a 2000 interview for the German documentary series *Holocaust*, he even said that *Der ewige Jude* was 'the most disgraceful example of anti-Semitism'.

Like Leni Riefenstahl and other makers of Nazi propaganda films, Hippler was unable to accept responsibility for his contribution to Nazi idealism. The film remains banned from public transmission in Germany except for use as an educational tool, and even then only under the condition that the exhibitors have formal education in 'media science and the history of the Holocaust'.[380]

Der ewige Jude's reputation exceeds its commercial failure. Goebbels had made two versions, one for the public with many of its more explicit scenes, such as the slaughtering of animals, taken out, while the full unexpurgated version was seen by party activists. The public were not drawn to it, even at a time when cinema attendance was at an unprecedented high; it was withdrawn in Dresden after less than a week. Goebbels, disappointed with its reception, did not even refer to its commercial failure in his diaries.[381]

By 1940 Hitler was at the peak of his power. He had gone from being a homeless drifter in 1914 to being ruler of the continent. But that was not enough for him. His goal was to extend the Reich to the Ural Mountains in western Russia, running from the Arctic Ocean to the Ural River and north-western Kazakhstan. It is the boundary between Europe and Asia, and everything on the western side of the border was to belong to him.

He looked westward, and at the beginning of April 1940 his forces swept into Denmark and Norway. A month later he marched against the old mortal enemy, France, then Luxembourg, Belgium and the Netherlands.

‡

Many Jews who had fled to those countries from Nazi Germany found themselves in the very trap they had attempted to escape. German singer and actress Dora Gerson, whose first husband was one of Hitler's favourite film directors, Veit Harlan – they married in 1922 and divorced in 1924 – was a star on screen, in cabaret and on record. After 1933 she began recording music for a small Jewish record company; she also recorded in Yiddish, her 1936 song 'Der Rebe Hot Geheysn Freylekh Zayn' (The Rebbe Has Bidden Us to Be Merry) being a favourite of European Jews in the 1930s. One of her most memorable recordings from this era was 'Vorbei' (Beyond Recall), an emotional ballad which subtly memorialised Germany before the rise of the Nazi Party.

In 1936 Gerson, her second husband Max Sluizer and her relatives fled Nazi persecution in Germany and settled in the Netherlands, but on 10 May 1940 the family was caught again in the Nazi net when Germany invaded the Netherlands. Jews there were subject to the same anti-Semitic laws and restrictions as in Germany. In 1942 the Gerson family attempted to escape, but they were seized trying to flee to Switzerland, and sent by rail to Westerbork and then to Auschwitz. On 14 February 1943 the family died in the gas chambers of Auschwitz: Dora Gerson at the age of forty-three, her husband and their two children, Miriam Sluizer, aged five, and Abel Juda Sluizer, not yet three.[382]

Stopping his advance through France outside of Dunkirk, allowing the main body of the British Expeditionary Force to escape across the Channel during May and June 1940, Hitler accepted the French plea for an armistice, signed on 21 June 1940, and then drove into Paris for his first view of the city. After driving for three hours through the silence of empty streets he left, but the dream of his lifetime, he said, had been fulfilled.

In a prison in Paris was the former owner of the Pathé studio, Bernard Natan; his real name was Natan Tannenzaft, but he changed it to hide his Jewish identity.[383] Born in Romania in 1886, he left after the First World War to settle in France to become involved in the film industry. In France he made so-called 'stag' films – hardcore pornographic shorts – but these were distinguished by their attention to plot, editing, costumes and overall production professionalism. He moved into mainstream cinema and worked as a publicity stringer for Paramount during the early 1920s. He developed his own production company, Rapid Film, and became a member of the executive committee of the Cinematographic Employers' Federation. By 1926, his film laboratory was highly regarded, and he established a marketing firm.

Natan was, despite his rather sordid beginnings, a pioneer of modern cinema. He is credited with having laid the foundation for the modern film industry in France, and helped revolutionise film technology around the world.[384] In 1928, he predicted that sound would have a major impact on the film industry and, realising that none of the big French studios were prepared for it, bought out the financially troubled Pathé-Cinéma, renaming it Pathé-Natan, and equipped it to produce talkies. He built two sound stages, and also financed and produced films for other studios.[385] Many of his films attracted attention for their political content, such as his 1934 film *The Last Billionaire*, which ridiculed Hitler and caused rioting among French Nazi sympathisers. The French press attacked

Natan for his stewardship of Pathé, and there were veiled references to Natan's homosexuality.[386]

Pathé-Natan did well under Natan despite the world economic crisis. As well as investing in technology for sound films, he also launched two new cinema-related magazines, *Pathé-Revue* and *Actualités Féminines*, to help market Pathé's films. He also funded the research of Henri Chrétien into the development of the anamorphic lens – this later became the technology that became known as Cinemascope, followed by Panavision, and is still the most widely used system of creating widescreen pictures, in the cinema, on DVD and on TV.

He even established France's first television company in 1929, Télévision-Baird-Natan. A year later, he purchased a radio station in Paris and formed a holding company, Radio-Natan-Vitus, to run what would become a rapidly increasing radio empire.

In order to finance the company's continued expansion, Pathé's board of directors, which still included Charles Pathé, voted in 1930 to issue shares worth 105 million francs. But with the depression deepening, only 50 per cent of the shares were purchased. One of the investor banks collapsed, and Pathé was forced to follow through with the purchase of several cinema chains it could no longer afford to buy. The company began to lose more money than it could make.

In 1935 Pathé was bankrupt, and the French authorities indicted Bernard Natan on charges of fraud. He was accused of financing the purchase of the company without any collateral, of bilking investors by establishing fictitious shell corporations, and negligent financial mismanagement. He was even accused of hiding his Romanian and Jewish heritage by changing his name. He was imprisoned in 1939, and was behind bars when France fell to Hitler.

He was freed in September 1942, but almost immediately the French government handed him over to the Nazis, who were rounding up Jews for deportation. Natan was sent to Auschwitz on 25 September, and died there the following month. Hitler had his revenge for Natan's 1934 film *The Last Billionaire*.

After France fell, Leni Riefenstahl sent Hitler a telegram of congratulations: 'With indescribable joy, deeply moved and full of warm gratitude, we are experiencing with you my *Führer* yours and Germany's great victory. Offering congratulations is not enough to express to you the feelings that move me.'[387]

Hitler returned to Germany in triumph; his entry into Berlin was greeted with flowers and jubilation. For many Germans the war had seemed senseless at first, but Hitler's victories resulted in an almost unanimous flood of adoration and adulation, and also respect, for this was the man who had eradicated the humiliation of the First World War.

This was to be the last triumphal procession of his career.

France, in German hands, had become the place to see and be seen. Zarah Leander went to Paris in 1940 to be filmed signing autographs for the occupying German troops. Photographs of her posing with German soldiers and officers were seen back in Sweden.[388] Winifred Wagner also went to Paris in 1940 on an official mission along with singers from her opera house and conductor Herbert von Karajan to perform Wagner's works in celebration of Hitler's victory – a musical conclusion of a six-week campaign of warfare that would engulf much of the world;[389] Richard Wagner appearing right at the heart of the Second World War. He was even hijacked by Charlie Chaplin in his film *The Great Dictator*, which was premiered in New York in September 1940 to great acclaim and went on achieve to big box office. While Goebbels had been supervising the making of *Der ewige Jude*, Charlie Chaplin had been making *The Great Dictator* in Hollywood. Chaplin's film opened in the UK in December; the British government now welcomed his satire on Hitler as essential propaganda.

In one of the film's most famous scenes, Hynkel dances with a large, inflatable globe while dreaming of being Emperor of the world and listening to the Prelude to Act I of Wagner's *Lohengrin*. Suddenly the globe pops, and the music ends. Chaplin was prophesying the downfall of Hitler as the great bubble burst to the strains of Wagner. Hitler was incensed, but Chaplin's name was already marked for death. Chaplin's prophecy proved more powerful than the one Hitler received from Wagner.

The Great Dictator might never have been made if Chaplin had not begun work on it as early as he did; he later stated that he would not have made the film had he known the true extent of the Nazis' crimes.[390] But Hitler feared Chaplin's masterpiece because he understood the power of the moving picture. With Goebbels, he would respond with a film even more powerful, but one which would be reviled for decades to come.

CHAPTER SEVENTEEN

A REFLECTION OF HITLER

'Hitler knew the power of films,' observed Wolfgang Preiss. 'He was probably the first leader of a country to use the medium of moving pictures to inspire and even indoctrinate. Joseph Goebbels too knew the power of film, and that movie *Jud Süß* became the opinion of the German nation. The strength of power that a film can have is terrifying.'[391]

In November 1939 Goebbels commissioned a new film adaptation, *Jud Süß*. It originated from an 1827 novella of the same name by Wilhelm Hauff, a writer of historical romances. His original story was based on the true tale of Joseph Süß (or Suss) Oppenheimer, a Jewish financial advisor to Duke Karl Alexander of Württemberg in Stuttgart. Oppenheimer established a duchy monopoly on the trade of salt, leather, tobacco and alcohol, and founded a bank and a porcelain factory;[392] in the process he made many enemies. When Duke Alexander died, Oppenheimer was arrested and accused of fraud, embezzlement, treason, lecherous relations with the court ladies, accepting bribes, and trying to re-establish Catholicism. The Jewish community unsuccessfully tried to ransom him, but at his trial, despite no evidence being offered against him, he was sentenced to death. He refused to convert to Christianity and was led to the gallows on 4 February 1738, where he was given a final chance to convert to Christianity but refused.[393]

The short story was turned into a full-length novel by German-Jewish playwright and novelist Lion Feuchtwanger, and it was translated into English as *Power*. There followed a 1927 stage production in Germany, which was then translated into Yiddish and produced by Maurice Schwartz for New York's Yiddish theatres in 1929. There was also a 1920 London production, by Ashley

Dukes, a Broadway play in January 1930, and then a new Berlin production in 1930 by Paul Kornfeld. None of the published stories or stage productions was anti-Semitic.

The first film version, based on Feuchtwanger's novel, was made in Britain in 1935. *Jew Süss* starred Conrad Veidt, Emmy Göring's former co-star, as Oppenheimer, and was directed by Lothar Mendes. While the film condemned anti-Semitism, the British censors did not allow it to criticise persecution of the Jews; knowing that anti-Semitism was growing in Germany under the Nazis, Britain did not want the film to become a diplomatic incident. It found little success in America or Europe, and was banned in Vienna. The world at that time cared little about the plight of the Jews. Goebbels was adamant that 'a new film version had to be made'.[394]

When Goebbels set his mind on turning *Jud Süß* into a Nazi anti-Semitic propaganda picture, he commissioned Ludwig Metzger to write the screenplay, but he found Metzger's draft of the script to be insufficiently anti-Semitic. He assigned playwright Eberhard Wolfgang Möller to work with Metzger; Möller's task was to ensure that the script met Goebbels's ideological objectives.

Veit Harlan was assigned to direct the film. Harlan had not been directing for long, and in fact had started out as an actor who studied under Max Reinhardt and made his stage debut in 1915 aged just sixteen. In 1922 he married Jewish actress and cabaret singer Dora Gerson (who later died at Auschwitz with her family, as documented in the previous chapter). After she left him to marry a Jew, Harlan married actress Hilde Körber, with whom he had three children. They divorced over political differences when he supported National Socialism. After directing Swedish actress Kristina Söderbaum in two films, he married her in 1939.

Söderbaum had left Sweden in 1933, after both her parents had died, to enrol in a theatre school in Berlin. She became a top star of German cinema, specialising in Aryan maiden roles. Harlan completely possessed her; she made films only for him, and in almost all of their films together he made her perform dangerous stunts that most other actors would have baulked at. Filming *Opfergang* (*The Great Sacrifice*), he waited until the waves of the North Sea were big enough, then made her ride into it on her white horse; it was November and the sea was freezing. In the same film, she rode a horse into a cage containing six tigers. 'He gave her personal feelings scant regard in his professional life,' said Harlan's son Casper.[395]

Goebbels appointed him as one of his leading propaganda directors in 1937, when Harlan made *Der Herrscher* (*The Ruler*), which laced drama with ideological content and propagated the Nazi cult of the genius. It starred Germany's most famous actor, Emil Jannings, who taught Hitler how best to use his voice when speaking to an audience. His character spoke of the state as being 'our national community', and of a conviction that from among the common workforce would come the man 'who is born to lead, [who] needs no other teacher than his own genius.' It was a direct reference to Hitler.

After reading Harlan's script ideas for *Jud Süß*, Goebbels wrote on 15 December 1939, 'Harlan reworked brilliantly the Jew Süss film. This will be *the* anti-Semitic film.'

There was no question that Kristina Söderbaum would play the female lead because she was Harlan's wife and she was in all his films. She also had considerable box office appeal. As the archetypal naive, childlike woman with natural blond hair and Aryan looks, Söderbaum had become one of the highest paid female stars of German cinema. She embodied purity, and Harlan exploited her qualities and charisma to enhance the kind of dramatic, sentimental and somewhat gloomy films he leaned towards. Her characters usually died, and Söderbaum was nicknamed 'the water corpse' because in 1938's *Youth*, she made a beautiful corpse found lying in a river; in *Jud Süß*, her body was ferried across the river by boatmen; then in *The Great Sacrifice* in 1942, her spirit appeared to pass through gates into a heavenly ocean.

Her son Casper Harlan felt Söderbaum should not be reproached for her part in *Jud Süß*. She had 'gone through thick and thin with

[Veit Harlan] and done everything that he told her to,' he said. 'My mother's strengths didn't include her intellect or her analytical abilities. She had no idea what she had done there.'[396]

Söderbaum, however, said that she *did* understand, and was shocked by Harlan's decision to make *Jud Süß*. She recalled, 'He came home, pale in the face, said, "I'll tell you about it later." And then he told me that night, after lights out. He said, "Yes! I have to make the film." And I sat up straight and said, "You simply cannot do this!"' Over the years following *Jud Süß*, she was at pains to emphasise that she was not anti-Semitic: 'It was a well-known fact that anti-Semitism was present in Germany. And it was after 1938 and I began experiencing those terrible things. I wasn't in Berlin on *Kristallnacht*, but it was 1938 and even if you'd seen nothing, you still knew that people were being persecuted.'[397]

Harlan's claim that he was 'coerced' by Goebbels to make *Jud Süß* was dismissed by his own granddaughter, Jessica Jacoby, who believed her grandfather hoped that by fulfilling this commission he would be allowed to continue making films: 'It wasn't fear that drove him,' she said. 'He was working with material that meant something to him, and he moulded it to perfection because of this … Scruples? No, he certainly had none.' Harlan's son Jan described him as 'an ambitious man who got himself the career he wanted.'[398] After the war, Harlan would claim that he rewrote the script so that it was less anti-Semitic than the Metzger/Möller script; but it was Harlan's idea to add an important sequence designed to increase the audience's hatred for Süß in which he is responsible for the execution of a blacksmith.[399] Despite this, Casper Harlan said his father 'was certainly not anti-Semitic. And certainly not a Nazi. He spoke so derogatorily about Nazis. He can't have been one.' Harlan's daughter Maria Körber said her father had many Jewish friends. 'They loved him. Our doctor was Jewish. We had Jews all around us.'[400]

Yet Jessica Jacoby said, 'I believe that [Veit Harlan] really had a huge problem with Jewish culture and with the Jewish religion.' When his first wife Dora left him and married a Jew, 'this hurt his ego.' For *Jud Süß*, 'He draws on all of the anti-Jewish imagery and depictions throughout the centuries. Thus all his resentment and rejection of this culture finds expression this way.' Veit Harlan, and his reasons for making *Jud Süß*, remains an enigma for his whole family.

The lasting controversy split Harlan's family. Another son, Thomas, believed his claim that he made the film against his will, but he could not understand why his father coerced his wife to make a film he felt to be 'reprehensible'. 'Why put her in a position where she will do something immoral that I want to avoid?' asked Thomas Harlan. 'She's a free woman. Goebbels can't give her orders.' But Goebbels *could* order any actor to be in a film, or suffer the consequences. Ferdinand Marian, who played Joseph Süß Oppenheimer, was forced to play the vile title role.

Marian led a private, very secretive life which belied the image he built as a Nazi supporter and ardent anti-Semite. The son of a Viennese opera singer, he abandoned his studies to be an engineer to work as an extra in theatres in Austria and then Germany. His first film was 1933's *Der Tunnel* (*The Agitator*), by which time he was thirty-one, but his big breakthrough was in *La Habanera* in 1937 with Zarah Leander. His career was completely overshadowed by *Jud Süß*, in which he gave a highly exaggerated performance of the caricatured materialistic, immoral, cunning and untrustworthy Jew Joseph Oppenheimer.

Marian's personal life bore no resemblance to his role in *Jud Süß*, or the appearance such a role gave him. He had a half-Jewish daughter from his first marriage to Jewish pianist Irene Saager. His second wife Maria Byk's former husband, theatre director Julius Gellner, was also Jewish, and Marian and Byk protected him from reprisals by hiding him in their home at great risk to themselves. Marian's only reason for taking on the role in *Jud Süß* was fear of reprisals which would have probably led to his secret being uncovered.[401]

While Ferdinand Marian's Oppenheimer was shaven and wore gentile clothing, all the other Jewish characters were visually stereotyped to look 'alien' – that is, non-German – such as the character of Rabbi Loew, as played by Werner Krauß (Krauss). Krauß was a classical actor, famous for his sensational demonic portrayal of the title character in *The Cabinet of Dr Caligari* in 1920, and for his Shakespearean roles on stage. In 1933 he performed with the Vienna *Burgtheater* in *Campo di Maggio* (*100 Days of Napoleon*), which was written by Giovacchino Forzano and Benito Mussolini, another dictator who considered himself an artist. Krauß was subsequently received by Mussolini and became acquainted with Joseph Goebbels, who appointed him Vice President of the *Reichskulturkammer* theatre department and also gave him the title of *Staatsschauspieler* – State Actor. A dedicated Nazi, Krauß was personally appointed by Hitler to be his cultural ambassador. He played a succession of stereotypical Jewish characters, which led to his casting as Rabbi Loew in *Jud Süß*, and in 1943 he played a 'particularly loathsome' Shylock in *The Merchant of Venice* at the *Burgtheater*.[402]

If it is true that Veit Harlan made the film because he was ordered to by Goebbels then, as Thomas Harlan wondered, 'Why did he have to make it so well?'[403] Veit Harlan exploited the Jews of the ghettos of Prague and Lublin for crowd scenes, and sent a postcard from Lublin to Thomas saying, 'You can't imagine how glad the Jews are to work with me.' Thomas later wondered if his father 'really believed that those people who were soon to be killed would have been so happy to be allowed to celebrate their religion in peace one last time? What did they know of their end? What did my father know of it?'[404]

Jud Süß opened in September 1940 and was seen by around twenty million Germans, and another twenty million people watched it throughout Europe. A week after the premiere, Heinrich Himmler released an official communiqué demanding that all SS and policemen see the picture: 'I wish that measures be taken to ensure that all SS men and policemen see *Jew Süss* during the winter. *Reichsführer-SS*, Heinrich Himmler.'

Lion Feuchtwanger was incensed at the way in which his novel had been manipulated and distorted, calling the film a '*Schandwerk*'

('shameful work'). In 1941 he wrote an open letter to the film's leading actors, expressing his shock that they would agree to participate
in Goebbels's propaganda film.[405] Jessica Jacoby called *Jud Süß* 'a call
to persecute and kill the Jews in Germany and the rest of Europe'.
Thomas Harlan said the film 'became a murder weapon'.[406] While
Wagner was the driving force behind Hitler's madness, *Jud Süß* was
part of the Nazi programme to drive German people to intense
hatred of the Jews; in German cinemas, audiences yelled 'Kick
the Jews out!' when Oppenheimer introduced Jews into Stuttgart,
which they found threatening to their way of life. The film is
considered the most reviled film in cinema history.

There is much more to *Jud Süß* than a controversy and hate-
stirring. Like most – if not all – of the films commissioned by
Joseph Goebbels from the late 1930s to the end of the war, it is a
reflection of Hitler: his deluded belief in his own infallibility, his
philosophies that sprang more strongly from Wagner than from
any other inspiration, and his penchant for covering up the truth
with the biggest of lies.

CHAPTER EIGHTEEN

KILLING HITLER

Basking in the glory of his victory over France, Hitler went to the Bayreuth Festival for the final time in July 1940. He stayed for just one performance of *Götterdämmerung,* which had come to symbolise his love of destruction. Winifred Wagner's own joy in the victory was short lived; she had lost her daughter Friedelind because of Hitler, and now she found that he had virtually no time for her; and she felt the distance growing between them.[407]

On 19 July 1940, Hitler summoned the *Reichstag* and appointed Göring as *Reichsmarschall*, and created twelve new field marshals whom he put into planning Operation Sea Lion, the invasion of Britain. But he hesitated because he hoped to make peace with Britain by political means so that his forces would be free to march on Russia, which was his next target – he had never intended to go to war with Britain; he was fighting the wrong war. But Britain had been deceived and betrayed by Hitler too often to trust him again and, finally, when it was clear Churchill would not compromise, the *Luftwaffe* began bombing airfields in the south of England on 13 August. The battle for Britain was on.

While the Battle of Britain raged on, Olga Tschechowa visited a *Luftwaffe* fighter wing base in Normandy, where she was honoured with a parade led by a band. She signed autographs for the men and was photographed by the pilots of Messerschmitt 109 fighter aircraft. Because of heavy losses to the *Luftwaffe* and bad weather conditions, the Battle of Britain was brought to a close on 16 September. Admiral Raeder informed Hitler that the German navy was ready to take Britain from the sea a few days before the *Luftwaffe* withdrew, but Hitler, still uneasy, abandoned Operation Sea Lion.

In October, Olga Tschechowa played at the *Théâtre des Champs-Elysées* in Paris, attracting many German troops occupying France, and a photograph of her surrounded by soldiers appeared on the front cover of *Das Illustrierte Blatt*. She visited German army bases in Brussels, and when in Lille she was invited for a drink in a restaurant by the town commandant. A young *Luftwaffe* captain came into the restaurant and approached her, saying, 'I knew I would meet you.' She was immediately attracted to this young officer who was 'tall and sure of himself, but without a trace of arrogance'.[408]

His name was Jep, a squadron commander in General Adolf Galland's fighter group. He was around fifteen years her junior, but she was still very beautiful, and they became lovers. Separated by war for much of the time, most of their contact was by telephone and letter. He told her about aerial dogfights over England and the Channel, and she told him the latest studio gossip.[409]

Through the war, her films became increasingly pro-Nazi – or anti-British – such as *Der Fuchs von Glenarvon* (*The Fox of Glenarvon*). Set during the First World War in Ireland, Tschechowa played an Irish patriot supporting the fight for independence. The German Propaganda Ministry graded the film 'artistically valuable', an attribute given to movies which fulfilled special aesthetical criteria and which allowed cinemas showing them to pay less tax. Goebbels was enthused by the film and wrote on 22 April 1940, 'Now it's great and very useful for our propaganda.'

She then starred in *Menschen im Sturm* (*In the Eye of the Storm*), an anti-Serbian film in which she played a woman of German origin being persecuted by Yugoslavs. While trying to escape to Germany, she is shot by them and dies a martyr with the final words, 'We are going home.' With her morale-boosting visits to the troops, a love affair with a *Luftwaffe* officer, and Nazi propaganda films, Tschechowa gave the strong impression that she had forsaken her love for Mother Russia and given her heart to the Fatherland. But appearances were deceiving.

In November 1940, Soviet Foreign Minister Vyacheslav Molotov arrived in Berlin with his interpreter Valentin Berezhkov, his deputy

Vladimir Dekanozov, and 'diplomat' Vsevolod Nikolayevich Merkulov, who was responsible for the massacre of Polish officers in the Katyn Forest. Unknown to the *Abwehr*, Dekanozov was the head of NKVD's Foreign Intelligence Department, assisting Merkulov 'to assess personally the operational situation in Germany'.[410]

On 13 November 1940, Molotov gave a reception in honour of his Nazi hosts at the Soviet embassy in Berlin. Hitler did not attend, but Joachim von Ribbentrop, Rudolf Hess and Hermann Göring did. So did Olga Tschechowa. She was one of the very few NKVD agents in Berlin, and during the evening she was introduced to Merkulov. Just as the gathering was raising glasses for the first toast, the sirens warned of an impending air raid by the British Royal Air Force. The Nazis evacuated the embassy to head for their shelters, but because the Soviet embassy had none, the Russian contingent and Olga remained to discuss matters freely as bombs rained down on Berlin.

It was hoped that Olga would be in a position to help Merkulov and Dekanozov, who were following Stalin's orders to discover 'Hitler's source of strength' within Germany, and to identify influential people in Germany opposed to an attack on the Soviet Union. The Russians overestimated Olga's contacts, having assumed from a widely circulated photograph of her sitting next to Hitler at Ribbentrop's garden party that she was a confidante of the *Führer*. She almost certainly continued her role as a 'sleeper' agent and was rewarded with a message from Lev reassuring her that her family in Moscow was being protected.[411] Tales had reached the Knipper family that Olga was associating with Nazi leaders and that Hitler himself had introduced Olga to Molotov as his hostess. They had no idea that between them, Olga and Lev were ensuring the family remained safe.

Goebbels had managed to regain Hitler's confidence by indulging the *Führer* in his pet projects, such as his new vegetarian religion, and his plan to build a huge naval base at Trondheim in Norway. Hitler also planned to kill those who were mentally ill. To Hitler's mind, when Darwin taught that only the fittest survived in nature, he was also saying that the weakest of human beings should die in secret. By January 1941, 40,000 'incurably mentally ill' adults and children were put to death, with another 60,000 awaiting their turn. Rumours of this euthanasia programme caused public unease, so Goebbels commissioned a 'film on euthanasia', *Ich klahe an* (*I Accuse*). Directed by Wolfgang Liebeneir, it told the story of a woman suffering from multiple sclerosis who pleads with doctors to kill her. Her husband gives her a fatal overdose and is put on trial, during which arguments are put forward that prolonging life is something contrary to nature and that death is a human right. The film culminates in the defendant reproaching his accusers' cruelty for trying to prevent such deaths. Established within the framework of a love story and the courtroom drama, the pro-euthanasia message was subtly presented; but the weakness of the argument was that the German people were expected to assume that anyone with mental or physical disabilities wished to die.

When *Ich klahe an* was released in cinemas in 1941, the SS reported that churches were uniformly negative about the film. Opinion among the medical profession was more positive, and the general population was supportive; it was seen by more than fifteen million Germans.[412] Like *Jud Süß*, *Ich klahe an* was a reflection of Hitler; in the film lies an image of a man deranged by his own genetic weaknesses, of his deluded beliefs in Wagner and his own infallibility, and of his increasing penchant for mass killing.

On 6 April 1941 Hitler launched the invasion of Yugoslavia. The Royal Yugoslav Army surrendered unconditionally on 17 April; there followed the annexation and occupation of the region by the Axis powers and the creation of the Independent State of Croatia – the *Nezavisna Država Hrvatska*, or NDH. Its new laws prohibited Jews from working. One of Croatia's biggest film stars was Lea Deutsch, who was called the 'Croatian Shirley Temple'. Her popularity as a child star had spread through Europe.[413]

‡

Just fourteen years of age when *Nezavisna Država Hrvatska* was created, Lea Deutsch was banned by its laws from the theatre where she performed and from the school she attended because she was Jewish. In an attempt to save the family from the horrors to come, her father converted them to Catholicism, not knowing that would not save them.

On 5 May 1941 Heinrich Himmler came to Zagreb and pressed NDH leader Ante Pavelić to round up all the Jews for deportation. Members of the national theatre intervened to try to help Lea Deutsch and her family; its famous actors, including Tito Strozzi, Vika Podgorska and Hinko Nučić, and the theatre's director, Dušan Žanko, all attempted to save Lea's life by organising the Deutsch family's escape to Karlovac where they would meet up with partisans, but they failed to make contact with their rescuers, and so they had to return to Zagreb, where they hid in the lower floor of their house.

They were discovered in May 1943 and deported to Auschwitz. Out of the seventy-five people crammed into the cattle wagon for the six-day journey without food and water, twenty-five died. Lea Deutsch was one of them. She was sixteen. Her mother and brother were killed in Auschwitz, but her father survived the Holocaust and lived until 1959. In 2003, a Lauder Jewish elementary school in Zagreb was named after Lea Deutsch.

The invasion of Yugoslavia was followed quickly by the invasions of Greece and Crete in May. On 22 June 1941, Hitler launched Operation Barbarossa, the attack on the Soviet Union. Initial gains were made that brought German forces within 15 miles of Moscow by 2 December. After the euphoria among the Nazi leadership over this initial success, there was the sudden rush to seek a solution to the 'Jewish question' because millions of Jews of the western Soviet Union were about to come under German control.[414]

A few weeks after Barbarossa, Magda Goebbels invited Olga Tschechowa for a Sunday lunch at Schwanenwerder. Olga was collected by a ministry car and arrived to find more than thirty guests including actors, diplomats and Propaganda Ministry officials. Joseph Goebbels proclaimed to them all that Moscow would fall and, turning to Olga, announced, 'We've got a Russian expert here, Frau Tschechowa.' Then he asked her whether she agreed that the war with Russia would be finished before winter and they could all celebrate Christmas in Moscow. She replied, 'No.'

'Why not?' Goebbels demanded.

She reminded him of the fate that befell Napoleon, to which Goebbels replied, 'There's a huge difference between us and the French. We've come to Russia as liberators. The Bolshevik clique is going to be overthrown by the new revolution.' Olga warned that in the face of new danger the Russians would show solidarity as never before. Goebbels asked her, 'Does this mean that you do not believe in German military power? You are predicting a Russian victory.'

'I am not predicting anything, Herr Minister. You just asked me whether our soldiers will be in Moscow by Christmas and I just expressed my opinion, which may prove right or wrong.'[415] It may be that Goebbels made a tactical error in revealing to Tschechowa German plans to attack Moscow, and Hitler may even have let slip – presumably in one of his bragging monologues – that he was going to launch a massive armoured attack on Kursk, the site of the biggest tank battle of the war; the implication is that Olga Tschechowa warned the Kremlin.[416]

Olga later claimed that this conversation resulted in her being blacklisted; Goebbels often berated anyone publicly who mentioned the possibility of defeat as cowards and traitors. But far from being blacklisted, Tschechowa went on to make another eight films before the end of the war, and continued to receive invitations from Goebbels,[417] including one to a celebration of the 500th performance of *Aimée* at his country house at Lanke. Magda and the children were away on holiday in Austria as a temporary escape from the heavy bombing raids on Berlin.

Olga asked Goebbels if he intended to extend his house, which by Nazi standards was quite small and unpretentious. He replied,

'The land does not belong to me but to the local town, and in any case, for whom should I carry on building? If I am no longer alive, should my children take on the burden of the hatred directed at me?' He had become extremely preoccupied by the future of his children in the event of a defeat, and to hear Goebbels even discussing the possibility of a defeat was shocking. Like Hitler, he usually insisted that the war was still theirs to win,[418] but perhaps Goebbels knew it was a fantasy and simply managed to keep up the pretence most of the time.

Olga did eventually fall from Goebbels's good graces when her mother Lulu publicly snubbed him at a theatre.[419] Goebbels had a new favourite to fawn over, Marika Rökk, a blonde Hungarian singer, dancer and actress born in Cairo to a Hungarian architect, Eduard Rökk, and his wife Maria Karoly. Marika had danced at the Moulin Rouge in Paris as one of the Gertrude Hoffman Girls, and the troupe toured several American cities and performed on Broadway, leading to Marika's film debut in the American movie *Sailors Leave Home* in 1930. Soon after, she signed a contract with UFA to star in several operettas including *Leichte Kavallerie* (*Light Cavalry*), but her breakthrough was in *Kora Terry*, directed by Georg Jacoby, whom she married. The film featured several dance routines which were quite revealing for the time – perhaps that's why Goebbels fixated upon her. What he didn't know, however, was that she was funnelling information to Soviet intelligence.[420]

He decided Rökk would be the first female star to appear in a film using Germany's new Agfacolor system, designed to compete with Hollywood's Technicolor. It produced a dream-like pastel quality, emphasising golden and warm tones. *Frauen sind doch bessere Diplomaten* (*Women Are Better Diplomats*) was the first Agfacolor film, and proved to be a tremendous success; it cost 2.8 million marks to make and earned 7.9 million when released in 1941.

There is no evidence that Marika Rökk had an affair with Goebbels, but he would have undoubtedly attempted to encourage her to grace his casting couch, as he did with all the starlets who came to UFA and were known as '*Goebbels-Gesfielinnen*' –

Goebbels's playthings. Insiders joked that he did not sleep in his own bed but in his own big '*Klappe*', the slang word for 'mouth' which also meant 'clapperboard'.

During the war years Heinz Rühmann, the non-political actor and Zarah Leander's friend, finally gave in to pressure from Goebbels to make a film that would be of use to the Third Reich. Under the direction of *Reichsfilmkammer* President Carl Froelich, Rühmann played the title role in *Der Gasmann*, about a gas meter reader who is suspected of foreign espionage. Rühmann was a favourite actor of Anne Frank, who pasted his picture on the wall of her room in her family's hiding place in Amsterdam during the war, where it can still be seen today.

On 16 July 1941, Hitler addressed a meeting of his ministers, including *Reichsmarschall* Hermann Göring, to discuss how the occupied Soviet territories were to be administered. Hitler declared that the Soviet territories west of the Urals were to become a 'German Garden of Eden', and that 'naturally this vast area must be pacified as quickly as possible; this will happen best by shooting anyone who even looks sideways at us.'[421]

Göring and *Reichsführer-SS* Heinrich Himmler understood this to mean they had the authority to proceed with the *Endlösung der jüdischen Frage* – the Final Solution of the Jewish Question. *SS-Obergruppenführer* Reinhard Heydrich, chief of the Reich Main Security Office, received written authorisation from Göring to draw up and submit a 'comprehensive draft' of a plan for the Final Solution.[422]

Goebbels's predictions that German troops would be in Moscow by Christmas were looking more realistic as Moscow was bombed for the first time on 22 July 1940. Field Marshal von Bock's Army Group Centre with 1.5 million men swept towards the Russian capital, and within days food was short in Moscow. There, Olga's uncle Vladimir Knipper, one of Moscow's leading opera singers, received a free lunch of soup and potatoes each day at the Central House of Workers in the Arts.[423] He had the chance to leave Moscow with a group of actors from the Moscow Art Theatre, including

Aunt Olya Knipper-Chekhova, which was being evacuated to the Caucasus. Knipper refused to leave his precious piano and books behind, and he stayed.

In Germany, Hitler was planning the rest of his war against Russia; his inspiration was still *The Lives of a Bengal Lancer*. He said in 1941, 'Let's learn from the English who, with 250,000 men in all, including 50,000 soldiers, governed 400 million Indians. What India was for England, the territories of Russia will be for us.' It was hardly a realistic approach to modern warfare, but he was so caught up in his own fantasy that he pressed on. On 30 September, Operation Typhoon was launched against the Russian capital.

With the enemy at the gates, Lev Knipper urged Uncle Vladimir to evacuate, but Vladimir still refused to leave his beloved piano and books. Meanwhile Lev and his wife, NKVD agent Mariya Melikova, were assigned a special mission that would involve Lev's movie star sister. The mission was to kill Hitler.

Expecting the Germans to occupy Moscow, Lev and Mariya were to 'defect' if the opportunity arose, with Lev claiming that he had been persecuted for being a German and an artist, and declaring he longed only to work with the liberators and most especially to be reunited with his sister, the famous German film star Olga Tschechowa. All Olga had to do was verify Lev's story about his German background and perhaps appear in Moscow at the same time as Hitler. With eleven men especially assigned to him, all equipped with remote control grenades, explosives and guns, Lev was to use Olga to get close enough to Hitler to kill him. It was like a plot out of a movie, but this was a real plot – to kill Hitler, and Olga Tschechowa was the star. That was really the extent of Olga's participation, and it is very likely that she never knew what Lev intended to do, or that she was even being used, because Moscow didn't fall. Siberian divisions and tanks which had been held in reserve launched a series of counter-attacks, and the Germans fell back.

Apart from this being the moment when Moscow was saved and the tide of the war turned against Hitler, it also meant that Hitler would never come to Moscow. The trap set by Lev and his men was cancelled. Nevertheless, Lev and Mariya received medals from the NKVD for the defence of Moscow. (Only after the war was it discovered that had Moscow fallen, Hitler never had any intention of visiting Moscow.)[424] An alternative plan was drawn up to assassinate Hitler, and as before it involved Olga Tschechowa. Lev and Mariya would 'defect' and make their way to Berlin, where they would use Olga to get close enough to Hitler to kill him.

Olga later claimed that everyone – and that would include the Russians – greatly overestimated her close links with Hitler, yet less than a year earlier, on 23 December 1940 when she was in France to see Jep, she received a large Christmas parcel from Hitler via the German embassy in Paris. The parcel contained cakes, chocolate, assorted nuts and gingerbread, plus a card bearing his portrait, with the message 'Frau Olga Tschechowa, in sincere admiration and veneration, Adolf Hitler' and personally signed by the *Führer*.[425] There was every chance that at some point she would find herself at another Nazi reception which Hitler would attend, and Lev must have hoped that as her brother and a celebrated musician, he would be able to meet Hitler in person, then kill him.

While Soviet forces were driving the *Wehrmacht* back by over 200 miles in the harsh condition of the Russian winter, Goebbels, unable to bring himself to note in his military situation reports the retreat of some of General Guderian's men,[426] was in Vienna for the 150th anniversary of Mozart's death. In his speech at the State Opera on 5 December, he declared that Mozart's music was one of the things 'our soldiers were defending from the wild onslaught of eastern barbarism'.[427] Culture and celebrity were major factors in Hitler's war.

The next day, Goebbels listened to the Mozart *Requiem* as conducted by Wilhelm Furtwängler in rehearsal with the Vienna Philharmonia and Opera Choir, and instantly decided it could not be broadcast. 'Right now we need funeral music which is heroic, but not Christian or certainly not Catholic,' he thought.[428] Goebbels could manage his cult of death, but not Christian faith.

In America, isolationists had long campaigned to keep America out of the war. In Germany, efforts were made to assure Americans that the Nazis were not the enemies of the United States, and that they even counted some Brits among their friends. As proof, they presented celebrated British writer P. G. Wodehouse on Berlin radio.

It was in June 1941 that the voice of Wodehouse was heard over the radio in America, broadcasting from Berlin. When his broadcasts, in which he recounted with humour his time in an internment camp with seemingly friendly German guards, were heard in Britain, he was immediately denounced as a traitor and a Nazi sympathiser in Parliament. British Foreign Secretary Anthony Eden accused Wodehouse of having lent his services to the Nazi war propaganda machine, and Conservative MP Quintin Hogg compared him to William Joyce, the Brit nicknamed 'Lord Haw-Haw' who made pro-Nazi broadcasts. Wodehouse's works were banned by the BBC, and public libraries withdrew all his books.[429] It certainly seemed to anyone hearing his broadcast or reading the texts that he was on friendly terms with the Germans and possibly a Nazi sympathiser, but the truth was not that cut and dried.

Wodehouse and his wife Ethel had been living in Le Touquet in France since 1934, long before the war, but the speed of the German advance in May 1940 had taken them by surprise, and they were arrested and interned in Tost in Upper Silesia in Poland; he later quipped, 'If this is Upper Silesia, what must Lower Silesia be like?'[430]

He was released from internment shortly before his sixtieth birthday – the Geneva Convention ensured that civilians aged sixty be freed – and taken to Berlin, where he made five broadcasts based on the witty stories with which he had entertained his fellow civilian inmates. He believed that in doing so he would be admired as showing himself to have 'kept a stiff upper lip' during his intern-ment,[431] but instead he proved to be 'mistaken, foolish and naive',[432] and had been unwittingly manipulated.

Dr Paul Schmidt, the head of the private office of German

Foreign Secretary Ribbentrop, thought that releasing Wodehouse a few months early would please the Americans, show that Germans were civilised and help keep America out of the war, but Goebbels refused to agree to Wodehouse's release.

Another Paul Schmidt, director of the German Foreign Office's American department and an admirer of Wodehouse's novels, had recently read the article 'My War with Germany', which Wodehouse had written for the *Saturday Evening Post*. Schmidt thought a broadcast by Wodehouse to America along the same light-hearted lines as the article would serve the German Foreign Office's purpose, and this time Goebbels agreed. Wodehouse knew nothing of all this, only that on 21 June 1941, he was released quite unexpectedly and taken to Berlin. He had received many letters and food parcels from American fans and believed the broadcasts would allow him to thank America. But Goebbels had decided to portray Wodehouse as a Nazi sympathiser, and he began a campaign to persuade all neutral, foreign journalists in Berlin, especially American and Swedish ones, that this was the case. Goebbels also rebroadcast the talks to the United Kingdom, without the knowledge of the German Foreign Office.

The Wodehouses lived in Germany under supervision for just over two years, in the Hotel Adlon in Berlin during the winters, and for the rest of the year with friends in Degenershausen in the Harz Mountains. In September 1943, Wodehouse and his wife were allowed to move to Paris, where they stayed unsupervised at the Hotel Bristol until the Allies liberated Paris in August 1944.[433]

Wodehouse's reputation never fully recovered from accusations that he had agreed to the broadcasts in return for his freedom, and he went into exile in America; he was still vilified by some when he died in 1975, but he was a victim of his own naiveté and, most of all, of Joseph Goebbels, who knew how to make the greatest profit from his cult of celebrity.[434] Wodehouse's was not the only voice heard on American radio speaking of Germany. Winifred Wagner's daughter Friedelind had left Germany in 1939 in protest at Hitler's regime, and in 1941 went to America to agitate against him. Speaking to Germans on American radio, she said, 'German listeners, you may find it strange that I am speaking to you from New York. But believe me, I didn't leave Germany lightly. I only went away when the murderous intentions of the current German regime had become clear.' She urged all Germans to resist Hitler. Those who agreed with her either remained silent or were sent to concentration camps.[435]

At around the same time the Japanese launched their attack on Pearl Harbor, effectively bringing America into the war. Meanwhile, in Moscow, Lev Knipper and his wife Mariya were preparing to make their way to Germany via Iran, Turkey and Bulgaria, feigning defection and using Lev's role as a composer as cover; their intention was to establish themselves in Berlin, persuade Lev's famous sister Olga to use her contacts and influence to enable them to help them come into contact with Hitler, and kill him at close range.

As Stalin began to realise that Hitler was now facing defeat from east and west, he began to imagine that Hitler's death might mean the Western Allies would prefer to make peace with a new German regime and leave the Soviet Union to fight a massive European and American armed force. He cancelled Lev's mission. Had he not done so, Lev and Mariya would have failed because Hitler, brooding over his dire circumstances and wondering what destiny really had in store for him, made the decision to cut himself off from the world of movies and film stars altogether. There would be no more star-studded functions or even private affairs at which the likes of Olga Tschechowa would be present – and without Olga Lev and Mariya had no chance of getting up close to their target.

Olga's lover Jep was still flying missions over England in his Messerschmitt. He always took with him a small case she had given him, containing a photograph of her. 'The case with the little photograph gives me such happiness, because I always take it with me,' he wrote to her.[436] He must have had it with him when he was shot down and killed over England in December 1941.

CHAPTER NINETEEN

TIME IS BROKEN

Hitler had learned a trick from Wagner, who had tried to disguise his anti-Semitism in his operas by never actually mentioning Jews by nature or by name. Hitler never gave a direct order for the extermination of the Jews, but made his wishes known by inference or private and unrecorded dictates. However, when on 18 December 1941 *Reichsführer-SS* Heinrich Himmler asked Hitler, 'What do we do with the Jews?' Hitler replied, '*Als Partisanen auszurotten*' – 'exterminate them as partisans'. Israeli historian Yehuda Bauer commented that this remark is probably as close as historians will ever get to a definitive order from Hitler for the genocide of millions of Jews.[437]

Mass killings of some one million Jews had already occurred before the plans of the Final Solution were fully implemented in 1942, but it was only with the decision to eradicate the entire Jewish population that the extermination camps were built for the industrialised mass slaughter of Jews.

Hitler announced he would no longer watch movies. Eva Braun tried to change his mind. He told her, 'I can't watch films while the war is on, when the people have to make so many sacrifices and I must make grave decisions. I must also save my sensitive eyes for reading maps and reports from the front.'[438] He wanted it sound as if he was making a great sacrifice, but he continued to watch movies in his private cinema at the Berghof.

Films took on a new role for Hitler's people, becoming more than just entertainment or even propaganda. They were a diversion from the terrible truth. 'The films made by UFA were not propaganda,' said Wolfgang Preiss:

They were melodramas, romantic with many songs. They were not political pictures. Goebbels used films to make the German people happy so that they would not think and know they were losing the war. The newsreels were propaganda. They made us believe we could not lose. You were not to *think*.[439]

If the people didn't *think*, they wouldn't *wonder* what was really happening on the war fronts, and they wouldn't *know* that Germany was heading for defeat after the *Führer* had promised them total victory. It was more important for Hitler to maintain his image than for the German people to know the truth, that their *Führer* was not infallible after all.

In Britain and America, films were being made to boost morale and lift spirits; in Germany, they were simply to stop you thinking. Wolfgang Preiss was in one such film, his first – *Die Große Liebe* (*The Great Love*), starring Zarah Leander as singer Hanna Holberg whose lover Paul, a *Luftwaffe* pilot, played by Viktor Staal, must leave for the war, causing Hanna much emotional suffering and giving her the chance to sing several emotional songs. Preiss had a supporting role as Paul's best friend Etzdorf, who goes with him to the Eastern Front. Etzdorf is killed but Paul returns home from the war and marries Hanna. The final shot of the film is of the happy couple looking to the skies as squadrons of German bombers fly past. It was a film designed to stop the German people from even wondering whether the war was won or lost. 'Most never knew how bad things were going because of the propaganda that told us we were winning,' Preiss recalled. 'So you lived.' He, like all Germans, had no idea the war was lost: 'I only know from history. At the time we were not told anything other than Germany was winning the war. The plans were being set in 1941–42 to make the film. Germany was triumphant then. Later – no!'[440]

The film's musical score has a peculiar and secretive history. Michael Jary wrote the melodies and Bruno Balz the lyrics. Jary's real name was Maximilian Michael Jarczyk, but because his name made people think he was a Polish Jew, he went into hiding for a while and emerged as Michael Jary to become a respected composer of popular music.

Bruno Balz was arrested several times because of his homo-sexuality. After one spell in prison, he was released in 1936 on the condition that his name would not be credited on any songs he wrote. He also had to marry, and took a wife called Selina. He was arrested again in 1941 – apparently he was found with a Hitler youth – and tortured by the Gestapo. He was about to be sent to a concentration camp, but Michael Jary and possibly Zarah Leander persuaded somebody important – probably Joseph Goebbels – that Balz could write songs to aid the war effort.[441] It is said that within a day of his release, he had written his two greatest songs, 'Davon geht die Welt nicht unter' (That Is Not the End of the World) and 'Ich weiß, es, wird einmal ein Wunder gescheh'n' (I Know That Someday a Miracle Will Happen). Zarah Leander sang them both in the film and on record, and they became especially popular with the German troops who were fighting a losing war, which they had been told by Hitler they could still win. Zarah never considered them to be propaganda songs, but actor Will Quadflieg thought 'Ich weiß, es, wird einmal ein Wunder gescheh'n' was 'propaganda in its best and worst sense because everyone longed for that mira-cle'.[442] Many Germans listening to the song believed it told them that their *Führer* would defeat the enemy no matter what, because it was Zarah Leander who was singing it. The irony was that Balz had written the lyrics of both songs to reflect his own circumstances, and the songs became underground anthems for homosexuals in concentration camps.

As for *Die Große Liebe* itself, Goebbels allowed its direc-tor, Rolf Hansen, to take all the time he needed; it took from September 1941 to March 1942 to make, but it wasn't as much of a 'no expense spared' movie as it might seem. To save money, Hitler's own SS bodyguard were used as extras, and in the most extraordinary way: Wolfgang Preiss recalled, '[Leander] had a scene singing surrounded by women with wings. But they were all men from Hitler's SS bodyguard. They were not paid, so this was cheap to do.'[443]

Saving money was not the only consideration in using the SS as extras. Zarah Leander had arrived in German films with very un-German-like curves, and had grown curvier. 'She grew heavy, not fat,' said Preiss. 'They had to disguise her growing figure with carefully designed clothes and flattering camera angles – and they made it look as though she was not so big after all.' Surrounding her with burly SS men dressed as women had the effect of making Zarah look smaller. 'They had big arms, big shoulders, and they were tall because Zarah was tall. It was carefully filmed, and the only one the audience looked at was Zarah.' Preiss was shocked when he first saw the SS guards dressing up:

Oh, grotesque! I came into the room where the regiment was changing. I was in the uniform of a lieutenant – that was my part in the film – and the sergeant saw me and shouted '*Achtung!*' They all jumped to attention in their dresses. Wigs were slipping off, with make-up on or partly on. It was a grotesque sight.[444]

While Goebbels kept a tight rein on the budget – their dwindling funds were being sunk into the war effort – he also insisted on reshoots for some scenes which he felt were inappropriate. 'That is an example of how Goebbels could control a film,' Preiss recalled.

We had to reshoot an entire scene – a party. Goebbels saw the scene and said, 'A German woman doesn't live like that,' so we spent four days filming it again in a smaller room, with fewer people and with German sparkling wine instead of French champagne, because this was 1942 and Goebbels didn't want the people to see someone in a film who was living the high life.[445]

‡

It was during the making of the film that Wolfgang Preiss first heard mention of a 'Hitler film':

> When Goebbels had it in mind to make a picture about Hitler, he told Zarah he wanted her to be in it. The film was intended to portray Hitler as 'the saviour'. But bigger than Christ. I am facetious of course, but it's true. It's what many thought of him. He was of divine providence. It was to be the greatest story ever told.

Several prominent filmmakers were given the privilege of trying to get a screenplay completed, and at least three directors would work on the 'Hitler film'. Rolf Hansen was one of those; he told Preiss he wanted him in it, playing an officer in the *Wehrmacht*.[446]

The Hitler film was to have been Goebbels's cinematic masterpiece, and the conclusion of all his work – the immortalisation of Hitler. 'He was like Selznick and *Gone with the Wind*,' said Preiss. 'This movie had to be bigger than *Gone with the Wind*.' Rolf Hansen informed Preiss that he had been working on a treatment: 'Hitler is born – Hitler saves Germany – Hitler saves the world – a three-act drama of Wagnerian dimensions. And music by Wagner. That was decided.'[447]

No doubt it was to be filmed in Agfacolor and very possibly in 70mm, twice the size of conventional film, producing a much bigger and wide high-definition image which the Fox Film Corporation in Hollywood had dabbled with in a number of films including John Wayne's first film, *The Big Trail*, in 1930. Hitler loved film technology and kept a sharp eye on everything Hollywood was producing in regard to special effects and anything new that was technological, such as *King Kong*, which was among his very favourite films and which he had a print of in his collection. He was rumoured to also have a copy of Disney's *Snow White and the Seven Dwarfs* because he was captivated by the new animation technology. He also happened to love cartoons. One film he was said to dislike was *Gone with the Wind*, and the morning after treating all his staff to a screening of one of his favourite films – probably a war film or an action adventure – he was heard to gently chide one of his secretaries, who might have been Eva Braun, 'I understand you didn't like the movie last night? I know what you want. You want *Gone with the Wind*.'[448]

As well as Leni Riefenstahl and Rolf Hansen, Veit Harlan was also attached to the Hitler film project at some point. On 8 April 1942 Goebbels issued Harlan with a special ID card, allowing him through the back door of the Ministry of Propaganda in Wilhelmplatz in Berlin any time of day or night, making him part of an elite group of people given almost unlimited access to Goebbels. Strong themes throughout Harlan's films were the cult of death and the cult of fate. In his first colour film, *Die Goldene Stadt* (*The Golden City*) in 1942, a mother dies on the moors, and her daughter feels she has no choice but to follow her mother by killing herself; the film had a profound effect when, in the real world, German families were losing loved ones. Through such films, they were comforted with the thought that death had a real significance.

The problem with the Hitler film was that it could not be realised until Germany had won the war, and so it simmered along. Wolfgang Preiss thought Zarah Leander was to play Eva Braun, although all of the popular actresses of the time were probably considered. Leander was Rolf Hansen's choice, suggesting he planned to give the film its romantic touch. Exactly what shape the film would have taken remained a mystery, certainly to Preiss. 'Who knows?' he said. 'Who knows what was in the mind of Hitler or Goebbels?'

Hitler proved to be very fussy about how he was to be immortalised, especially in regard to who was to play him. 'That was a big problem,' said Preiss. 'No one could play Hitler but Hitler. And one day Hitler would say he would play himself. The next he said it must be a great actor. Then he said nobody could play the part because it was too big, too *great*. No actor was great enough. It drove Goebbels insane, I think.'[449] This might have been enough of a nightmare for Goebbels to omit any references from his diary – though he was thought to have written everything down of importance, he would not criticise his *Führer*, even in his diaries, which he no doubt expected to publish at some time in the future when the war was won and his place in German history secured.

With or without Goebbels's enthusiasm or participation, the film milled around for years within the film community, surfacing again during the final stages of the war; but later, after the war, no one owned up to it. Meanwhile, *Die Große Liebe* became a sensational hit when it had a double premiere in Berlin on 12 June 1942 at the German-Palast Cinema and the UFA-Palast-am-Zoo Cinema. It went on to be seen by twenty million people and took eight million marks, having cost three million to produce. The Film Censor's Office deemed it 'politically valuable', 'artistically valuable' and 'valuable for the people', and it became the most commercially successful film of the Third Reich era, making Zarah Leander a bigger star than ever.[450] 'The people loved her,' Wolfgang Preiss recalled. 'Wherever she went there were great crowds of fans, so she was mobbed.'

Incredibly, films and music were often the most important matters for discussion between Hitler and Goebbels even at a time when Germany was facing its most testing time since the outbreak of war – the RAF were attacking Lübeck and Rostock as well as launching the first 'thousand bomber raid' on Cologne. Perhaps buoyed by the success Rommel was enjoying in north Africa, Goebbels brought Hitler news of the great box office success of Veit Harlan's *Der Große König* (*The Great King*), which featured Otto Gebühr in his final portrayal of Frederick the Great. Hitler was also delighted with the new magnetic tape recordings of Germany's leading orchestras which Goebbels had given him in May, and they agreed that the Berlin Philharmonic was better than the Vienna Philharmonic.[451] Goebbels was pleased to report that book sales were up, noting, 'Never has German cultural life bloomed as now in the third year of the war.'[452] All that seemed far more important than what was really going on at the fronts. Culture, they seemed to believe, would solve all problems and bring success. The future of Germany lay in its cult of celebrity.

These were men whose deluded fantasies disguised the terrible truth; the summer of 1942 turned into a season of calm and contentment for Hitler and Goebbels, both men finding peace in their shared delusions. On 23 June, Goebbels visited Hitler and was joined there by Martin Bormann and Robert Ley, head of the German Labour Front. The four sat in the garden and enjoyed relaxed conversation. 'What glorious weather!' wrote Goebbels. 'We sit in the garden the whole afternoon, and one has the impression of the most profound peace.'[453]

By the summer of 1942 Operation Reinhard, the systematic extermination of the Jews, began, while in north Africa Hitler's forces were defeated at El Alamein, thwarting his plans to seize the Suez Canal and the Middle East. In Europe he was faced with the onslaught from American, British and Canadian forces as well as fighters from occupied territories, while in the east he had to defeat Stalin at all costs. He was dragged from his indolence back to a form of reality to personally manage the war, ignoring all advice from his generals. He was confident that Russia would quickly capitulate. But the battles raged on through the severe Russian winter, and the German forces, lacking proper winter clothing and supplies, began to retreat in the face of a Soviet counter-attack. The war took its toll on thousands of civilians inside Moscow, including Olga Tschechowa's uncle Vladimir Knipper, who had stubbornly remained there, dying on 12 November 1942.

After a massive defeat at Stalingrad during the winter of 1942–1943, 90,000 German troops, including the field marshal commanding them, surrendered; Hitler had ordered them all to fight to the death and, incensed at their betrayal, blamed them for the change in his fortunes. Increasingly, he was losing not just the war but also his grip on reality.

The Propaganda Ministry encouraged a number of celebrities to attend Goebbels's important speech on 18 February 1943 at the Berlin *Sportpalast*, to hear him respond to the defeat at Stalingrad in front of a carefully selected audience. At home, millions listened on radio as Goebbels spoke about the 'misfortune of the past weeks' and an 'unvarnished picture of the situation'. Why Goebbels was speaking and not Hitler was due partly to Hitler having taken to hiding at the Berghof.

Goebbels warned that if the *Wehrmacht* was no longer able to hold back the Soviets, the German Reich and then the whole of Europe would fall to Bolshevism. He blamed Germany's failure on the Jews, warning, 'We cannot overcome the Bolshevist danger unless we use equivalent, though not identical, methods – total war.' He screamed at his audience: 'Do you want total war? If necessary, do you want a war more total and radical than anything that we can imagine today?'[454]

‡

His audience cried out for total war, and the *Deutsche Wochenschau* newsreel cameras captured the reactions of the various celebrities in the audience. Olga Tschechowa buried her head in her hands in disbelief; that clip was never shown in the final edition of that newsreel.[455]

Goebbels's concept of 'total war' was nothing more than a phrase he had used often since 1939. He had read a book called *Total War* – he had not even thought up the term himself. Books, music, films, the cult of celebrity, the adulation of stars of screen and opera, of the concert hall and the stage, and the fantasy and delusions that sprang from it all – these were the inspiration behind the men who brought the greatest devastation and murder on a near-global scale in the middle of the twentieth century. These were amateur artists who became amateur generals. The German people had no desire for 'total war', which would have meant the mobilisation of every man, woman and child, and all areas of industry being devoted to war, meaning the closing of all cinemas, theatres, museums and other places of cultural interest.

Goebbels's 'total war' speech has been recorded as some kind of historic moment in the Second World War, but it turned out to be little more than a footnote in history because his vision was never fully realised. Civil building projects and cultural plans continued, many individuals maintained their lifestyles, and Hitler himself ignored the concept by insisting that cinemas, theatres, opera houses and museums stay open. Goebbels kept the film studios open and working; he believed that every film somehow served the war effort, and he still hoped to make the Hitler film. His attentions were diverted away from the realities of war, and he played the role he had created for himself as Germany's most prominent film producer, who was as much of an amateur in that field as he was at managing a world war.

On 27 February 1943 the deportation began of all the Jews still working in German industry – over 10,000 – to the death camps in Poland.

It might seem as though there was a huge gulf between the Final Solution, the Hitler film and Goebbels's 'total war' concept, but they were all aspects of one basic concept: the glorification of Hitler. The Final Solution *had* to be implemented to fulfil the prophecies of both Hitler and Wagner; otherwise they would both prove to be false prophets. The Hitler film *had* to be made, to become a lasting legacy of the life and career of Germany's star-Messiah – Hitler and Goebbels believed that cinema was the modern medium that would survive the centuries. 'Total war' *had* to be waged in order to ensure the previous two concepts were fulfilled, because to do otherwise would result in defeat and total failure. Without world conquest, Hitler's fame would become only infamy. But Germany had not the heart to wage true total war.

Even though funds for making films were dwindling, Goebbels kept pouring Reichsmarks into productions he took a particularly personal interest in. He even tolerated star tantrums and bad behaviour – the cult of celebrity remained one of his priorities. One of the most popular stars was Hans Albers, still depressed over losing his Jewish girlfriend Hansi. He drowned his sorrows in the bottle, which brought out the worst, and sometimes the foolhardy, in him. When, in the spring of 1943, Hitler invited Bulgaria's King Boris III to Munich, Albers refused to vacate the state visitors' hotel suite for the king, saying, 'I myself am king.' He was taken for interrogation, which he treated as if it were a performance, asking his interrogators, 'What do I owe the honour?' After hearing a succession of accusations, he said, 'And that was all you have to tell me?' He then took his hat and left. No further action was taken against him.[456]

Feeling virtually invincible, he declared, 'I am God!' Goebbels considered him so invaluable that he personally approved Albers being cast in the title role of *Münchhausen*, one of Goebbels's most ambitious film projects, which he had begun before the *Sportpalast* speech. He had insisted on a first-class screenplay and producer Eberhard Schmidt obliged by breaking Nazi laws and hiring blacklisted writer Erich Kästner.

Kästner was famous for his poems and children's literature, most notably *Emil und die Detektive* (*Emil and the Detectives*) and its sequel *Emil und die Drei Zwillinge* (*Emil and the Three Twins*). A pacifist who was opposed to the Nazi regime, Kästner was interrogated by the Gestapo several times. The Writers' Guild excluded him, and his books were among those burned on 10 May 1933 because of the 'culturally Bolshevist attitude in his writings'. Kästner moved to Switzerland where he wrote apolitical, entertaining novels, such as *Drei Männer im Schnee* (*Three Men in the Snow*) in 1934, and it was from Switzerland that he wrote the screenplay *Münchhausen* under the pseudonym Berthold Bürger. Goebbels never knew.

Goebbels ordered the production of *Münchhausen* to celebrate the twenty-fifth anniversary of the UFA film studio; he hoped the film would compete with Technicolor Hollywood fantasy family films like *The Wizard of Oz*. It was surprisingly devoid of Nazi politics, although Kästner did successfully slip in one political statement which was obviously lost on Goebbels: Münchhausen, while on the moon, experiences a time warp, and says, '*Nicht meine Uhr ist kaputt, die Zeit ist kaputt!*' (My watch is not broken; it's time that is broken!). Time was broken in the real world and could not be mended until Hitler was defeated or dead.

Albers did not attend the premiere of *Münchhausen* in March 1943, a month after the *Sportpalast* speech, but the German people flocked to see it, and for a few hours forgot about the war and Goebbels's 'total war' speech.

In 1943, extraordinarily heavy air raids hit German cities: Duisburg on 14 May, Dortmund on 25 May, Elberfeld on 25 June – razing 870 acres of the city centre to the ground – and Hamburg on the night of 27 July. Despite these indications of the disaster to come, Goebbels maintained his cultural interests, and in advocation of the Nazi cult of celebrity, he had been thrilled to have as a guest at his home one of the authors who he most idolised, Knut Hamsun. Goebbels had been reading the 84-year-old Norwegian writer's works since his childhood, and was delighted to record, 'The wisdom of his age is written in his face. His belief in the German victory is completely unshakeable.'[457] But either the great author's wisdom was faltering, or, more likely, Goebbels was lost in his world of illusion, only able to see and hear what he wanted to see and hear.

The first attack on Berlin, by 600 British bombers, came on 24 August. They returned on 1 September and 3 September; then they hit Hanover and Kassel.

Zarah Leander suddenly disappeared from Germany. She had become increasingly pressured by Hitler and Goebbels to become a German citizen, but had always refused. When her villa in the fashionable Berlin suburb of Grunewald was hit in a British air raid, she decided it was time to leave Germany. She departed in secrecy, returning to Sweden to live in a mansion at Lönö, not far from Stockholm, which she had bought with her money earned in Nazi Germany.

Goebbels was furious when he learned she had abandoned the country that had made her a star, and called her a traitor; while in Sweden she was condemned as a Nazi collaborator, and only the Communist Party, to the puzzlement of most Swedes, described her as a 'true democrat'. By the time she was back in Sweden, her work for the NKVD was over because Germany was losing the war. Also over, it seemed, was her career. Nobody wanted to work with her. She was already reaping all she had sowed in Hitler's cult of celebrity.

CHAPTER TWENTY

THE PRICE

While the war became something from which Hitler wanted to hide, Wagner remained first and foremost on his mind, and when he heard that Winifred wanted to close down her company, he demanded it stayed open and arranged for all of her singers and musicians to be relieved of war service. He became a vital lifeline for Frau Wagner whenever she discovered that any of her performers and musicians had suddenly gone missing; she only had to call him, and he invariably managed to have them returned, although she never enquired where they had been exactly.[458]

One of her greatest stars was Max Lorenz, famous for his roles as Tristan, Siegfried and Walther. Lorenz was a homosexual, and to mask his sexuality, from 1932 he was married to Charlotte Appel, who was Jewish. When he was arrested because of an affair with a young man, Winifred contacted Hitler, who advised her that Lorenz would not be suitable for the Bayreuth festival. She replied that without Lorenz she might as well close the Festival because, without him, 'Bayreuth can't be done'. Hitler withdrew his objections and Lorenz was released.

Lorenz was foolishly open about being married to a Jewish woman, provoking the SS, which had been ordered to turn a blind eye. When he was away from his house, the SS burst in and tried to take Charlotte and her mother, but were foiled at the last moment when Charlotte was able to make a phone call to the sister of Herman Göring, and the SS was ordered to leave the two women alone. Göring stated in a letter of 21 March 1943 that Lorenz was under his personal protection and no action should be taken against him, his wife or her mother.[459]

Winifred Wagner helped a number of people in danger of being interned. In the late 1930s, a letter from her to Hitler prevented Hedwig and Alfred Pringsheim, whose daughter Katia was married to Thomas Mann, from being arrested by the Gestapo.[460] Winifred's Jewish builder and his family were also protected by her, as were others who were of special interest to her, especially if they were musicians. It was often done with a simple phone call or telegram to Hitler, and many sought her help at the outbreak of war, hoping that she would have both compassion and influence. She recalled, 'When war broke out, lots of people were put into concentration camps. I was sent vast numbers of petitions. The ones that seemed reasonably believable to me and also worthy of help, I passed them on.'[461] She was selective about who was worthy of help. Although Hitler obliged, she never saw him again as he no longer went to Bayreuth, and she stayed away from Berlin, afraid of the bombs.

Sometimes the cult of celebrity could save lives; at other times, it took them. Ottilie Metzger-Lattermann was a celebrated German Jewish contralto and a performer of Wagner who sang at the Bayreuth Festival, was first contralto with the Hamburg Opera, and performed as a *Lieder* recitalist, often accompanied by Richard Strauss and Hans Pfitzner. In 1933 she gave concerts under Bruno Walter in Berlin and Otto Klemperer in Dresden. But after Hitler came to power, she performed only for Jewish audiences. In 1939 she and her daughter fled to Brussels, but were later rounded up by the Nazis and sent to Auschwitz in 1943. The exact dates of their deaths are unknown, but Ottilie Metzger-Lattermann was probably around sixty-five when she was murdered by the Nazis.

Richard Breitenfeld, a German baritone, sang the role of the count in Act II of Franz Schreker's *Der ferne Klang* (*The Distant Sound*) at its world premiere at the Frankfurt Opera in 1912. The contralto was Magda Spiegel. Fame didn't save either of them; both were Jewish. Breitenfeld was murdered in 1944 in Theresienstadt, aged seventy-five; Magda Spiegel died in Auschwitz the same year, aged fifty-seven.

Henriette Gottlieb, a German Jewish soprano, made a name for herself with her performance in the Wagnerian role of Brünnhilde in the *Théâtre des Champs-Élysées* in Paris during the performance of *Der Ring der Nibelung* in 1928, when she was still a promising young newcomer. She was famous for her numerous performances and recordings of Brünnhilde, but that did not save her from dying in the Łódź ghetto on 2 January 1942, aged fifty-eight.

Hitler would have known of Gottlieb and her work, as he would have also known of others which his delusions, which were born out of his love for opera, sent to their deaths. Hans Tobias Erl was a German operatic bass who, in 1918, began a fifteen-year engagement with the Frankfurt Opera as the first bass, but because he was Jewish he was dismissed from the opera in June 1933 and forced, with other Jews, to gather in the *Festhalle Frankfurt*, where he was made to sing 'In diesen heil'gen Hallen' ('In These Hallowed Halls'). He was deported in 1942 to Auschwitz, and died, probably in the same year.

Grete Forst was an Austrian soprano, who made her operatic debut in Cologne in 1900 in the title role of *Lucia de Lammermoor*, repeating the role three years later at the Vienna State Opera where she was made a member of the company by Gustav Mahler. In an effort to save herself from deportation, she converted to Catholicism in 1940, but on 27 May 1942 she was sent to the Maly Trostenets extermination camp in Belorussia and was murdered on 1 June 1942.

Hitler would also have known of Erhard Eduard Wechselmann, the great German baritone who, on at least one occasion, sang for a Jewish audience with the contralto Ottilie Metzger-Lattermann who, like him, was murdered in Auschwitz.

The Nazi cult of celebrity could, in its twisted irony, save celebrities from the gas chambers, even within the confines of Auschwitz, as in the case of Alma Rosé, an Austrian Jewish violinist from a dynasty of classic musicians. Her father was the violinist Arnold Rosé, who was the leader of the Vienna Philharmonic Orchestra for fifty years from 1881 to 1931, and of the Vienna State Opera orchestra and the legendary Rosé String Quartet. Alma's mother was Gustav Mahler's sister, Justine, making Alma Gustav Mahler's niece.

In 1930 Alma married Czech violinist Váša Příhoda, one of the great violin virtuosi of the twentieth century, but they divorced in 1935. She continued to follow a highly successful career, and in 1932 founded the women's orchestra *Die Wiener Walzermädeln* (The Waltzing Girls of Vienna), which undertook concert tours throughout Europe. When Austria was annexed to Germany, she and her father escaped to London, but Alma chose to perform in Holland and found herself trapped there when the Germans occupied the Netherlands. A fictitious marriage to a Dutch engineer named August van Leeuwen Boomkamp did not save her; nor did her conversion to Christianity, and she went on the run, managing to reach France late in 1942. Upon trying to escape to Switzerland, she was captured by the Gestapo.

After several months in the internment camp of Drancy she was deported in July 1943 to Auschwitz, where she was quarantined and became very ill. She was recognised and allowed leadership of the *Mädchenorchester von Auschwitz* (Girl Orchestra of Auschwitz), a pet project of *SS-Oberaufseherin* Maria Mandel. The ensemble largely consisted of amateur musicians, and its primary function was to play at the main gate each morning and evening as the prisoners left for and returned from their work assignments. The orchestra also gave weekend concerts for the prisoners and the SS, as well as entertaining at SS functions.

As the conductor of the orchestra, Alma Rosé had the status of a *Kapo* in the camp, with privileges and comforts including additional food and a private room. The other musicians lived less luxuriously, but were adequately clothed and spared hard manual labour. Thanks to her musical prowess, Alma was held in high esteem by Maria Mandel and Josef Mengele.

The orchestra included two professional musicians, cellist Anita Lasker-Wallfisch and vocalist and pianist Fania Fénelon, each of whom wrote memoirs of their time in Auschwitz. Fénelon's account, *Playing for Time*, which became a play by Arthur Miller and was later made into a film, depicted Rosé as a cold-hearted autocrat who kowtowed to the Germans for her own self-interest. She also claimed that Alma was abusive to the musicians. But other members of the orchestra, including Anita Lasker-Wallfisch, disputed Fénelon's account, maintaining that Rosé's interest was in protecting the well-being of the women in her orchestra, which not only required that Rosé establish and maintain a high musical standard by any means possible, but also that she placated her Nazi captors. As evidence of her success, her supporters note that, under her residence, not one member of the orchestra was killed, and musicians who fell ill were treated at the hospital, which was unheard of for Jewish prisoners at Auschwitz.

Alma Rosé died in Auschwitz in 1944 aged thirty-eight, probably as a result of food poisoning, though typhus is another possibility. Fénelon alleged that she was deliberately poisoned, but few believe that. Arnold Rosé, grief-stricken by news of his daughter's death, did not survive long after the war.

In 1943 the Bayreuth Festival played host to wounded soldiers from the front. They arrived in Bayreuth to be welcomed by a *Wehrmacht* band as the League of German Girls handed them bunches of flowers. For Hitler this was Wagner playing his part in the *Führer*'s war. He didn't consider whether or not any of the soldiers actually wanted to be force-fed Wagner while they recuperated; it was not their decision – it was *his*. Frau Wagner mothered the soldiers, and she saw to it that each and every one of them was well fed and comfortable.

In the festival book, she wrote a short prayer: 'May Wagner's music give our soldiers fanatical faith in the victory of our guns.' Music had become a weapon of war;[462] it was the realisation of Hitler's dream, that his great idol Richard Wagner become the weapon by which he, as the Messiah/*Führer*, would fulfil his destiny that Wagner had himself prophesied through *Rienzi*.

Leni Riefenstahl had gone back to making feature films, and in 1940 had resumed work on a project she had abandoned when Hitler persuaded her to make *Triumph of the Will*. *Tiefland* (*Lowland*) was set in the Spanish Pyrenees, but because there were no people with the requisite Mediterranean looks in Germany to act as extras, she used Roma and Sinti Gypsies interned in Maxglan, Austria. She later claimed she had never been in the Maxglan camp, but one of the gypsies, Rosa Winter, remembered that Riefenstahl came into the internment camp 'with the police detective' to choose her extras.[463]

Filming was laboriously slow, beginning in 1940 on location in Mettenwald in Austria. In the autumn of 1941 the scenes involving the gypsies were finally finished, and the Roma and Sinti were returned to the camp in Maxglan. In 1943 that camp was disbanded and most of the gypsies went to Auschwitz, others to a small part of the Lackenbach camp in Burgenland. Virtually all those who were sent to Auschwitz died there.[464] In later years, Riefenstahl made a public statement that all the extras survived and that she had met them again after the war. In 2002 she attempted to sue documentary filmmaker Nina Gladitz for alleging that she did not meet the survivors and that she must have known the gypsies would be sent to a death camp. The suit was dropped.[465]

Filming of *Tiefland* continued into 1944; Riefenstahl was only able to carry on because Hitler made sure Goebbels, who did not consider her film essential to his plans, gave her all the finance and any other help she needed. When snow fell, she asked Goebbels to send a company of soldiers to sweep it from the roofs; Major Peter Jakob, upon arriving with his men and discovering why they had been sent, told her, 'You must be crazy! You want my men and me to shovel snow?' Despite his initial anger, he fell for her, and they married on 21 March 1944; the union lasted only two years. Just before they married, she introduced him to Hitler at the Berghof where she noted that her *Führer* seemed depressed; it was the last time she saw him.

Hitler had a great deal to be depressed about. On 10 July 1944 the Allies had landed in Sicily, opening a new front to the war and leading to the deposition of Mussolini by Pietro Badoglio. On 30 August the city centre of Rheydt, Goebbels's home town, was destroyed by British bombing. Goebbels pressed Hitler to speak to the nation, but Hitler continued to lose himself in his own fantasies and delusions while the war was being lost. On 8 September 1943 the new Italian government surrendered unconditionally to the Allies, and Hitler's Germany became ever more isolated.

Goebbels urged Hitler to negotiate with Stalin, but Hitler still believed he could negotiate with the British. Finally Goebbels persuaded Hitler to deliver a speech by radio, and on 10 September 1944 the German people heard their *Führer's* voice for the last time. Goebbels now came to the same conclusion as Hitler, that they could negotiate with the British, who would surely prefer that Germany remained a National Socialist state than become a Communist one under Stalin. They failed to understand the loathing they had engendered throughout Europe and America.

Perhaps it was impending doom that reunited Goebbels and Magda; their relationship improved while Germany's situation declined. Perhaps they both knew that the inevitable outcome would result in them sharing a destiny, along with their children, celebrating the cult of death which he and Hitler had so carefully designed and nurtured. Whether or not they yet harboured those thoughts which would certainly occupy them in time, they both maintained a public belief in the final victory, and she dutifully performed for the cameras by doing some work in a factory to contribute to the 'total war' effort.

Goebbels maintained his position as the arbiter of taste and banned a 1944 film, *Die Feuerzangenbowle* (*The Fire Tongs Bowl* or *The Punch Bowl*), for 'disrespect for authority'. Based on the book by Heinrich Spoerl, who also wrote the screenplay, it was the tale of a famous writer, during the time of the Wilhelminian Empire in Germany, going undercover as a student at a small town secondary school after his friends tell him he missed out on the best part of growing up by being educated at home. It was a nostalgic comedy of mistaken identities, but Bernhard Rust, Secretary of Education and a former high school teacher, complained about the way the movie poked fun at teachers, and the premiere of the film was cancelled.

The film starred one of Germany's most popular actors, Heinrich Rühmann; determined to save the film, he used his contacts with Nazi leaders to go over Goebbels's head and have the picture screened for Herman Göring, who then made a direct appeal to Hitler to have the ban lifted. Hitler cared nothing for schoolteachers, and to Goebbels's chagrin he ordered the film be released. To save face, Goebbels insisted that scenes be reshot to make every scene, in his opinion, perfect. It was to become one of the most popular films of Rühmann's career, described by critic Georg Seeßlen a 'masterpiece of timeless, cheerful escapism'.[466] As an ironic footnote, because the film's premiere was delayed so long, by the time the movie was on general release, the German army had suffered massive casualties and some of the actors in the film had been drafted and killed on the battlefield.

At a time when the men of Germany were being called upon to sacrifice their lives on the war fronts, certain film stars were put on a list of 'indispensable actors', called the *Gottbegnadeten* list ('God-gifted' list). Assembled in September 1944 by Goebbels and Hitler, it was a 36-page list of artists considered crucial to Nazi culture which excused certain individuals from military service during the Second World War. A total of 1,041 artists, architects, music conductors, singers, writers and filmmakers appeared on it. Goebbels listed about 640 motion picture actors, writers and directors on an extended version of the list, including Willi Fritsch and Werner Johannes Krauß, who had played Rabbi Loew in *Jud Süß*. Among the musicians included were Richard Strauss, Hans Pfitzern, Carl Orff, Wilhelm Furtwängler and the Wagnerian baritone Rudolf Bockelmann. Each listed artist received a letter from the Nazi Propaganda Ministry certifying his or her status. The only non-German on the list was Dutch actor Johannes Heesters.[467] Heinrich Rühmann was on the list, but Goebbels ordered him to take basic training as a pilot in revenge for going over his head. Rühmann was spared having to take part in the war effort, possibly due to intervention by Göring. But while the cult of celebrity had its perks, it was also rife with danger – Goebbels was not someone to be crossed.

The Soviet Union continued to steadily push Hitler's forces into retreat along the Eastern Front throughout 1944. On 6 June that year the Western Allied forces landed on the Normandy beaches of France. Many leading officers in the German military knew that defeat was inevitable, and some even conspired to remove the *Führer* from power. A plot involving some of Germany's highest-ranking officers was hatched; but on the day Hitler should have died, 20 July 1944, the suitcase bomb planted in Hitler's headquarters in Poland, the *Wolfsschanze* (Wolf's Lair), was accidentally moved underneath a heavy conference table so when it exploded, the table deflected much of the blast away from Hitler. He was injured, but survived to order reprisals and inform the people over the radio that providence had ensured his survival. He now found a new form of entertainment: he ordered that the executions of all those found guilty of the plot to kill him – they were hanged from meat hooks – be filmed so he could watch them in his private cinema in the Berghof.

The 'Hitler film' project remained a curiously open secret – and one to be completely forgotten, denied and buried for many years – but it continued to surface within the state-run film industry from time to time. Wolfgang Preiss was reminded of it again in 1944.

> I was making *The Crew of the Dora* – the director was Karl Ritter, and he had written it – he wrote many screenplays and produced many films. It was about Germany winning the war and yet the war was lost. He also had a treatment of the Hitler picture, or an idea for it. I said to him, 'If we lose the war, will Goebbels still want this [Hitler film] made?' He said, 'If we lose the war we will not be allowed to make another film again because we have told Nazi lies and we will not be forgiven. But if all is lost, Hitler will want his story told as one who fought to the end.' And I think that is true because he refused to surrender, and like a character in a Wagnerian opera he sacrificed himself.[468]

The purge on those who did not embrace the cult of celebrity continued. In 1944 stage and screen actor Kurt Gerron, who had starred in *Der Blaue Engel* (*The Blue Angel*) opposite Marlene Dietrich, was interned at Theresienstadt where he made what would prove to be his last film – as a prisoner. The Nazis forced him to feature in a propaganda film to demonstrate how humane conditions were at the concentration camp.

Gerron had been a military doctor in the First World War, and became an actor in 1920; he was famous for originating the role of 'Tiger' Brown in the Berlin premiere production of *Die Dreigroschenoper* (*The Threepenny Opera*), in which he sang 'Mack the Knife'. A Jew, he had escaped Nazi Germany in 1933 with his wife and parents, travelling first to Paris and later to Amsterdam where he kept on working as an actor at the *Stadsschouwburg*; he also directed films. He was offered work in Hollywood several times at the behest of Peter Lorre and Joseph von Sternberg, but kept refusing and remained in Amsterdam. After the Nazis occupied the Netherlands, he was held in the transit camp at Westerbork and then sent to Theresienstadt where he ran a cabaret called *Karussell* to entertain the inmates. His final film is alternatively known as *Theresienstadt: Ein Dokumentarfilm aus dem jüdischen Siedlungsgebiet* (*Terezin: A Documentary Film of the Jewish Resettlement*) and *Der Führer schenkt den Juden eine Stadt* (*The Führer Gives the Jews a City*); it remains the only film made by the Nazis inside a concentration camp.

Theresienstadt, promoted as the 'model' ghetto, was established by the Nazis in 1941 in Terezin, a town in the former Czechoslovakia. Goebbels intended to use the film as evidence to show to the International Red Cross and the world that Jews were well treated in the camps. But it was an elaborately staged hoax, presenting a completely false picture of camp life, and upon its completion the director and most of the cast of prisoners were put on the camp's final transport to Auschwitz,[469] among them Kurt Gerron and the members of jazz pianist Martin Roman's Ghetto Swingers. Gerron was killed immediately upon arrival at Auschwitz on 15 November 1944. Orders from Heinrich Himmler closed the gas chambers at Auschwitz the next day. Pianist Martin Roman and guitarist Coco Schumann survived the Holocaust.

Also in the Theresienstadt camp was Czech composer Viktor

Ullmann, who might have hoped that the fact he was a Roman Catholic would have spared him – his Jewish parents had converted to Roman Catholicism before Viktor's birth. Educated in Vienna, Ullmann's musical talents led him to Prague where he was mentored by Alexander von Zemlinsky, under whose direction he served as a conductor at the New German Theatre of Prague until 1927. His composition for piano *Schönberg Variations* brought him the Kertzka Prize. He spent time in Stuttgart but was forced to flee Germany in 1933 and returned to Prague. By the time he was deported to the Theresienstadt concentration camp, on 8 September 1942, his list of works had reached forty-one opus numbers and contained an additional three piano sonatas, song cycles on texts by various poets, operas, and the piano concerto Op. 25, which he finished in December 1939, nine months after the entry of German troops into Prague. Only thirteen printed items survive, which he published privately and entrusted to a friend for safekeeping.

He remained active at the camp as a composer and pianist, and performing concerts with other prominent musicians interned there such as Gideon Klein and Hans Krása. Ullmann wrote, 'By no means did we sit weeping on the banks of the waters of Babylon. Our endeavour with respect to arts was commensurate with our will to live.'[470]

The Nazis cynically promoted the artistic achievements and activities in the camp to deceive the International Red Cross. Once the inspectors left, most of the inmates were sent to their deaths, as was Viktor Ullmann, who was deported to the camp at Auschwitz-Birkenau where, on 18 October 1944, he was murdered in the gas chambers. Most of the work he completed in Theresienstadt was preserved and continues to be performed at concerts around the world.

The camp's first commandant, Rudolf Höss – not to be confused with Rudolf Hess – testified at the Nuremberg trials that up to three million people had died there: 2.5 million gassed, 500,000 from disease and starvation,[471] a figure since revised to 1.1 million; around 90 per cent of them were Jews.[472] Others deported to

Auschwitz included 150,000 Poles, 23,000 Roma and Sinti, 15,000 Soviet POWs, about 400 Jehovah's Witnesses and tens of thousands of people of diverse nationalities.[473] Those not killed in the gas chambers died of starvation, forced labour, disease, individual executions and medical experiments.[474]

There is no definitive figure for how many died either in the extermination camps, from forced labour or in mass killings. According to the United States Holocaust Memorial Museum in Washington DC, in 1933 there were approximately nine million Jews in Europe; by 1945, the Nazis had reduced that number to about three million. As many as 200,000 Roma gypsies died, and the number of physically and mentally handicapped persons, homosexuals and Polish intellectuals accounted for at least another 200,000. This totals about 6,400,000 victims of the concentration camps.

The Nazis also killed between two and three million Soviet prisoners in labour camps or executions, as well as any number of non-Jewish Poles and Soviets who died in forced labour due to malnutrition, unsafe work conditions, disease and experimentation. In Russia and many other parts of the Soviet Union, many were killed in mass open-air shootings and buried in large pits. In Poland, large numbers of Jews perished in the ghettos.[475] More than sixty million people in total may have died during the Second World War. That was the human cost of Hitler's ambition to be an artist, and of his delusions of a divine calling that came through the operas of Richard Wagner. Hitler's Nazi cult of celebrity came at a price so obscene it is inconceivable.

CHAPTER TWENTY-ONE

THE FALL

For those in the camps, life was hell on earth. For Berliners, life in 1944 had become another kind of living hell, with constant air raids by day from the American Army Air Force and more by night from the RAF. The terror, as well as age and illness, took its toll on Olga Tschechowa's mother Lulu Knipper, and she died in Berlin on 9 May. Olga moved from her Kaiserdamm apartment in West Berlin to live in her wooden dacha at Gross Glienecke, where she could escape the worst of the bombing; she took with her the large stained-glass panel bearing the Knipper arms.

By late 1944, the Red Army had pushed German forces back into western Europe while the Western Allies advanced on Germany, stalled only by Germany's attempt to defeat them in the Ardennes. Even at this critical time, Hitler believed that films were so vital to the war effort – and to his personal image – that while he closed theatres – and also schools – in 1944, he decreed that cinemas remained open – which they did to the very end of the war. In Berlin, anti-aircraft units were posted especially to protect the city's cinemas. Few films were being made at Babelsberg because of the air raids, and food was running low in Berlin and throughout Germany, so most films were made elsewhere. In October, Olga Tschechowa escaped Berlin for a while to make *Melusine* in the ski resort of Kitzbühel in the Austrian Tyrol.

While dining at her hotel, Tschechowa met Hitler's personal adjutant, Julius Schaud, who regaled her with all the gory details of the attempted assassination of Hitler at the *Wolfsschanze*; Schaud had been there and was rendered almost totally deaf by the explosion. Olga was shocked to learn that supplies of food and ammunition were being delivered to the Berghof while Hitler's own people were going hungry.[476]

When she wasn't filming, Olga travelled from city to city throughout Germany, performing at theatres and raising morale. While in Cologne, her hotel was hit by a British bomb and burned down, leaving her without her belongings; she had to return to Berlin by train wearing her stage costume. Back home, she faced the same hardships of the less affluent Berliners, eating whatever was available and, worse as far as she was concerned, allowed only 3 gallons of car fuel each month. She asked Goebbels if she could have extra rations of fuel for her Fiat Topolino and was furious when he refused her request. Even Goebbels could do little to overcome national shortages for one of his favourite film stars, and she had to take the S-Bahn suburban train like everyone else. To get to work each day at the studio, she walked up to 6 miles.[477]

Her life was made bearable by the presence of a new young man, Albert Sumser. They met at a party in Wannsee near Potsdam, where he was serving as a signals officer. When he first saw her, he did not recognise her; he was the only man to stand up when she entered the room. He told author Antony Beevor that he 'did not even dare to think about making an advance towards this beautiful woman', but she came over to him and talked, gave him her card and invited him to call her. He arrived at her house bringing 'instead of red roses' a brace of wild duck he had shot. His good manners and practical gesture was much appreciated by Olga, and the two became lovers 'on her initiative'. When he fell ill, she walked the 6 miles through the Königswald forest to Potsdam to see him, bringing what food she could gather.[478]

The war was almost lost, though the Nazi government was not admitting it. In 1943, Goebbels had commissioned Veit Harlan with a film project intended to inspire Germans to fight to the end. *Kolberg* was an historical costume epic about the Pomeranian town's resistance against Napoleon in 1807. America had its Alamo, the British Empire had its Rorkes Drift, and Germany had its Kolberg. The film was a call to all Germans to never surrender to the enemy but to die as martyrs; this was Hitler's message, conveyed to the masses as entertainment, and it was Goebbels's own watchword – 'total war'. Goebbels believed the historical events in the film would make suitable propaganda for the circumstances Germany now faced.[479] The film glorified the ideal of fighting to the death, which is what Hitler and Goebbels hoped the people of Germany were prepared to do. Harlan later commented that Hitler and Goebbels were 'convinced that such a film was more useful than a military victory'.[480]

Despite the lack of materials, which were poured into the war, Goebbels gave Harlan virtually unlimited resources, including the use of an estimated 10,000 soldiers as extras for the huge battle scenes. It was the most expensive film made during Hitler's rule, costing eight million marks, and taking a year to shoot. Goebbels wrote on 2 December 1944, 'I tell the *Führer* about the new 'Kolberg' film, describe a few scenes from it, which move him almost to tears.'

The film that Hitler and the public eventually saw was not entirely the picture that Harlan had made. When Goebbels first saw the film, he had what Harlan described in a 1963 interview as 'a choleric fit' and called it 'a pacifist film', and in his delusional state told Harlan that 'pacifists are always ruled by non-pacifists'. What shook Goebbels were the scenes of the horror of war – scenes of doors being torn down to make coffins, of water contaminated by corpses, of a grenade exploding in a house where a woman has just given birth and the newborn is buried alive. To Goebbels this was sadism, and he demanded cuts in the film, to which Harlan objected: 'I can't portray heroics if I don't show how heroic people are and how terrible their circumstances.' Goebbels disagreed, and ordered the offending scenes be removed.[481]

It was the last film to be given a lavish Nazi premiere, which was held on 30 January 1945 at a temporary cinema in Berlin, following the last radio address Hitler ever gave. That evening it was screened privately for Hitler at the Reich Chancellery as well to the men serving at the naval base at La Rochelle. It was released in the cinemas still standing in Germany until the end of the war, when it was withdrawn and banned until 1965.

As Germany headed inexorably towards destruction, Hitler embraced the coming catastrophe, and on 18 January 1945 he returned to Berlin, a city in ruins, as was much of Germany, along with large areas of Europe and the Soviet Union. In mid-February, he took cover from the intense air raids in the shelters that he had ordered Albert Speer to build in 1941 beneath the bomb-damaged Reich Chancellery. It was a virtual catacomb divided into two sections – the ante-bunker and the so-called *Führer* Bunker, linked by a single short corridor. The ante-bunker was for staff accommodation, while the *Führer* Bunker was for Hitler. It had twenty small rooms, all sparsely furnished, including a living room, a study and several bedrooms. From the *Führer* Bunker, he managed the war towards its inevitable outcome. Those about him expected him to take full control, but what they observed was a man who was lethargic, who preferred playing for hours with his dog Blondi and who for much of the time seemed absent minded and unable to make decisions.

On 1 February 1945, Olga Tschechowa returned to Berlin from Prague where she had been filming[482] – by then many German films were being produced in Prague, which had remained virtually untouched by the war. That same day, the Red Army under Marshal Zhukov's 1st Belorussian Front crossed the frozen River Oder and seized bridgeheads on the west bank. With the Red Army within 60 miles of Berlin, Olga was naturally concerned for her family. Her daughter Ada had married gynaecologist Wilhelm Rust, and they had a four-year-old daughter, christened Olga but called Vera. Wilhelm had been called up to serve as a *Luftwaffe* doctor attached to the headquarters of General Stumpff in the north. Ada and Vera lived in Olga's Gross Glienecke house[483] while Olga stayed with her niece, Marina Ried – daughter of Olga's sister Ada Knipper – and her husband just outside of Berlin.[484]

On 7 March, Hitler made a final visit to his front line troops at the Ninth Army headquarters on the River Oder. Visibly ill and with his grip on reality loose, he ordered his troops to fight to their dying breath. That same day, Eva Braun arrived in Berlin to join him in the *Führer* Bunker, pledging her loyalty and refusing to leave as the Red Army closed in.

On 20 March Hitler was filmed for the very last time, decorating boys of the Hitler Youth for bravery. His left hand visibly shook, giving rise to speculation that he suffered from Parkinson's disease. He remarked on several occasions that his hands shook so much he could barely hold his pistol. 'If I was ever wounded,' he said, 'none of my staff would be willing to give me the *coup de grâce*.'[485]

His health was in a terrible condition. He suffered from irritable bowel syndrome, skin lesions and an irregular heartbeat as well as the tremors.[486] Some of his conditions may have been caused by the amount of medication he was given by his regular physician, Dr Theodor Morell, which included 'Dr Koester's Anti-Gas Pills', which contained strychnine and atropine – Hitler couldn't bear body odours and especially his own propensity for flatulence – as well as injections of pulverised bull testicles in grape sugar because Hitler feared impotence. Dr Morell prescribed massive doses of dexedrine, caffeine, cocaine, pervatin, prozymen and ultraseptyl.[487]

It was not just his left hand that shook but the entire left side of his body. When he sat, he held his right hand over his left, and kept his right leg crossed over his left to hide the constant shaking. When walking, he shuffled slowly, his posture bent forward. *Feldmarschall* Heinz Guderian wrote that Hitler's 'mind, to be sure, remained active – but there was something weird about this activity, for it was dominated by constant wanderings, a mistrust of humanity and dictated by the efforts to conceal his physical, mental and military collapse'.[488]

For much of his life Hitler had lived in fear of cancer, probably because it was the disease that killed his mother; his fear increased with age. He also suffered from terrible nightmares, and would sometimes wake up as if he were suffocating, possibly due to his fear of death. With thoughts of suicide now in his head, perhaps he concluded that not only would he attempt to induce his own

Götterdämmerung, but bring his increased mental and physical sufferings to an end too. While he feared death, he never feared suicide, and maybe that was because suicide would be of his own making, whereas death by illness or injury would only serve to prove he was mortal after all; that was the conundrum he couldn't live with. He turned his mind to one final objective: his own *Götterdämmerung* as he headed towards the abyss, hastened by the Soviet advance upon Berlin.

He began working for destruction with almost as much energy as he had worked for conquest. He fled from reality into the world of Wagner's operas; Hitler's caretaker Herbert Döhring remembered Hitler having around 500 gramophone records of Wagner in the bunker,[489] losing himself in the narcotic effect of the music he loved, disabling him of sympathy for anyone and of conscience for anything. *Götterdämmerung* became his own personal score for the coming apocalypse, and he wanted to take the whole world with him into the abyss.

He ordered that all essential supplies and foodstuffs throughout Germany be destroyed to prevent them falling into the hands of the Russians. He cared nothing for the suffering of ordinary Germans, or about the displacement of millions throughout Europe, as he had cared nothing for the millions of Jews, Slavs and other groups sent to extermination camps. He ordered the destruction of all German industrial infrastructure before it could fall into Allied hands. Believing that Germany's military failures had forfeited its right to survive as a nation, he executed his scorched-earth policy, the Nero Decree – his identification with Nero was about to be fulfilled. He entrusted this mission to Albert Speer, now his Armaments Minister, who secretly disobeyed the order.[490]

Almost at the last, Goebbels tried to demonstrate that he still had control over the lives of Germany's film stars by having Hans Albers blacklisted. Albers had starred in a film which the navy had requested as a memorial to their heroes, but the film's director, Helmut Käutner, had something different in mind. *Große Freiheit Nr. 7* (*Great Freedom No. 7*, or *Port of Freedom* as it was known in the UK) told of a 'singing sailor', Hannes Kröger, played by Hans Albers, who works in a Reeperbahn club close to Große Freiheit, a street in Hamburg in the St. Pauli red light district. Sailors were depicted as drunks, Hannes was dependent on the bottle, and the girl he loved smoked cigarettes and slept with shipyard workers.

Most of the film was shot in Prague's Barrandov Studios from May to November 1943 to escape the bombing on Berlin. Far from the German capital, Käutner was free to make a vastly different film to the one the navy and Goebbels had in mind, depicting the bitter farewells and melancholy of sailors on shore leave; there was not even a sign of a swastika until the very end, and even then it was hardly noticed on the flagpole of the windjammer *Padua*.

Grand Admiral Karl Dönitz was furious with the outcome, as was Goebbels, who demanded many changes. Despite a year of editing, the movie was deemed unsuitable and banned in Germany, although it was premiered in Prague on 15 December 1944. Goebbels, clearly looking for a scapegoat, held Hans Albers responsible for the fate of this film, which was to have honoured the navy, and banned him in April 1945 for 'insulting the German sailor' – as if any of that mattered by that point. Albers had survived Hitler, the Nazis and Goebbels. (Almost the moment the war ended he drove through the ruins of Berlin in his white limousine at walking pace, greeting people who were stumbling over the rubble; women swarmed around his car, calling his name and crying.)[491]

Olga Tschechowa's most pressing concern as Berlin was about to fall was for her son-in-law Wilhelm Rust. The field hospital where he was based had been withdrawn northwards towards Lübeck on the Baltic coast when the great offensive was launched against Berlin. Stalin had given orders to his army to take Berlin by 1 May so that his victory would be the triumphant conclusion of the May Day celebrations. He didn't trust the British or the Americans to keep their word that the Soviets could have the honour of taking Berlin, so he needed a speedy end to the war. Now the German population, which had hailed Hitler as their messianic *Führer* and had jubilantly rejoiced at the fall of France five years before, began to curse his name as they became crushed between the lines on every side of Germany's capital. The people wanted only an end to the carnage – probably no more than around 10 per cent of the population still supported Hitler[492] – but although the war was lost and further fighting futile, Hitler had decided there was to be no surrender.

Lübeck, where Wilhelm Rust found himself, was expected to fall to the Red Army. Olga and her daughter Ada discussed whether he should desert and hide out at the Gross Glienecke house, but decided instead that he should surrender at the first opportunity to the Soviets, whereupon Olga would arrange for guarantees for him using her NKVD contacts;[493] at last her role as a 'sleeper' agent would serve a practical purpose. To achieve all this, she had to have been able to make contact with her NKVD controllers so that the message that Wilhelm Rust was to be taken alive and treated well was passed down to the front line. The plan, however, was dependent on many factors way beyond anyone's control.

The onslaught on the Oder began on 16 April. Olga's neighbours, including her former lover Carl Raddatz and his wife, and the Afghan ambassador, asked if they could join Olga and her family when the Soviets arrived because she spoke Russian.[494]

Goebbels and Magda made a final visit to their lakeside villa at Schwanenwerder; she carried out an inventory of the house, knowing she would never return there, while her husband busied himself destroying all his correspondence and personal memorabilia. Among his belongings was a signed photograph of Lída Baarová which he had kept hidden in his desk. He showed it to a colleague who had come to say goodbye, saying, 'Look, that's a woman of perfect beauty.'[495]

On 19 April 1945, Goebbels summoned his staff in the ministry building and talked of the film *Kolberg* and its theme of a heroic resistance. Then he told them:

Gentlemen, in a hundred years' time they will be showing another fine colour film describing the terrible days we are living through.

Don't you want to play a part in this film, to be brought back to life in a hundred years' time? Everybody now has the chance to choose the part which he will play in the film a hundred years hence. And for the sake of this prospect it is worth standing fast. Hold out now, so that a hundred years hence the audience does not hoot and whistle when you appear on the screen.[496]

Even as defeat stared him in the face, Goebbels had not given up his delusion of a legendary Hitler film.

On 20 April 1945, Hitler celebrated his fifty-sixth birthday in the bunker, and for one last time Goebbels praised his *Führer* on the radio in what might be described as a fanatical eulogy. 'He was born from the womb of the German people. They raised him onto their shield in a free election: a man of truly secular greatness, of unparalleled courage; of a steadfastness that uplifts and loves hearts and spirits.' Goebbels and other high-ranking Nazis, including Ribbentrop and Göring, who had just arrived from blowing up his house at Karinhall with dynamite, gathered for the last time in the Reich Chancellery to wish Hitler a happy birthday.

Olga Tschechowa did not even think of Hitler on his birthday, but thought only of her lover Albert Sumser, and as Hitler turned fifty-six, she walked to the Potsdam barracks and told Sumser that if he would desert, she would hide him. He later escaped from the barracks on an army motorcycle, just before his unit marched off to defend Potsdam.[497]

By 21 April, Georgy Zhukov's 1st Belorussian Front had broken through the last defences of General Gotthard Heinrici's Army Group Vistula during the Battle of the Seelow Heights. Facing little resistance, the Soviets advanced into the outskirts of Berlin, which was now surrounded by over a million Soviet troops. Shells began to hit the government buildings in the administrative district of the city. Hitler heard the guns for the first time when he was woken by his manservant at 9.30 a.m., and asked where the gunfire was coming from. He had not believed the Russians were so close so soon. From that moment on his only real concern was his place in history.

Albert Speer had once advised Hitler that when the curtain fell, he should be centre stage, and Hitler took this literally, fantasising about a theatrical finale with magnificent spectacle in the manner of a Wagnerian opera; he found these thoughts comforting at a time when everything was lost. He imagined being buried in a sarcophagus, high above the new city of Linz in Austria, of which he had a model in the bunker. He would die on an altar, if not in Linz then in Berlin. His *Götterdämmerung*. He would have considered this end more fitting than a victory, for as Joachim Fest said, 'What would he have done with a victory? The end suited him. It was a logical consequence of everything he had ever thought, wished or hoped for.'[498] To his mind, he would not have been a failure.

Now he would conclude his personal drama with *Götterdämmerung* and turn a humiliating defeat into a heroic catastrophe.

On 22 April the Goebbels family moved into the bunker to die. Joseph and Magda were willing to sacrifice their lives for the ideology of National Socialism, and for their *Führer*. Magda had no compulsion about taking her children with her, though the children didn't know that was the purpose of moving in with Uncle Adolf. They were each allowed to bring one toy and some nightclothes. For Goebbels, this act of total loyalty completely finalised his reunification with Hitler since the Lída Baarová scandal.

Field Marshal Keitel drove to the front line to personally relay an order to Wenck – 'Liberate Berlin and get the *Führer* out.' The plan was for Wenck to turn his army, currently facing the Americans to the west, and move east towards Berlin, where it would link up with the 9th Army and break through to the city. Keitel told Wenck that it was now up to him to save Germany. Wenck knew he would be sending his soldiers into Berlin to be slaughtered, but rather than betray his true thoughts to Keitel, he told him he would do his best. The army began to move east, not to rescue the city but to pick up thousands of wounded soldiers.

When news arrived that the 12th Army had reached Ferch, south-west of Berlin, Hitler became excited and turned hopefully towards General Albert Krebs, who said, 'My *Führer*, Ferch is not Berlin.'[499] But to Hitler this was providence – a last-minute rescue, almost exactly as it had happened to Frederick the Great in 1762. A portrait of Frederick hung in Hitler's study, and he stood looking at it for some time as if it would help bring a miracle to pass. Although he had long given in to the thought that his death would be the war's inevitable conclusion, he craved victory as long as there was a chance, and this news of imminent rescue shook him into a state of desperate hope – a drowning man clutching at straws. The miracle never happened. Those in the bunker had privately admitted defeat, but were forbidden from even thinking of surrender and were ordered by Hitler to keep fighting 'in an irrational hope for victory,' said Bernd Freytag von Loringhoven, adjutant in the bunker.[500]

At 7 o'clock in the morning of 26 April, a fine dust made its way into the bunker through the ventilation system. It came from the barrage outside as the Soviet artillery fired directly at government buildings, but those inside the bunker didn't know exactly where the Red Army soldiers were. Radio communications were down so random phone numbers were dialled, and whoever answered was asked if they knew where the Soviet troops were; this was the only method by which those in the bunker could find out how much time they had left. A guard came running in and announced that the Russians were firing at the entrance, and it seemed the end had come; but then it was discovered to be a false alarm, and Hitler again hoped for a miracle.[501]

That same day the Red Army arrived at the house where Olga Tschechowa and her niece Marina and husband lived; Albert Sumser was also there. Upon discovering that Olga spoke Russian, the first Russian soldiers sent for a large female commissar, who almost immediately grabbed her by the throat and screamed that she was a traitor. A colonel arrived, demanding to know what the trouble was; Olga explained who she was, and the colonel immediately turned on the commissar, yelling at her that she was stupid for not knowing the name Chekhova. He sent her out and ordered two soldiers to stay in the house to take care of the family.[502]

Olga immediately wrote to her Aunt Olya in Moscow that they were 'alive and in good health – miracles do happen. I'm so excited, I can hardly breathe.'[503] For Olga and her family, the Red Army came as liberators, while to most Berliners they came as rapists and killers; they were the very last soldiers the women of Berlin wanted to fall into the hands of, and the last that German soldiers wanted to surrender to. (Olga Tschechowa later wrote a highly melodramatic and largely fictitious account of their 'liberation', claiming a wounded Russian soldier staggered into their house, aimed his gun at them, but fell dead, after which the family were marched off believing they were all going to be shot.)[504]

On 27 April, Berlin was completely cut off from the rest of Germany, and as the Soviet forces closed in, Hitler's followers urged him to flee to the mountains of Bavaria to make a last stand. But he was determined to either live or die in the capital. 'It is over, gentlemen,' he announced. 'I will stay in Berlin and shoot myself when the time comes. Whoever wishes to leave is free to do so.'[505] He arranged for all the women in the bunker to be evacuated to his mountain retreat near Berchtesgaden, but Eva Braun, having dedicated her life to Hitler, refused to leave. Hitler's secretary Traudl Junge saw Hitler kiss Eva, which he had never done before in front of witnesses. Junge and the other two secretaries decided they would stay as well. Hitler still commanded loyalty from a few who responded to what they perceived to be his nobility and even kindness towards them.

There can be nothing admirable to be found in Hitler. He starved his own people during the final weeks of the war, caring nothing for them because, to his mind, by losing the war the nation had shown itself to be the weaker of the nations, and he said he would not shed a tear for it.

Although he knew the war could not be won, he was obsessed with having it end differently to the way the First World War had.

There was to be no repeat of 1918, and above all else he had to perpetrate his own myth by fighting to the very end, against all the odds while betrayed on all sides, abandoned by all, standing heroically alone at the last; this was how he wanted to be remembered in posterity. If ever there was to be a Hitler film, this is how it would portray him.

Outside the bunker was chaos. German soldiers trying to surrender to the Soviets were shot by SS officers. The citizens sought any kind of food, often carving up dead horses in a frenzy, desperate to avoid starvation. The German people no longer cared about Hitler or the Third Reich or National Socialism.

On the evening of 28 April, a staff car with two Soviet officers pulled up outside Olga Tschechowa's wooden house at Gross Glienecke; to the officers she was Olga Chekhova. She said goodbye to her daughter Ada, granddaughter Vera and her lover Albert, who thankfully had not been taken away as a POW, and was driven off into the night.

After midnight on 29 April, Hitler and Braun were married in a small civil ceremony in the bunker. As long as there had been a future, Hitler had not wanted to marry Eva, or anyone else – except Winifred Wagner, and then only when he was still a rising star – but the time had come to reward Eva for her unending loyalty. Eva's cousin Gertraud Weisker was of the opinion that Hitler was 'no longer in a position to refuse or resist [marrying her]. He had no reason to [resist] any more. He'd been married to Germany, and now there was no Germany.'[506]

The event was witnessed by Goebbels and Martin Bormann. Afterwards, Hitler hosted a modest wedding breakfast with his new wife, then he took Traudl Junge to another room to dictate his last will and testament.[507]

Junge later said she had hoped that Hitler's last will and testament would finally explain 'why this war is ending the way it is, and why things went the way they did'; but all he dictated was a document full of arrogant gratification and unrestrained hatred of the Jews. He claimed he never wanted the war and blamed others for starting it. Junge noted that the document contained 'no regrets, no explanation as to why he had not surrendered. The testament was one huge disappointment for me.'[508]

After signing the documents at 4 a.m., Hitler went to bed. That afternoon, he was informed of the assassination of Italian dictator Benito Mussolini. That same day, the US Army was liberating the concentration camp at Dachau and witnessing firsthand the horror of Hitler's Final Solution. Dead bodies were heaped into piles. Those who were still alive when the US soldiers opened the gates were like walking skeletons. Thirty thousand people were murdered in Dachau. The German people were now faced with the full extent of the evil that had been unleashed with their support. More than thirty years later Wolfgang Preiss commented, 'What happened to the Jews is a guilt we must bear. It isn't enough to say "I didn't know", because, of course, you did know *something*. Who could believe a whole nation could be murdered?'[509]

On 29 April Hitler said goodbye to his loyal staff members in the conference hall. His impending suicide was no surprise to those around him. Traudl Junge recalled that Eva often said, 'The *Führer* will tell us when he's going to kill himself.' That day Eva told them all, 'You'll cry later today,' and they knew that the time had come.[510]

On 30 April 1945, Soviet troops were within a block or two of the Reich Chancellery. Hitler gave one last prediction – that he would be cursed by millions – then he and Braun committed suicide. Braun bit into a cyanide capsule; Hitler possibly did likewise, but also shot himself in the head with his Walther PPK 7.65mm pistol, said to be the same pistol that his niece Geli Raubal had used in her suicide.

Hitler had wanted to ensure that when his time came he would die without fail, and he knew that some people who had shot themselves in the head sometimes survived, such as Unity Mitford, and he didn't want to. He had consulted the SS surgeon Ernst Gunther Schenck about the best method of committing suicide; Schenck recommended hydrogen cyanide. The army medical service had been ordered to produce these capsules in vast quantities since

November 1944. To be sure that a cyanide capsule would work, Hitler tested it on his dog Blondi, who promptly died.

The bodies of Hitler and Eva Braun were carried up the stairs and through the bunker's emergency exit to the bombed-out garden behind the Reich Chancellery where they were placed in a bomb crater, doused with petrol and set alight. It was hardly the twilight of the gods he had envisioned. His death was announced over the radio as if it were a heroic end. 'The *Führer*'s headquarters have announced that our *Führer* Adolf Hitler this afternoon in the Reich Chancellery, fighting to the last breath against Bolshevism, fell for Germany.'

Still alive inside the bunker were Joseph Goebbels and his family. Magda believed that, without Hitler and National Socialism, the world was not one where she and her children should live. Her adulation of Hitler and her belief in his messianic teachings compelled her to take the lives of all of her children. She put them to bed in the room the children shared inside the bunker, drugged them with morphine and then poisoned them with cyanide. The mother of Hitler's Germany had murdered her own children – the Holy Mother had become Herod, massacring the innocents. Then she and Goebbels took poison, and the Nazi Holy Family came to an ignominious end.

On 2 May, Berlin surrendered.

When a newspaper reporter called Winifred Wagner with the news that Hitler had married Eva Braun, she responded, 'That's a typical journalist's lie.' She could accept his death, but not the fact that he had married someone other than her.[511]

American troops entered Bayreuth, which had finally become victim to bombing and shelling; Villa Wahnfried was partially reduced to rubble. Wagner's city became occupied, and a GI discovered the Master's grand piano with no one to play it now. Winifred called it 'desecration' and fled to her country house.[512]

The end, when it finally came, was only a mere reflection of the grand operatic finale Hitler had envisaged for himself, but in his own mind he probably thought it really was *Götterdämmerung*. Sir Ian Kershaw reflected on 'this really macabre end':

It does seem as if you've written a script for it and it ends up with *Götterdämmerung* and with this all going up in flames in the bunker. If you had been trying to write a film about Hitler, this is how you would have wanted it to end, I presume.[513]

It wasn't the way Hitler had wanted it. He had wanted his great sacrifice to end in glorious flames. Instead he came to a squalid and sordid end. He had made one final prediction, that he would be cursed, which did come true, though not as he must have meant it – he was cursed by millions, not because they misunderstood him but because he misunderstood himself. He thought himself 'the martyr deserted by everyone,' said Preiss. Perhaps in his own mind, Hitler really had burned on a pyre like a legend. 'I am sure he would have wanted that made as a picture, but there was no one to make it.'[514]

CHAPTER TWENTY-TWO

THE FINAL CUT

On the night of 29 April 1945, when Olga Chekhova was collected by two Soviet officers and driven into the night, she was taken straight to the headquarters of Marshal Zhukov's 1st Belorussian Front, based in the former military engineers school at Karlshorst on the other side of Berlin. She spent the night there, then in the morning she was interrogated by Colonel Shkurin of SMERSH, the Soviet counter-intelligence organisation. Later that day, 30 April, she was put aboard a plane and flown to Moscow. She finally arrived home twenty-five years after leaving.

Viktor Abakumov, head of SMERSH, put her into an NKVD safe house in central Moscow. Abakumov was later charged of ignoring 'Communist moral principles' because he used these safe houses for illicit affairs with 'actresses, cheating wives, secretaries and foreign visitors';[515] he was obsessed with film stars, but there is no evidence that Olga slept with him, though it is possible she did, under duress or otherwise; she later wrote to him, addressing him as 'Dearest Vladimir Semyonovich' – Vladimir was his pseudonym – and asking, 'When are we going to meet?'[516] She spent time playing chess with the officers, who looked after her and escorted her to her interrogation sessions where they hoped to discover what she could tell them about Hitler; Stalin was obsessed with finding out the source of Hitler's power over the German people.

Tschechowa knew that if she wrote a diary it would be discovered by agents, and so she began to write one specifically so she could record:

Rumours circulating about me are worthy of a novel. Apparently, there's information about me being intimate with Hitler. My God,

I laughed a lot about it. How come and what are all these intrigues about me? Incredible and mean slander? When one's conscience is clear, nothing can affect one. And how wonderful it is to speak the truth. Time will show whether they will believe me or not.[517]

It isn't known whether she was ever told about Lev's plan to use her in his unrealised mission to assassinate Hitler, but for the rest of her life she neither saw Lev nor communicated with him in any way. Although she had been treated well, the six weeks spent in Moscow were a considerable strain upon her, and when she was flown back to Berlin during the last week of June she looked 'exhausted and shaken', according to Albert Sumser.[518]

In recognition of her services, the SMERSH chief in Berlin, General Vadis, saw to it that she was given a large house, Spreestrasse No. 2 in the town of Friedrichshagen east of Berlin: its previous owner had been moved out by an armed brigade. From her new home, she looked out over water and willows.

On 24 July her son-in-law Wilhelm Rust simply turned up at Olga's house where her daughter and sister and their families all lived. He had been captured by the British and interned in a POW camp in Denmark, where he had worked as a doctor, then was transferred, at his own request, to a British POW camp at Braunschweig in Germany. There the British provided him with documents, an ambulance, medical supplies and a medical assistant who was also a POW, and he drove back to Berlin to be reunited with Ada and daughter Vera.[519]

Olga maintained contact with the NKVD, and in 1949 she and her family were suddenly moved to a new apartment in Charlottenburg in the western sector.[520] She continued making films, retired in 1974, and published her memoirs. She died in Berlin on 9 March 1980.

In Sweden, Zarah Leander's fortunes slowly improved. At first she was shunned, but gradually she managed to land engagements on the Swedish stage, and eventually toured Germany and Austria, giving concerts, making new records and acting in musicals. She was always met by an eager audience who had not forgotten her. She also appeared in a number of films and television shows.

She was often asked about her years in Nazi Germany, and although she willingly talked about her past, she stubbornly rejected allegations of her having had sympathy for the Nazi regime, insisting that her position as a German film actress had been that of an entertainer working to please an enthusiastic audience in a difficult time. She repeatedly described herself as a 'political idiot' and, like Olga Tschechowa, never revealed her connections to the Soviet secret service. She continued to be very popular in Germany for many decades after the Second World War, and was interviewed several times on German television. She died of a stroke on 23 June 1981. In 2003, Värmland Opera House erected a bronze statue in her home town of Karlstad, where she began her career. After many years of discussions, the town government accepted this statue on behalf of the first local Swedish Zarah Leander Society.

Lída Baarová had been living and working in Prague since she fled there following her affair with Joseph Goebbels, but in April 1945 she decided to move back to Germany to live with her current lover, Hans Albers, in his house on the shores of Lake Starnberg. She never arrived because she was arrested by American military police and imprisoned in Munich.

Hans Albers had been expecting Lída, but after she failed to appear, he settled into an uncertain future, banned from working, as were most who had worked under Nazi rule and were considered Nazi sympathisers. Then in 1946, his former girlfriend Hansi Burg, in a British army uniform, returned to Germany, and the couple were reunited. In 1947 Albers was allowed to return to work, as was his friend Willy Birgel, and the two of them continued to be among Germany's top stars into the 1950s, making several films together. Albers and Hansi Burg remained together until his death in 1960.

While Albers found happiness again, Lída Baarová was extradited to Czechoslovakia, where she was tried for her life for working with the Nazis. She escaped death when she was able to prove that she had been working in Germany before the war broke out. She was sent to prison where she was visited often by an infatuated fan,

Jan Kopecký, who was related to an important Czech politician. Through his connections he was able to arrange for her release in 1949. They married and moved to Austria, but when she fell ill he emigrated to Argentina, while she stayed behind to recuperate in a sanatorium. When she had recovered she attempted a comeback, but her co-star Anton Walbrook, an ardent anti-Nazi, refused to work with her, and she fled to Argentina to join her husband. But the marriage was all but over, and she lived alone and in poverty. She settled in Italy in 1952 where she resumed her film career, and divorced Kopecký in 1956 and married a Swedish physician; they divorced in 1980. In 1995 she made a documentary about her life, *Lída Baarová's Bittersweet Memories*, which was also the title of her autobiography. She suffered from Parkinson's disease and died in Salzburg in 2000.

As soon as the war was at an end, the victors looked for those responsible. The generals, the ministers, and everyone who had a hand in the Nazi regime and especially the death camps, were rounded up and put on trial. American screenwriter Budd Schulberg, who had been assigned by the US Navy to the Office of Strategic Services (OSS) for intelligence work while attached to John Ford's documentary unit, was the officer sent to arrest Leni Riefenstahl at her chalet in Kitzbühel, Austria. He really only wanted her to identify the faces of Nazi war criminals in German film footage captured by the Allied troops. She claimed she was unaware of the nature of the internment and extermination camps, but when she stated she had been forced to follow Goebbels's orders under threat of being sent to a concentration camp, Schulberg asked her why she should have been afraid if she did not know concentration camps existed. When shown photographs of the camps, Riefenstahl reportedly reacted with horror and tears.

The officer who interrogated her, Irving Rosenbaum, remembered her as 'a broken woman', observing that 'she did not fit the picture that we might have had of her as a Nazi collaborator, as a friend of Goebbels or Hitler.' But the officer was not convinced by her performance of one who knew nothing. His impression was that she understood everything but rejected it, 'and in rejecting it I think she partly thought she vindicated herself to herself'.[521]

From 1945 to 1948 she was held in various American and French detention camps and prisons, and was for a while under house arrest. She was tried four times by various postwar authorities, but was never convicted for her alleged role as a propagandist or for the use of concentration camp inmates in her films. Branded 'a Nazi sympathiser', for the rest of her life she felt she was unjustly persecuted; she argued that she was only an artist. 'It destroyed me,' she said in 1998. 'It's horrible. When one likes working, as I do, and is so obsessed, and keeps trying to find new ways and is boycotted. I couldn't make a film for half a century. It's like a death.'[522]

She tried unsuccessfully to resume her career as a filmmaker. In 1956 she started work on *Black Freight*, planning to play the lead herself as well as direct. While scouting locations, she almost died from injuries received in a truck accident. She woke up from a coma in a Nairobi hospital and finished writing the script there; but filming was thwarted by uncooperative locals, the Suez Canal crisis and bad weather. She only made some test shots before the financiers pulled the plug.

She later said that her biggest regret was meeting Hitler: 'It was the biggest catastrophe of my life. Until the day I die people will keep saying "Leni is a Nazi", and I'll keep saying "But what did she do?"' She won more than fifty libel cases against people accusing her of having any knowledge of or anything to do with Nazi crimes, and maintained her innocence until she died on 8 September 2003.

Veit Harlan paid the penalty for making films for the Third Reich, especially *Jud Süß*. In May 1945 he had been named the number one Nazi film director by both international and German newspapers; this came as an honour from newspapers at home, but as an accusation from newspapers abroad. Towards the end of the war Harlan did not want either the accusation or the acclaim, so he wrote a 23-page statement claiming that his life and that of his wife had been under threat from the Nazis to ensure his compliance, and that he had been under an 'obligation to obey orders'. This remained his defence during his trials after the war ended, when the denazification commission banned him from making films; he directed several plays under a pseudonym.

In 1948 he was prosecuted in Hamburg for making *Jud Süß*; he was the only filmmaker charged with committing Nazi crimes. His defence was that he had been forced to make *Jud Süß* and had no choice. This was very much like the scenario he had presented in the film in which Oppenheimer made the same kind of defence, saying, 'I am merely the faithful servant of my master.' In the scene, Oppenheimer was laughed at. Harlan was despised but cleared of all charges related to *Jud Süß*, because the court could find no direct connection between the film and Nazi war crimes. Allegedly the judge, Dr Tyrolf, had been a Nazi. Having been found innocent, Harlan was free to make films again, but public opinion was against him, and his personal appearances and premieres were met with protests and boycotts. He defended himself at every opportunity, stressing that he'd been used by the Nazis and by the 'demonic Goebbels'.

He returned to work with smaller budgets, but using themes and styles that were stuck in the 1930s. He attempted to make a statement about judgement in *Hanna Amon* in 1951, in which Kristina Söderbaum played a character devoted to her brother who finds that the whole village where she lives has wrongly judged her to be incestuous. The persecution Harlan faced during the 1950s helped him to maintain his view that *he* was a victim of the Nazi era.

Over time, Harlan and his family were able to maintain a relatively normal and prosperous existence in a Bavarian village where they lived and where friends from the film industry came to visit. But the shadow of *Jud Süß* never lifted, and Söderbaum admitted that the film ruined their lives. The couple was often met with demonstrations on the street and sometimes pelted with eggs.[523] When they went to the *Hamburger Kammerspiele Theater* in Hamburg, which until 1941 had been used by the *Jüdischer Kulturbund* – the Cultural Federation of German Jews – they were seen in the audience by actress Ida Ehre, who had reopened the theatre on 10 December 1945. Ida Ehre was Jewish and had attempted to escape Germany with her husband and daughter, but their ship, bound for Chile, was forced to return to Hamburg because of the outbreak of war. Ehre was eventually arrested by the Gestapo and sent to a concentration camp at Fühlsbüttel.[524] When she realised that Veit Harlan and Kristina Söderbaum were in the audience, she stood on stage and ordered them to leave.

Harlan died from heart failure at the age of sixty-four on 13 April 1964 while holidaying on Capri. Kristina Söderbaum died aged eighty-eight on 12 February 2001. Her acting career never recovered after the war, but she was successful as a fashion photographer. Her last film appearance was in *Night Train to Venice* in 1994 opposite Hugh Grant.

Almost everyone associated with *Jud Süß* suffered the consequence of being a part of the most reviled film of all time. Ferdinand Marian was banned from working until August 1946, when he celebrated the news that he had been given permission by US film officer Eric Pleskow to work again. On 7 August he borrowed a car and drove towards Munich to collect his denazification papers, and was killed when he crashed near the village of Dürneck in Bavaria.

His *Jud Süß* co-star Werner Johannes Krauß, who had delighted Goebbels and many of the anti-Semites in Germany with his portrayal of loathsome Jewish characters, lived out his days following the war in virtual obscurity in Vienna, and made only three more films before he died in 1959.

Among other actors who were blacklisted was Willy Birgel, but only until 1947. Wolfgang Preiss was another. 'I didn't work in pictures after the war for a few years because all of us who worked in films in the Third Reich were banned. I did some theatre.' From 1949 he worked as a voice actor, dubbing many English-language films into German; he returned to the screen in 1954, playing the role of Von Stauffenberg, the officer who tried to kill Hitler, in the film *Der 20. Juli.* 'It was made by Alfred Weidenmann who had been also banned, until in 1954 he made in Germany *Canaris Master*

Spy, which was anti-Nazi; and so he was allowed to work, and he gave me a part [in *Der 20. Juli*] which really began my career.'[525] Preiss enjoyed a long and successful career in international films, but is best remembered by English-speaking audiences for his roles in Second World War films such as *The Longest Day*, *The Train*, *Is Paris Burning?* and *A Bridge Too Far*.

The actors who faced just a ban were luckier than Heinrich George. He had been a star of silent films, such as Fritz Lang's *Metropolis* in 1927, and enjoyed continuing success with the advent of sound. Before the Nazi takeover he had been active in the Communist Party, but like many others he agreed to toe the Nazi Party line in order to work, and appeared in several blatant propaganda films including *Jud Süß* and *Kolberg*. He and his wife Berta Drews were imprisoned by the Soviet Army in June 1945, first in Berlin-Hohenschönhausen, then in the Speziallager Nr. 7 Sachsenhausen concentration camp in Oranienburg. It had been used primarily by the Nazis for political prisoners from 1936 to May 1945, when the Russians took it over for their own purposes. Over 4,200 prisoners of the Soviet Union were forced to live in densely crowded conditions. Sanitation was horrific and nutrition wholly insufficient. Prisoners suffered from the cold in unheated conditions and were not supplied with blankets. Many internees fell ill or died. According to official Soviet information, 886 people died between July 1945 and October 1946, but it is estimated elsewhere that more than 3,000 people died. Their bodies were buried in bomb craters and in rubbish heaps near the camp.

Basis for internment was a 1945 Soviet order according to which spies, subversive elements, terrorists, NSDAP activists, members of the police and secret service, administration officials and other 'hostile elements' in Germany were arrested. It is believed that most of those who were arrested were marginally involved in the Nazi system, and some not at all. Unsubstantiated denunciations led to many arrests, as in the case of Heinrich George,[526] who died in the camp on 25 September 1946. The Soviets said he died from complications following an appendix operation, but there is speculation that he starved to death.[527] In 1994, after the collapse of Communism and the removal of Soviet occupation troops from Germany, thousands of bodies were found in a forest near Sachsenhausen in unmarked graves, and one of them was identified as Heinrich George by comparing his DNA with his son's. His remains were buried in the *Städtischer Friedhof Berlin-Zehlendorf*.

Winifred Wagner was brought to trial, and at her court hearing, her first statement was that she never slept with Hitler. Witnesses for and against her appeared, and ultimately the Chamber concluded that she had not benefited from the party, while stressing her friendship with the top party officials. She was sentenced to 450 days of special labour – picking bilberries in Warmensteinach – while 60 per cent of her assets were confiscated.[528]

The Bayreuth Festival was revived without her; her two sons took it over, and most of the musicians and singers remained to continue performing Wagner. Winifred remained a devotee of Hitler, explaining, 'We old Nazis invented a new code name after the war because we couldn't talk about him in public. When we wanted to do that we called him "USA". That stands for "*Unser Seliger Adolf*" (Our blessed Adolf).'[529]

She never lost her admiration – perhaps even love – for Hitler, and said in 1975, 'If Hitler came in through the door today I'd be as happy as ever to see him and have him here. And everything that is dark about him, I know it exists, but it doesn't for me.'[530] She never regretted her relationship with Hitler or being a Nazi. In her own way she kept alive the legend that still shone bright in the memories of hardcore Nazis, his muse to the last.

The glory that was Hitler's Nazi Germany was a curse on humanity. It was fleeting, lasting just twelve years, from 1933 to 1945, barely a blink of an eye compared to the thousand years Hitler predicted the Third Reich would endure. Yet Hitler's immortality is assured, but not the way he had hoped. Evil has its own cult of celebrity, and there can be few in history, or in the millennia to come, who can compare to Hitler; as a consequence of his obsession with his own celebrity, more than sixty million died.

He was not an evil genius – he never had a brilliant idea of his own in his life. He mostly gambled and won at moments in his life when he had no plan, merely an idea that he was being led by providence. In the end, he was defeated not only by overwhelming military might and brains, but by a life-long identity crisis – or, more correctly, a *multiple* identity crisis: artist, writer, architect, a new Wagner, a new Messiah, Emperor of a new Roman Empire, the bringer of the end of the gods. He was one step away from becoming God Himself; had Germany won the war, mankind would have been forcibly converted to his new vegetarian religion.

That Hitler was evil is without question; where evil comes from is debatable. Could Hitler have been any different? He was born with deficient genes as a result of intra-family procreation, creating mental and physical instabilities in some of the children of Alois and Klara Hitler. Socially deficient as a child, he sought friendship by trying to lead but where no one would follow. Sexually repressed, he discovered erotic relief in his relationship with the masses which became an addiction, and also in sadism and masochism. His adulation of Wagner and the extreme emotional effect of Wagner's music upon him ignited his delusions, at first that he was the one who prepared the way for Wagner's white knight, then, that he was the Messianic Knight himself. And behind it all was one simple and overwhelming dream – to be celebrated. If he couldn't be an artist, he would be a celebrity any way he could.

He became a politician only because it served his cravings. He had no interest in serving his country, only his celebrity. He had no idea how to govern Germany, and thought it could be done through culture; by applying the arts, especially music and cinema, to Fascism, he thought to shape a people and a Europe to his image. Then he could be considered the supreme artist, greater even than Wagner.

As he began to earn plaudits, he basked in his small grow-ing fame, and in his deluded sense of his divine importance he raised himself, with help from others equally deluded like Joseph Goebbels, onto the highest pedestal – the evolution of the Nazi cult of celebrity. But it was all a performance, and he played out his life as though the world was his stage, or his own silver screen; no wonder film historian Eric Rentschler commented, 'Hitler's regime can be seen as a sustained cinematic event.'[531] He learned how to perform as Adolf Hitler in what must be the most terrifying and most convincing performance of pure evil there has ever been.

Is evil anything other than a form of abnormality? Hitler was born into abnormality, carrying genes that may have contributed in some part to his mentality, but that can never excuse the deaths of more than sixty million people for which he was responsible and can never be forgiven. The awful irony is that Hitler's immortality has been assured by those millions. But he didn't get the ending he wanted. His *Götterdämmerung* was merely smouldering remains; a more ignominious ending is hard to imagine for the man who dreamed he would bring about the Twilight of the Gods. I wonder whether, when he sat with Eva Braun in that room in the *Führer* bunker, about to end their lives, he thought to himself, 'This isn't how it was supposed to end', like an actor finding himself in a scene he never imagined, demanding, 'Where's the writer? This wasn't in the script.' Goebbels, if he could, would have deleted that scene and, to complete his final cut of Hitler's life, would have had the ending reshot – a flaming pyre high above the new city of Linz and the downfall of the other gods, the whole set to stirring strains of Wagner, which is how it all started.

NOTES

1   Interview with Zeissler, Shofar FTP Archive File online. (Zeisler's name was
     misspelt in the interview and in the title of the article, which is available to
     view online.) The story is one that emerged in 1943 from an interview the
     Office of Strategic Services (OSS) conducted with Alfred Zeisler; he had
     left Germany in 1935 to escape Nazism and was making an anti-Nazi film in
     Hollywood about Joseph Goebbels called *Enemy of the People*.

2   Curd Jürgens interview with MM, Pinewood Studios, 1976. Curd Jürgens
     (1915–1982), billed as 'Curt Jürgens' in English-speaking countries, was
     acknowledged as one of the most successful European film actors of the
     20th century; among his most famous English-language films are *The Enemy
     Below* (1957), *The Inn of the Sixth Happiness* (1958), *The Longest Day* (1962)
     and *The Spy Who Loved Me* (1977). Although he was born in Bavaria in
     Hohenzollern Imperial Germany, he abandoned Germany and became an
     Austrian citizen in 1945 because he had been sent to a concentration camp
     for 'political unreliables' in 1944 due to his anti-Nazi opinions (an experi-
     ence he refused to speak about when interviewed).

3   Interview with Zeissler, Shofar FTP Archive File online.

4   Walter C. Langer (1889-1981) was a psychoanalyst who drew up a psycho-
     analytical profile on Hitler for the Office of Strategic Services in which he
     predicted Hitler's suicide was the 'most plausible outcome' among several
     possibilities identified. Langer also identified the possibility of a military
     coup against Hitler. Langer's report was published in book form, with new
     material including a foreword, introduction and afterword, published as *The
     Mind of Adolf Hitler*.

5   Langer, Walter C., *The Mind of Adolf Hitler: The Secret Wartime Report*,
     Meridian-New American Library, 1985, p. 88.

6   Interview with Zeissler; Shofar FTP Archive File online.

7   Langer, W. C., pp. 175–176; see also *The Hitler Source-Book* – interview with A. Zeissler, Hollywood, California, 24 June, 1943, p. 921; also Interview with Zeissler; Shofar FTP Archive File online.

8   Langer, W. C., p. 176.

9   Interview with Zeissler; Shofar FTP Archive File online.

10   Langer, W. C., p. 176.

11   Pope, Ernest R., *Munich Playground*, G. P. Putnam's Sons, 1941, pp. 5–9.

12   Maser, Werner, *Hitler: Legende, Mythos, Wirklichkeit*, Bechtle, 1971; trans. *Hitler: Legend, Myth & Reality*, Harper & Row, 1973, p. 110; also Jenks, William Alexander, *Vienna and the Young Hitler*, Columbia University Press, 1960, p. 14; Zoller, Albert, *Hitler privat: Erlebnisbericht seiner Geheimsekretärin*, Droste-Verlag, 1949, p. 58.

13   Kershaw, Ian, *Hitler 1889–1936: Hubris*, Penguin, 1999, p. 21. Sir Ian Kershaw is a British historian of twentieth-century Germany whose work has chiefly focused on the period of the Third Reich, and is regarded by many as one of the world's leading experts on Hitler and Nazi Germany, and is particularly noted for his monumental biography of Hitler.

14   Kubizek, August, *Adolf Hitler, Mein Jugendfreund*, Stocker, 1953, p. 195. August Kubizek (1888–1956) and Hitler shared a small room in Vienna in 1908. As the only son of a self-employed upholsterer, August was expected to take over his father's business, but Hitler persuaded Kubizek's father to let his son go to the metropolis to attend the conservatory. Kubizek completed his studies in 1912 and was hired as conductor of the orchestra in Marburg on the Drau, but his musical career was cut short by the beginning of WWI, and after the war he accepted a position as an official in the municipal council of Eferding. In 1933 he wrote to Hitler to congratulate him on having become Chancellor, and six months later received a reply. In 1938 Hitler offered Kubizek the conductorship of an orchestra, which Kubizek politely refused. Hitler insisted on financing the education of Kubizek's three sons at the Anton Bruckner Conservatory in Linz. In 1938, Kubizek was hired by the Nazi Party to write two short propaganda booklets called *Reminiscences* about his youth with Hitler. Kubizek had avoided politics all his life but became a Nazi in 1942 as a gesture of loyalty to his friend, and after the war was arrested and imprisoned for sixteen months. In 1951, he published *Adolf Hitler, mein Jugendfreund*.

15 Jenks, W. A., pp. 89–95.

16 Kubizek, A., p. 198.

17 Ibid., p. 83.

18 Ibid., p. 195.

19 *Monologe*, pp. 25–26, p. 234, January, 1942 (trans).

20 Oechsner, Frederick, *This is the Enemy*, Little, Brown & Co., 1942, pp. 86–87.

21 Kershaw, I., p. 43.

22 Kubizek, A., pp. 106–109; also Jetzinger, Franz, *Hitlers Jugend*, Europa-Verlag, 1956, pp. 166–168.

23 Adorno, Theodor, *In Search of Wagner*, Verso Books, 2009, pp. 34–36.

24 Brando, Marlon, with Lindsey, Robert, *Brando: Songs My Mother Taught Me*, Century, 1994, p. 218.

25 Langer, Walter, C., *The Mind of Adolf Hitler: The Secret Wartime Report*, Meridian-New American Library, 1985, p. 100.

26 Smith, Bradley, *Adolf Hitler, His Family, Childhood and Youth*, Hoover Institution on War, Revolution, and Peace, 1967, p. 103.

27 Larry Solomon website; Larry Solomon is a musicologist.

28 *Neue Zeitschrift für Musik*, 1850

29 see Wagner, Richard, 'Prose Works', *Das Judenthum in der Musik* (*Judaism in Music*), 1850.

30 Wagner, Richard, *Art and Politics* Vol. 4, University of Nebraska Press, 1995, pp. 149–170.

31 Rose, Paul Lawrence, *Wagner, Race and Revolution*, Yale University Press, 1992, p. 71. Paul Lawrence Rose is a professor of European history and Mitrani Professor of Jewish Studies at Pennsylvania State University, specialising in the study of anti-Semitism, German history, European intellectual history and Jewish history.

32 Rauschning, Hermann, *Gespräche mit Hitler*, Europa-Verlag, 1940, p. 230. It should be noted that some historians have cast doubt on Hermann Rauschning's account of his discussions with Hitler between 1932 and 1934. Shortly after Rauschning's death in 1982, Swiss researcher Wolfgang Hänel declared that *Gespräche mit Hitler*, which is the original German title, was a fraud. Professor Ian Kershaw also dismisses Rauschning's account, but other historians have not been convinced by Hänel's research. David Redles

attacked Hänel's method, which consisted of 'pointing out similarities in phrasing of quotations from other individuals in Rauschning's other books and those attributed to Hitler in *Voice of Destruction* (Rauschning). If the two are even remotely similar, Hänel concludes that the latter must be concoctions. However the similarities, which are mostly slight, could be for a number of reasons ... [they] need not stem from forgery.' (David Redles, *Hitler's Millennial Reich: Apocalyptic Belief and the Search for Salvation*, New York University Press, 2005, p. 195.) Eberhard Jaeckel also concluded that, although Rauschning's book cannot be regarded as a true verbatim account, it remains a good guide to Hitler's world view from someone who conversed with him. Rauschning came 'to the bitter conclusion that the Nazi regime represented anything other than the longed-for German revolution.' (Phelan, p. 66.) Rauschning wrote several books, some of which are sourced by Joachim C. Fest in his 1973 book *Hitler*.

33 Rose, P. L., *Wagner, Race and Revolution*, Yale University Press, 1992.

34 Zalampas, Sherree Owens, *Adolf Hitler: A Psychological Interpretation of His Views on Architecture, Art, and Music*, Bowling Green University Popular Press, 1990, p. 48.

35 Wagner, Richard, *My Life*, trans. Andrew Gray, Da Capo Press, 1992, p. 171.

36 Gutman, Robert W., *Richard Wagner: The Man, His Mind and His Music*, Harvest Books, 1990, p. 406.

37 Wagner, Cosima, *Diaries*, 19 December 1881, trans. Geoffrey Skelton, Collins, 1980.

38 Wagner, Richard, *Sämtliche Briefe*, 13 December 1834, eds Strobel & Wolf, Breitkopf and Härtel, 1987, p. 177.

39 Wagner, Richard & Liszt, Franz *Correspondence of Wagner and Liszt*, 18 April 1851, ed. F. Hueffer, Greenwood Press 1969.

40 Wagner, G., *Twilight of the Wagners: The Unveiling of a Family's Legacy*, Kiepenheuer & Witsch, 1997, p. 66.

41 Kubizek, A., pp. 98–101.

42 Langer, Walter C., *The Mind of Adolf Hitler: The Secret Wartime Report*, Meridian-New American Library, 1985, p. 109.

43 Ibid., p. 114.

44 Ibid., p. 112.

45 Ibid., p. 116.

46 Ibid., pp. III, II2.

47 ibid, p. II2.

48 Fest, Joachim C., *Hitler*, trans. Winston, Richard & Clara, Harcourt Brace Jovanovich, 1974, p. 29. Joachim Clemens Fest (1926–2006) was a German historian, journalist, critic and editor, best known for his writings and public commentary on Nazi Germany, including an important biography of Hitler, and a major documentary, *Hitler – A Career*.

49 Langer, Walter C., *The Mind of Adolf Hitler: The Secret Wartime Report*, Meridian-New American Library, 1985, p. 119.

50 Ibid, p. 119.

51 Ibid, p. 159.

52 Hamann, Brigitte, *Hitler's Vienna: A Dictator's Apprenticeship*, trans. Thomas Thornton, Oxford University Press, 1999, p. 176.

53 Fest, J. C., p. 34.

54 Hitler, Adolf, *Mein Kampf*, trans. Ralph Manheim, Sentry, 1943, p. 16.

55 Ibid., p. 19.

56 Fest, J. C., p. 44.

57 Hitler, A., *Mein Kampf*, p. 20.

58 Fest, J. C., p. 46.

59 Fest, J. C., p. 48.

60 Zalampas, Sherree Owens, *Adolf Hitler: A Psychological Interpretation of His Views on Architecture, Art, and Music*, Bowling Green University Popular Press, 1990, p. 110.

61 Kubizek, August, *Adolf Hitler, Mein Jugendfreund*, Stocker, 1953, p. 195.

62 Waite, R. G. L., *The Psychopathic God*, Basic Books, 1977, p. 113.

63 Kubizek, A., p. 75.

64 Hanisch, R., *New Republic*, 5 April 1939, pp. 239–242, plus 12 April 1939, pp. 270–272, plus 19 April 1939, pp. 297–300; also Fest, p. 71. (Reinhold Hanisch published articles on Hitler, with whom he had lived in 1910.)

65 Kubizek, August, *Adolf Hitler, Mein Jugendfreund*, Stocker, 1953, p. 56.

66 Fest, J. C., p. 73.

67 Interview with Zeissler; Shofar FTP Archive File online.

68 Langer, Walter, C., *The Mind of Adolf Hitler: The Secret Wartime Report*, Meridian-New American Library, 1985, p. 77.

69 Zalampas, Sherree Owens, *Adolf Hitler: A Psychological Interpretation of His Views on Architecture, Art, and Music*, Bowling Green University Popular Press, 1990, p. 110.

70 Hitler, Adolf, *Mein Kampf*, trans. Ralph Manheim, Sentry, 1943, p. 42.

71 Hitler, A., *Mein Kampf*, as quoted by Langer, W. C., p. 55.

72 Fest, J. C., p. 71.

73 Fest, J. C., p. 80.

74 Fest, J. C., p. 169.

75 Fest, J. C., p. 171.

76 Hitler, A., *Mein Kampf*, p. 355.

77 Fest, J. C., p. 177.

78 Langer, W. C., p. 155.

79 Rauschning, Hermann, *Gespräche mit Hitler*, Europa Verlag, 1940; *Voice of Destruction*, (US) G. P. Putnam's Sons, 1940; *Hitler Speaks*, (UK) Thornton Butterworth, 1939, pp. 66–67.

80 Wiegand, Karl von, 'Hitler Foresees His End', *Cosmopolitan*, May 1939, p. 48.

81 Voigt, Frederick Augustus, *Unto Caesar*, G. P. Putnam's Sons, 1938, p. 261.

82 Curd Jürgens, interview with the author, Pinewood Studios, 1976.

83 'Interview with Zeissler', Hollywood, California, 24 June 1943; Shofar FTP Archive: people/h/hitler.adolf/oss-papers/text/oss-sb-zeissler (note: Zeisler is misspelled).

84 Hanfstaengl, Ernest, *Hitler: The Missing Years*, Eyre and Spottiswoode, 1957, pp. 68 & 87; see Zalampas, S. O., p. 42.

85 'Winifred Wagner: The Muse', *Hitler's Women*, Annette Tewes & Christian Deick, ZDF Enterprises, the History Channel, SBS, 2001.

86 Ibid.

87 Ibid.

88 Ibid.

89 Ibid.

90 Rose, Paul Lawrence, *Wagner: Race and Revolution*, Yale University Press, 1992, p. 48.

91 Wagner, Friedelind, *The Royal Family of Bayreuth*, Eyre and Spottiswoode, 1948. p. 9.

92 'Winifred Wagner', *Hitler's Women*.

93 Ibid.

94   Fest, Joachim C., *Hitler*, trans. Winston, Richard & Clara, Harcourt Brace Jovanovich, 1974.

95   Zalampas, Sherree Owens, *Adolf Hitler: A Psychological interpretation of His Views on Architecture, Art, and Music*, Bowling Green University Popular Press, 1990. p. 48.

96   'Winifred Wagner', *Hitler's Women*.

97   *Hitler – A Career*, Joachim Fest, Werner Rieb Produktion, 1977.

98   'Uneven Romance', *Time* magazine, 29 June 1959. The world would never have known anything about Maria Reiter were it not for Paula Hitler, who, in March 1959, casually mentioned to a German reporter, Günter Peis, that she had recently visited with 'perhaps the only woman my brother ever loved', Günter Peis investigated further and discovered that the woman in question was Maria Reiter, then forty-seven and living quietly in a Munich suburb. Reluctant at first, she finally revealed to Peis her long-kept secret of her romance with Hitler. And she had letters to prove it. The story was first printed in the German publication *Stern* in 1959, and the world learned of the bizarre and almost tragic love story about the girl born in Berchtesgaden on 23 December 1911, the daughter of the co-founder of the Social Democratic Party, a sworn enemy of the National Socialists, a political secret which Hitler, as well as Maria, had to keep to themselves.

99   Ibid.

100 Rosenbaum, Ron, *Explaining Hitler: The Search for the Origins of His Evil*, Macmillan, 1998, pp. 114–116.

101 Interview with Zeissler; Shofar FTP Archive File online.

102 Langer, Walter, C., *The Mind of Adolf Hitler: The Secret Wartime Report*, Meridian-New American Library, 1985, p. 96.

103 Kubizek, August, *Adolf Hitler, Mein Jugendfreund*, Stocker, 1953, p, 237.

104 Wiegand, Karl von, 'Hitler Foresees His End', *Cosmopolitan*, May 1939, p. 158.

105 Kubizek, A., p. 237.

106 Hitler, Adolf, *Mein Kampf*, trans. Ralph Manheim, Sentry, 1943, p. 63.

107 Langer, W. C., p. 157.

108 'Eva Braun', *Hitler's Women*.

109 Ibid.

110 Ibid.

111 Fröhlich, Elke (ed.), *Die Tagebücher von Joseph Goebbels: Teil I, Aufzeichnungen 1923–1941*, Saur, 1998–2006, 14 volumes, Volume 1/I, pp. 326–327.

112 Ibid., p. 365.

113 Thacker, Toby, *Joseph Goebbels: Life and Death*, Palgrave Macmillan, 2010, p. 12. Dr Toby Thacker is a lecturer in modern European history, specialising in music and politics in Germany after 1945, the denazification and the Allied occupation of Germany, and propaganda and culture in Germany 1919–1990. Author of books on Joseph Goebbels, the Third Reich and culture in Germany.

114 Thacker, T., p. 21.

115 Fröhlich, E., p. 29.

116 Thacker, T., p. 37.

117 Ibid., pp. 108–109.

118 Fröhlich, E., p. 106.

119 Ibid., p. 108.

120 Langer, Walter C., *The Mind of Adolf Hitler: The Secret Wartime Report*, Meridian-New American Library, 1985, p. 44.

121 Hitler, Adolf, *My New Order*, Reynal & Hitchcock, 1941, p. 26.

122 White, *Scribner 9*, April 1932.

123 Langer, p. 45.

124 Huss, Pierre J., *The Foe We Face*, Doubleday, Doran & Co., 1942, p. 210.

125 Fröhlich, E., pp. 124–125.

126 Ibid., pp. 202–206.

127 Ibid., pp. 208–209.

128 Thacker, p. 46.

129 Fröhlich, E., pp. 374–375.

130 'Winifred Wagner: The Muse', *Hitler's Women*, Annette Tewes & Christian Deick, ZDF Enterprises, the History Channel, SBS, 2001.

131 Fröhlich, E., pp. 82–84.

132 Ibid., p. 95.

133 *Die Fahn Hoch! Der Angriff. Aufsätz aus der Kampfzeit* , Zentravlverlag der NSDAP, 1935, pp. 268–271; also Calvin German Propaganda, online.

134 Cecil, Robert, *The Myth of the Master Race: Alfred Rosenberg and Nazi Ideology*, Dodd, Mead, 1972, p. 97.

135 Fest, Joachim C., *Hitler*, trans. Winston, Richard & Clara, Harcourt Brace Jovanovich, 1974.

136 Fröhlich, Elke (ed.), *Die Tagebücher von Joseph Goebbels: Teil I, Aufzeichnungen 1923–1941*, Saur, 1998–2006, 14 volumes, Volume 2/II, p. 233.

137 'Winifred Wagner: The Muse', *Hitler's Women*, Annette Tewes & Christian Deick, ZDF Enterprises, the History Channel, SBS, 2001

138 Ibid.

139 Ibid.

140 Ibid.

141 Ibid.

142 Fröhlich, E., p. 277.

143 Meissner, Hans Otto, *Magda Goebbels, First Lady of the Third Reich*, Sidgwick and Jackson, 1980, p. 61.

144 Ibid., p. 77.

145 Ibid., p. 82.

146 Fröhlich, E., p. 334.

147 Ibid., p. 346.

148 Ibid., p. 362.

149 Thacker, Toby, *Joseph Goebbels: Life and Death*, Palgrave Macmillan, 2010, p. 121.

150 Fröhlich, E., p. 98.

151 Ibid., p. 100.

152 see Sage, Steven F., *Ibsen and Hitler: The Playwright, the Plagiarist, and the Plot for the Third Reich*, Carroll & Graf Publishers, 2006

153 quoted in Waite, Robert G. L., *The Psychopathic God: Adolf Hitler*, Basic Books, 1977.

154 see Waite, *Psychopathic God*.

155 'Eva Braun: The Mistress', *Hitler's Women*, Stefan Brauburger and Oliver Halmburger, ZDF Enterprises, the History Channel, SBS, 2001.

156 Langer, Walter, C., *The Mind of Adolf Hitler: The Secret Wartime Report*, Meridian-New American Library, 1985, p. 87.

157 Heiden, Konrad, *Adolf Hitler*, Europa Verlag, 1936, pp. 279–280.

158 Price, George Ward, *I Know These Dictators*, Harrap, 1937, pp. 119–120.

159 Ibid., p. 79.

160 see Knopp, Guido, *Hitler's Women*, Routledge, 2003.

161 Interview with Friedelind Wagner, *The Hitler Source Book*, p. 937.

162 Fröhlich, E., p. 133.

163 Thacker, p. 126.

164 Rauschning, Hermann, *Gespräche mit Hitler*, Europa Verlag, 1940; *Voice of Destruction*, (US) G. P. Putnam's Sons, 1940; *Hitler Speaks*, (UK) Thornton Butterworth, 1939, p. 5.

165 Fest, Joachim C., *Hitler*, trans. Winston, Richard & Clara, Harcourt Brace Jovanovich, 1974, p. 581.

166 Langer, Walter C., *The Mind of Adolf Hitler: The Secret Wartime Report*, Meridian-New American Library, 1985, p. 58.

167 'Winifred Wagner: The Muse', *Hitler's Women*, Annette Tewes & Christian Deick, ZDF Enterprises, the History Channel, SBS, 2001.

168 Fest, J. C., *Hitler – A Career*.

169 Macintyre, Ben, 'I Foresee a Troubled Future for Burmese Generals – a look at leaders who cling desperately to astrology and superstition', *The Times*, 28 September 2007.

170 'Hitler's Private World', *Revealed*, Channel Five, 2006.

171 Fry, Michael, *Hitler's Wonderland*, John Murray, 1934, p. 106.

172 'Cocksure Dictator Takes Timid Soul Precautions', *Newsweek*, 6 April 1935.

173 Flanner, Janet, *An American in Paris*, Simon & Schuster, 1940, pp. 414–415.

174 High, *Literary Digest*, 21 October 1933, p. 42.

175 Strasser, Otto, *Flight from Terror*, R. M. McBride and Co., 1943, pp. 24–25.

176 Fest, J. C., *Hitler – A Career*.

177 Curd Jürgens.

178 Gordon, Mel, *Hanussen: Hitler's Jewish Clairvoyant*, Feral House, 2001, p. 242.

179 Fest, J. C.,, p. 660.

180 Karney, Robyn (ed.), *Cinema Year by Year 1894–2005*, Dorling Kindersley, 2005, p. 236.

181 Friedman, Jonathan C. (ed.), *The Routledge History of the Holocaust*, Routledge, 2011, p. 92.

182 Wulf, Josef (ed.), *Musik im Dritten Reich: Eine Dokumentation*, Mohn Verlag, 1963, pp. 23–25.

183 Ibid., pp. 81–83.

184 see Geissmar, Berta, *The Baton and the Jackboot: Recollections of Musical Life*, Hamish Hamilton, 1944; also Potter, P., 'The Nazi "Seizure" of the Berlin

Philharmonic or the Decline of a Bourgeois Institution', in *National Socialist Cultural Policy*, ed. Glenn R. Cuomo, Palgrave Macmillan, 1995, pp. 39–66.

185 'Winifred Wagner', *Hitler's Women*.

186 'Eva Braun', *Hitler's Women*.

187 Harding, Luke, 'Leni Riefenstahl: Hand-held History', *The Economist*, 13 September 2003.

188 'Leni Riefenstahl', *Hitler's Women*.

189 Moore, Charles, 'Leni Riefenstahl', *Daily Telegraph*, 10 September 2003.

190 Williams, Val, 'Leni Riefenstahl', *The Independent*, 9 October 2003.

191 'Leni Riefenstahl: The Film Director', *Hitler's Women*, Sebastian Dehnhardt & Friederike Dreykluft, ZDF Enterprises, the History Channel, SBS, 2001.

192 James, Clive, 'Reich Star', *New York Times*, 25 March 2007.

193 *The Swastika and the Stage: German Theatre and Society, 1933–1945* (excerpt) online.

194 Ibid.

195 Isaacson, Walter, *Einstein: His Life and Universe*, Simon & Schuster, 2007, pp. 407–410.

196 Riefenstahl, Leni, *The Sieve of Time*, Quartet Books, 1992, pp. 132–133.

197 Fröhlich, Elke (ed.), *Die Tagebücher von Joseph Goebbels: Teil I, Aufzeichnungen 1923–1941*, Saur, 1998–2006, 14 volumes, Volume 2/III, p. 188.

198 Karney, Robyn (ed.), *Cinema Year by Year 1894–2005*, Dorling Kindersley, 2005, p. 236.

199 Thacker, Toby, *Joseph Goebbels: Life and Death*, Palgrave Macmillan, 2010, p. 157.

200 Wolfgang Preiss (1910–2002) appeared in many English-language films, most often as a German officer in WWII pictures. In Germany he was famous for playing the arch-villain Dr Mabuse in a series of films. He appeared in more than 100 films.

201 *Senses of Cinema*, issue 59.

202 Fröhlich, E., p. 260.

203 Ibid., p. 328.

204 Riefenstahl, pp. 132–133.

205 Riefenstahl, pp. 138–140. Some historians doubt this episode, but a small detail she included might add credibility to it simply because it is almost irrelevant to the story she is telling: when they got into the car, he took a

gun from his raincoat pocket and placed it in the glove compartment. After coming to a halt, he simply took the gun from the compartment and put it in his pocket.

206 Langer, Walter C., *The Mind of Adolf Hitler: The Secret Wartime Report*, Meridian-New American Library, 1985, p. 47.

207 Thacker, p. 157.

208 *Der Angriff*, 10 October 1933.

209 Herzstein, Robert Edwin, *The War that Hitler Won*, Putnam, 1978, p. 262.

210 Koonz, Claudia, *The Nazi Conscience*, Harvard University Press, 2003, p. 85.

211 Fröhlich, E., p. 286.

212 Ibid., p. 287.

213 Ibid., p. 288.

214 Hanfstaengl, Ernest, *Hitler: The Missing Years*, Eyre and Spottiswoode, 1957, p. 233.

215 Amberger, Cristoph writing in the German historical journal, *Einst & Jetzt*, 1991.

216 Riefenstahl, L., pp. 141–147. She dates this event to 13 October 1933, when Goebbels was actually in Geneva at the Disarmament Conference to announce Germany's withdrawal from the League of Nations. Why she chose this date is puzzling, but incorrect dates are by no means unusual in celebrity memoirs. It is unlikely that this event could have happened anywhere around October, because she spends time at Goebbels's home discussing the Horst Wessel controversy rather than being banished from his presence.

217 *Dr Mabuse: The Gambler*, Lang, F., Uco-Film GmbH, 1922.

218 Kalat, David, *The Strange Case of Dr Mabuse: A Study of the Twelve Films and Five Novels*, McFarland & Co., 2005, pp. 34–35.

219 Ibid., p. 36.

220 *Dr Mabuse: The Gambler*, 1922.

221 Kalat, pp. 34–35.

222 Elfriede Scholz Obituary, Osnabrück cultural website.

223 Wolfgang Preiss.

224 'Marlene Dietrich: The Opponent', *Hitler's Women*, Matthias Unterburg, ZDF Enterprises, the History Channel, SBS, 2001.

225 Ibid.

226 Ibid.

227 *So wahr ich der liebe Gott bin*, Zeit online.

228 Ibid.

229 Ibid.

230 'Zarah Leander: The Singer', *Hitler's Women*, Jörg Müllner & Ricarda Schlosshan, ZDF Enterprises, the History Channel, SBS, 2001.

231 Curd Jürgens.

232 Max Ehrlich Association, online.

233 Ibid.

234 Unger, Aryeh L., 'Propaganda and Welfare in Nazi Germany', *Journal of Social History* Vol. 4, No. 2, 1970–1971, pp. 125–140.

235 Beevor, Antony, *The Mystery of Olga Chekhova*, Penguin, 2005, p. 53. Antony James Beevor, FRSL (born 1946) is a British historian and author of several books on the subject of WWII, as well as several novels.

236 Ibid., pp. 82–84.

237 Ibid., pp. 106–107.

238 Ibid., p. 110.

239 Archive of the Moscow Art Academic Theatre Museum, K-Ch No. 2761, 16 March 1924.

240 Beevor, p. 116.

241 Knipper, Vladimir Vladimirovich, *Pora Galliutsinatsii, Spolokhi*, 1995, p. 10; see also Beevor, pp. 126–127.

242 Archive of the Chekhov house-museum at Melikhovo, V. V. Knipper Fond, file 22; also Beevor, p. 127.

243 Rees, Laurence, *The Nazis: A Warning from History*, New York Press, 1997.

244 Ibid.

245 Ibid.

246 'Ein ewig Rätsel bleiben will ich mir und anderen', from a letter dated 27 April 1876 to actress Marie Dahn-Hausmann, published in *Die Propyläen* 17, Munich, 9 July 1920.

247 Fest, Joachim C., *Hitler*, trans. Winston, Richard & Clara, Harcourt Brace Jovanovich, 1974, pp. 662–663.

248 Thacker, Toby, *Joseph Goebbels: Life and Death*, Palgrave Macmillan, 2010, p. 160.

249 Fröhlich, Elke (ed.), *Die Tagebücher von Joseph Goebbels: Teil I, Aufzeichnungen 1923–1941*, Saur, 1998–2006, 14 volumes, Volume 3/I, p. 33.

250 Ibid., p. 50.

251 'Leni Riefenstahl: The Film Director', *Hitler's Women*, Sebastian Dehnhardt & Friederike Dreykluft, ZDF Enterprises, the History Channel, SBS, 2001.

252 Ibid.

253 Ibid.

254 Ibid.

255 Ibid.

256 Ibid.

257 Ibid.

258 Behrend, Auguste, 'Meine Tochter Magda Goebbels' ('My Daughter Magda Goebbels'), *Schwäbische Illustrierte*, 26 April 1952.

259 Fröhlich, Elke (ed.), *Die Tagebücher von Joseph Goebbels: Teil I, Aufzeichnungen 1923–1941*, Saur, 1998–2006, 14 volumes, Volume 3/I, p. 211.

260 Gun, Nerin E., *Eva Braun*, Coronet Books, 1968, p. 165.

261 'Eva Braun: The Mistress', *Hitler's Women*, Stefan Brauburger and Oliver Halmburger, ZDF Enterprises, the History Channel, SBS, 2001.

262 Beevor, Antony, *The Mystery of Olga Chekhova*, Penguin, 2005, p. 129.

263 Wolfgang Preiss.

264 Curd Jürgens.

265 Fest, Joachim C., *Hitler*, trans. Winston, Richard & Clara, Harcourt Brace Jovanovich, 1974, pp. 659–660.

266 Heiber, Helmut (ed.), *Goebbels-Reden, Band I, 1932–1939*, Droste Verlag, 1971, p. 242.

267 Thacker, T., p. 170.

268 Ludwig, Hartmut, 'Das Büro Pfarrer Grüber 1938–1940', in *Büro Pfarrer Grüber Evangelische Hilfsstelle für ehemals Rasseverfolgte. Geschichte und Wiren heute*, Walter Sylten, Joachim-Dieter Schwäbl and Michael Kreitzer on behalf of the Evangelical Relief Centre for the Formerly Racially Persecuted, Berlin, 1988, pp. 1–23.

269 Richthofen, Felicitas Bothe-von, *Widerstand in Wilmersdrof* (*Memorial to the German Resistance*), Gedenkstätte Deutscher Widerstand, 1993, p. 140.

270 Russian State Archive for Literature and the Arts 2316/3/146, Moscow.

271 Fröhlich, Elke (ed.), *Die Tagebücher von Joseph Goebbels: Teil I, Aufzeichnungen 1923–1941*, Saur, 1998–2006, 14 volumes, Volume 3, p. 294; see also 5 May 1939, Part I, Volume 6, p. 338.

272 Beevor, A., p. 149.

273 Berezhkov, Valentin, *Diplomatic Mission to Hitler*, Allard, 1972, p. 109.

274 Zalampas, Sherree Owens, *Adolf Hitler: A Psychological Interpretation of His Views on Architecture, Art, and Music*, Bowling Green University Popular Press, 1990, p. 48.

275 "Leni Riefenstahl: The Film Director', *Hitler's Women*, Sebastian Dehnhardt & Friederike Dreykluft, ZDF Enterprises, the History Channel, SBS, 2001.

276 Ibid.

277 Fröhlich, Elke (ed.), *Die Tagebücher von Joseph Goebbels: Teil I, Aufzeichnungen 1923–1941*, Saur, 1998–2006, 14 volumes, Volume 3/II, p. 97.

278 'Eva Braun: The Mistress', *Hitler's Women*, Stefan Brauburger and Oliver Halmburger, ZDF Enterprises, the History Channel, SBS, 2001.

279 'More about Evi', *Time*, 18 December 1939.

280 Speer, Albert, *Inside the Third Reich*, Ishi Press International, 2009. p. 92.

281 'Eva Braun', *Hitler's Women*.

282 Wilson, Frances, 'The Eva Braun Story: Behind Every Evil Man', *The Independent*, 2 March 2006.

283 'Hitler's Private World', *Revealed*, Channel Five, 2006.

284 Ibid.

285 Kirkpatrick, Sir Ivone, *The Inner Circle*, Macmillan, 1959, p. 97.

286 Rees, Laurence, *The Nazis: A Warning From History*, New York Press, 1997.

287 Interview with Zeissler; Shofar FTP Archive File online.

288 Vanderbilt Jr, Cornelius, *Der Führer and the Brothers Marx*. This would be Cornelius Vanderbilt IV, one of the Vanderbilt dynasty which is reported as being the seventh wealthiest family in history. Cornelius Jr disappointed his parents by choosing to become a newspaperman and launching several newspapers in the early 1920s including the *Los Angeles Illustrated Daily News*, the *San Francisco Illustrated Daily Herald* and the *Miami Tab*, but his publishing company, Vanderbilt Inc., ceased operations after only two and a half years with losses amounting to nearly $6 million. He travelled as a roving reporter for *Photoplay*, the American film fan magazine, and found himself in Germany during the 1930s. After WWII he went to work as an

assistant managing editor of the *New York Daily Mirror*, and wrote numerous books including his memoirs, *Farewell to Fifth Avenue*, and a biography of his mother, Grace Graham Wilson, titled *Queen of the Golden Age*. He was a strong supporter of the newly created state of Israel.

289 'Hitler's Private World', *Revealed.*

290 Reimann, Viktor, *The Man Who Created Hitler*, Doubleday, 1976, p. 229.

291 Conradi, Peter, 'Goebbels's Mistress Tells Tales from the Grave', *The Times*, 31 October 2000.

292 Fröhlich, E., p. 180.

293 Potterton, Louise, 'Goebbels's Screen Goddess Dies Unforgiven', *The Times*, 31 October 2000.

294 Conradi, Peter, *The Times.*

295 Potterton, Louise, *The Times.*

296 Knipper, Vladimir Vladimirovich, *Pora Galliutsinatsii Spolokhi*, Moscow, 1995, p. 47; see also Beevor, Antony, *The Mystery of Olga Chekhova*, Penguin, 2005, pp. 129–130.

297 Beevor, p. 130.

298 Beevor, p. 138.

299 Ada Konstantinovna Chekhova to Olga Leonardovna Knipper-Chekhova, Brussels, 17 November 1937, Archive of the Moscow Art Academic Theatre Museum, K-Ch No. 2578; see also Beevor, p. 139.

300 Fröhlich, E., p. 93.

301 Beevor, p. 150.

302 'Marlene Dietrich: The Opponent', *Hitler's Women*, Matthias Unterburg, ZDF Enterprises, the History Channel, SBS, 2001.

303 Ibid.

304 Ibid.

305 Ibid.

306 'Zarah Leander: The Singer', *Hitler's Women*, Jörg Müllner & Ricarda Schlosshan, ZDF Enterprises, the History Channel, SBS, 2001.

307 Henriksson, Karin, SvD KULTUR, online.

308 'Zarah Leander', *Hitler's Women.*

309 Ibid.

310 Ibid.

311 Wolfgang Preiss.

312 'Zarah Leander', *Hitler's Women*.

313 Ibid.

314 Wolfgang Preiss.

315 'Zarah Leander', *Hitler's Women*.

316 Junge, Traudl, *Until the Final Hour: Hitler's Last Secretary*, Weidenfeld & Nicolson, 2003, p. 92.

317 Wolfgang Preiss; also 'Zarah Leander', *Hitler's Women*.

318 Henriksson, Karin, SvD KULTUR, online.

319 Boyes, Roger, 'Russia's Spying Stars Unmasked', *The Times*, 11 July 2003.

320 Wolfgang Preiss.

321 Ibid.

322 Ibid.

323 'Zarah Leander', *Hitler's Women*.

324 Wolfgang Preiss.

325 'Zarah Leander', *Hitler's Women*.

326 Wolfgang Preiss.

327 'Zarah Leander', *Hitler's Women*.

328 'Zarah Leander', *Hitler's Women*.

329 Archival evidence that Leander was recruited by Soviet intelligence was uncovered by Russian writer Arkadii Vaksberg; see also Roger Boyes, 'Russia's Spying Stars Unmasked', *The Times*, 11 July 2003.

330 Boyes, R., *The Times*, 11 July 2003. In 1996, shortly before he died, Pavel Sudoplatov made a startling confession to the effect that Leander was recruited before the war and given the codename Rose-Marie; see also Henriksson, SvD KULTUR, online.

331 'Zarah Leander', *Hitler's Women*.

332 Görtz, Franz J. & Sarkowicz, Hans, *Heinz Rühmann 1902–1994: Der Schauspieler und sein Jahrhundert*, Beck, 2001, p. 193.

333 Curd Jürgens.

334 'Winifred Wagner: The Muse', *Hitler's Women*, Annette Tewes & Christian Deick, ZDF Enterprises, the History Channel, SBS, 2001.

335 Ibid.

336 Thacker, Toby, *Joseph Goebbels: Life and Death*, Palgrave Macmillan, 2010, p. 224.

337 'Winifred Wagner', *Hitler's Women*.

338 Ibid.

339 Ibid.

340 Ibid.

341 Ibid.

342 Fröhlich, Elke (ed.), *Die Tagebücher von Joseph Goebbels: Teil I, Aufzeichnungen 1923–1941*, Saur, 1998–2006, 14 volumes, Volume 5, p. 323.

343 *Amtliche Mitteilungen der Reichsmuikkammer*, 1 June 1938.

344 Fröhlich, E., p. 393.

345 Fest, Joachim C., *Hitler*, trans. Winston, Richard & Clara, Harcourt Brace Jovanovich, 1974, pp. 771–772.

346 Beevor, Antony, *The Mystery of Olga Chekhova*, Penguin, 2005, p. 131.

347 Conradi, Peter, 'Goebbels's Mistress Tells Tales from the Grave', *The Times*, 31 October 2000.

348 Potterton, Louise, 'Goebbels's Screen Goddess Dies Unforgiven', *The Times*, 31 October 2000.

349 Conradi, *The Times*, 31 October 2000.

350 Potterton, *The Times*, 31 October 2000.

351 Fröhlich, E., pp. 44–45.

352 Henderson to Halifax, 17 August 1938, *Documents on British Foreign Policy 1919–1939, Third Series*, Vol. II, 1938 HMSO, 1949), p. 103; see also Thacker, Toby, *Joseph Goebbels: Life and Death*, Palgrave Macmillan, 2010, p. 201.

353 Fröhlich, E., pp. 122–124.

354 *Hitler – A Career*, Joachim Fest, Werner Rieb Produktion, 1977.

355 Fröhlich, E., p. 156–157.

356 Ibid., pp. 165–166.

357 'Leni Riefenstahl: The Film Director', *Hitler's Women*, Sebastian Dehnhardt & Friederike Dreykluft, ZDF Enterprises, the History Channel, SBS, 2001.

358 Leview, Werner, 'Arbeitsbericht des Jüdischen Kulturbundes in Deutschland e.V. vom 1.10.1938 – 30.6.1939' activity report rendered on 12 July 1939, Berlin, published in Akademie der Künste (ed.), *Geschlossene Vorstellung: Der Jüdische Kulturbund in Deutschland 1933–1941*, Edition Hentrich, 1992, pp. 321–340.

359 Seraphim, Hans Günther (ed.), *Das politische Tagebuch Alfred Rosenbergs*, Musterschmidt-Verlag, 1956, pp. 80–81.

360 Fröhlich, E., p. 245; see also Domarus, M., *Hitler: Speeches and Proclamations*, Vol. 3, p. 1449.

361 See Broder, Henryk M. & Geisel, Eike, *Premiere und Pogrom: der Jüdische Kulturbund 1933–1941*, Berlin: Wolf Jobst Siedler Verlag, 1992.

362 Braun, Bernd, 'Bücher im Schlussverkauf: Die Verlagsabteilung des Jüdischen Kulturbunds', published in Akademie der Künste, *Geschlossene Vorstellung: Der Jüdische Kulturbund in Deutschland 1933–1941*, (ed.) Edition Hentrich, 1992, pp. 155–168.

363 Kubizek, August, *Adolf Hitler, Mein Jugendfreund*, Stocker, 1953, p. 101; also Zalampas, Sherree Owens, *Adolf Hitler: A Psychological Interpretation of His Views on Architecture, Art, and Music*, Bowling Green University Popular Press, 1990, p. 14.

364 'Winifred Wagner', *Hitler's Women*.

365 'Hitler's Private World', *Revealed*.

366 Fröhlich, Elke (ed.), *Die Tagebücher von Joseph Goebbels: Teil I, Aufzeichnungen 1923–1941*, Saur, 1998–2006, 14 volumes, Volume 6, p. 337.

367 Ibid., p. 348.

368 Tschechowa, Olga, *Meine Uhren gehen anders: Erinnerungen*, F. A. Herbig Verlagsbuchhandlung, 1973, p. 190.

369 Beevor, A., p. 151.

370 'Nazi Propaganda Book Reveals Charlie Chaplin Was on Hitler's Death List', Mail Online, 27 February 2008.

371 Mitford, Deborah, 'My Sister and Hitler: Unity Mitford's War', *The Observer*, 8 December 2002; Yeoman, Fran, 'Did Unity Mitford Have Adolf Hitler's Love Child?', *The Times*, 12 December 2007; see also *Hitler's British Girl*, Richard Bond, Blakeway Productions, 2007.

372 Fest, Joachim C., *Hitler*, trans. Winston, Richard & Clara, Harcourt Brace Jovanovich, 1974.

373 Beevor, Antony, *The Mystery of Olga Chekhova*, Penguin, 2005, pp. 154–155.

374 Thacker, Toby, *Joseph Goebbels: Life and Death*, Palgrave Macmillan, 2010, p. 215.

375 see Friedlander, Saul, *The Years of Extermination: Nazi Germany and the Jews 1939–1945*, Phoenix, 2008.

376 Fröhlich, Elke (ed.), *Die Tagebücher von Joseph Goebbels: Teil I, Aufzeichnungen 1923–1941*, Saur, 1998–2006, 14 volumes, Volume 7, p. 138.

377 *Unser Wille und Weg* 10, 1940, pp. 54–55.

378 see Winkel, Roel Vander, 'Nazi Germany's Fritz Hippler', *Historical Journal of Film, Radio and Television*, vol. 23, no. 2, 2003.

379 'World War II: The Propaganda Battle', *A Walk Through the 20th Century with Bill Moyers*, PBS, 1983.

380 'The Eternal Jew – a Blueprint for Genocide', online.

381 Thacker, p. 226.

382 Joods Monument, online; also Schönfeld, Christiane & Finnan, Carmel (eds), *Practicing Modernity: Female Creativity in the Weimar Republic*, Königshausen & Neumann, 2006, p. 209.

383 see Waugh, Thomas, *Hard to Imagine*, Columbia University Press, 1996; also Slade, J., 'Bernard Natan: France's Legendary Pornographer', *Journal of Film and Video*, Summer–Fall 1993.

384 Slade, J., 'Bernard Natan: France's Legendary Pornographer'.

385 Willems, G., 'Rapid-Film et ses branches production', in Jacques Kermabon (ed.), *Pathé, premier empire du cinéma*, Paris: Centre Georges Pompidou, 1994; also Willems, G., 'Les Origines du groupe Pathé-Natan et le modèle américain', *Vingtième Siècle* 46, April–June 1995.

386 Slade, J., 'Bernard Natan: France's Legendary Pornographer'; also Willems, G., 'Les Origines du groupe Pathé-Natan et le modèle américain'; also Pierre-Jean Benghozi and Christian Delage (eds), *Une Histoire économique du cinéma français (1895–1995): regards croisés franco-américains*, Paris: Harmattan, 1997.

387 'Leni Riefenstahl: The Film Director', *Hitler's Women*, Sebastian Dehnhardt & Friederike Dreykluft, ZDF Enterprises, the History Channel, SBS, 2001.

388 'Zarah Leander', *Hitler's Women*.

389 'Winifred Wagner', *Hitler's Women*.

390 Brownlow, K., & Kloft, M., *The Tramp and the Dictator*, BBC, Photoplay, Spegiel TV and TCM, 2002.

391 Wolfgang Preiss.

392 Singer, Isidore & Adler, Cyrus (eds), *The Jewish Encyclopedia*, Funk & Wagnalls, 1912, p. 416.

393 Ibid., p. 416.

394 see Haines, B. & Parker, S. (eds), *Aesthetics and Politics in Modern German Culture*, Peter Lang Publications, 2010, p. 137.

395 *Harlan: In the Shadow of Jew Süss*, dir. Felix Moeller, 2008.

396 Ibid.

397 Ibid.

398 Ibid.

399 Haggith, Toby & Newman, Joanna (eds), *Holocaust and the Moving Image*, Wallflower Press, 2005, p. 78.

400 Ibid.

401 Curd Jürgens.

402 Ibid.

403 *Harlan: In the Shadow of Jew Süss*.

404 Ibid.

405 Wallace, Ian (ed.), *Feuchtwanger and Film*, Peter Lang Publications, 2009, p. 137.

406 *Harlan: In the Shadow of Jew Süss*.

407 'Winifred Wagner: The Muse', *Hitler's Women*, Annette Tewes & Christian Deick, ZDF Enterprises, the History Channel, SBS, 2001.

408 Tschechowa, Olga, *Meine Uhren gehen anders: Erinnerungen*, F. A. Herbig Verlagsbuchhandlung, 1973, p. 180.

409 Beevor, Antony, *The Mystery of Olga Chekhova*, Penguin, 2005, p. 157.

410 Andrew, Christopher & Gordievsky, Oleg, *KGB: the Inside Story of Its Foreign Operations from Lenin to Gorbachev*, Hodder & Stoughton, 1990, pp. 203–204.

411 Beevor, pp. 158–161.

412 Leiser, Erwin, *Nazi Cinema*, Macmillan, 1975, pp. 146–148; also Burleigh, Michael, *Death and Deliverance: 'Euthanasia' in Germany 1900–1945*, Cambridge University Press, 1994, pp. 209–219.

413 *Film o tragičnom usudu dječje zvijezde* Nacional online.

414 From minutes of the Wannsee Conference found by the Allies in Martin Luther's office. The minutes estimated the Jewish population of the Soviet Union as five million, including nearly three million in the Ukraine and 900,000 in Byelorussia.

415 Beevor, A., pp. 166–167.

416 Henrikkson, K., SvD KULTUR, online.

417 Beevor, A., p. 195.

418 Tschechowa, O., pp. 211–212.

419 Beevor, A., p. 196.

420 Boyes, Roger, 'Russia's Spying Stars Unmasked', *The Times*, 11 July 2003.

421 Browning, Christopher R., *The Origins of the Final Solution*, University of Nebraska Press, 2004, p. 309. (From Martin Bormann's minutes of the meeting, presented in evidence at the Nuremberg Trials.)

422 Ibid., p. 315.

423 Beevor, A., p. 167.

424 Ibid., p. 181.

425 Ibid., p. 162.

426 Thacker, Toby, *Joseph Goebbels: Life and Death*, Palgrave Macmillan, 2010, pp. 240–241; also Fröhlich, Elke (ed.), *Die Tagebücher von Joseph Goebbels: Teil II, Aufzeichnungen 1941–1945*, Saur, 1993–1998, 15 volumes, Volume 2, p. 240.

427 Thacker, pp. 434–437.

428 Fröhlich, E., p. 441.

429 Smith, David, 'Letter Reveals Wodehouse's Wounds over Nazi Broadcasts', *The Observer*, 3 June 2007; also 'P. G. Wodehouse – The Wartime Period', online.

430 Langton, David, 'Letter Reveals Wodehouse's Pain at Being Branded a Collaborator', *The Independent*, 2 June 2007.

431 Sproat, I., 'Wodehouse, Sir Pelham Grenville (1881–1975)', *Oxford Dictionary of National Biography*, Oxford University Press, September 2004.

432 'P. G. Wodehouse – The Wartime Period', online.

433 Ibid.

434 Smith, David, 'Letter reveals Wodehouse's wounds over Nazi broadcasts'.

435 'Winifred Wagner', *Hitler's Women*.

436 Tschechowa, p. 181.

437 Rees, L., *The Nazis: A Warning from History*, New York Press, 1997, pp. 148–149.

438 Junge, Traudl, *Until the Final Hour: Hitler's Last Secretary*, Weidenfeld & Nicolson, 2003, p. 70.

439 Wolfgang Preiss interview.

440 Ibid.

441 Knopp, Guido, *Hitler's Women*, Routledge, 2003, p. 248.

442 'Zarah Leander: The Singer', *Hitler's Women*, Jörg Müllner & Ricarda Schlosshan, ZDF Enterprises, the History Channel, SBS, 2001.

443 Wolfgang Preiss.

444 Ibid.

445 Ibid.

446 Ibid.

447 Ibid.

448 'Hitler's Private World', *Revealed*, Channel Five, 2006.

449 Ibid.

450 Leiser, Erwin, *Nazi Cinema*, Macmillan, 1975, p. 61.

451 Fröhlich, Elke (ed.), *Die Tagebücher von Joseph Goebbels: Teil II, Aufzeichnungen 1941–1945*, Saur, 1993–1998, 15 volumes, Volume 4, p. 408.

452 Ibid., p. 507.

453 Ibid., p. 610.

454 Calvin Edu German propaganda archive, online.

455 Beevor, Antony, *The Mystery of Olga Chekhova*, Penguin, 2005, p. 190.

456 *So wahr ich der liebe Gott bin*, online.

457 Fröhlich, E., p. 327.

458 'Winifred Wagner: The Muse', *Hitler's Women*, Annette Tewes & Christian Deick, ZDF Enterprises, the History Channel, SBS, 2001.

459 *Wagner's Mastersinger, Hitler's Siegfried: The Life and Times of Max Lorenz*, EuroArts, SF, Südwestrundfunk, Österreichischer Rundfunk, 2008.

460 Paterson, Tony, 'British Wagner Saves Jews from Her Friend Hitler', *Sunday Telegraph*, 25 June 2002.

461 'Winifred Wagner', *Hitler's Women*.

462 Ibid.

463 'Leni Riefenstahl', *Hitler's Women*.

464 'Nina Gladitz über Leni Riefenstahl und ihren Film', *Tiefland*, online.

465 United States Holocaust Memorial Museum, online.

466 Seeßlen, G., 'Die Feuerzangenbowle', *epd Film*, March 1994.

467 Klee, Ernst, *Das Kulturlexikon zum Dritten Reich: wer war was vor und nach 1945*, Fischer, 2007, p. 227.

468 Wolfgang Preiss.

469 Gerron, K., *The Führer Gives the Jews a City*, 1944.

470 *A Musical Postcard from the Eye of the Nazi Storm* online

471 Trials of the Major War Criminals before the International Military Tribunal, Nuremberg, 14 November 1945 – 1 October 1946, Volume 1, p. 251.

472 Memorial Museum Auschwitz-Birkenau, *Auschwitz and Shoah*, online; also Franciszak Piper, 'The Number of Victims', in *Anatomy of the Auschwitz Death Camp* edited by Y. Gutman & M. Berenbaum, Indiana University, with the US Holocaust Museum, Washington DC, 1994, pp. 68–70.

473 'Imprisoned for Their Faith', Memorial Museum Auschwitz-Birkenau, online.

474 Gutman & Berenbaum, p. 5.

475 United States Holocaust Memorial Museum, online.

476 Knipper, Vladimir Vladimirovich, *Pora Galliutsinatsii*, Spolokhi, 1995, p. 190.

477 Beevor, Antony, *The Mystery of Olga Chekhova*, Penguin, 2005, pp. 194–195.

478 Albert Sumser in Beevor, A., *The Mystery of Olga Chekhova*, pp. 197–198.

479 Leiser, Erwin, *Nazi Cinema*, Macmillan, 1975, pp. 122–123.

480 Harlan, Veit, *Im Schatten meiner Filme: Selbstbiographie*, Mohn, 1966, pp. 187–188.

481 *Harlan, in the Shadow of Jew Süss*, Felix Moeller, Zeitgeist Films, 2008.

482 Beevor, A., p. 197.

483 Ibid., pp. 198–200.

484 Ibid., p. 202.

485 *Hitler's Downfall*, History Media GmbH for ZDF Enterprises and The History Channel, 2005.

486 Butler, Ewan & Young, Gordon, *The Life and Death of Hermann Goering*, David & Charles, 1989, pp. 227–228.

487 Waite, Robert G. L., 'Afterword', in Langer, Walter C., *The Mind of Adolf Hitler: The Secret Wartime Report*, Meridian-New American Library, 1985, pp. 237–238.

488 Guderian, Heinz, *Erinnerungen eines Soldaten*, K. Vowinckel, 1951, p. 402.

489 'Winifred Wagner: The Muse', *Hitler's Women*, Annette Tewes & Christian Deick, ZDF Enterprises, the History Channel, SBS, 2001.

490 Sereny, Gitta, *Albert Speer: His Battle with Truth*, Knopf, 1995, pp. 498–504; also, Fest, Joachim C., *Hitler*, trans. Winston, Richard & Clara, Harcourt Brace Jovanovich, 1974, pp. 1085–1089.

491 *So wahr ich der liebe Gott bin*, Zeit, online.

492 *Hitler's Downfall*, 2005.

493 Beevor, A., pp. 198–199.

494 Ibid., p. 200.

495 Beyer, Friedemann, *Die Ufa-Stars im Dritten Reich: Frauen für Deutschland*, Heyne, 1991, p. 15.

496 Semmler, Rudolph, *Goebbels: The Man Next to Hitler*, Westhouse, 1947, p. 194.

497 Beevor, p. 201.

498 *Hitler's Downfall*, 2005.

499 Ibid.

500 Ibid.

501 Ibid.

502 Albert Sumser in Beevor, A., *The Mystery of Olga Chekhova*, p. 203.

503 Archive of the Moscow Art Academic Theatre Museum, K-Ch No. 2580, 26 April 1945.

504 Knipper, p. 180.

505 *Hitler's Downfall*, 2005.

506 'Eva Braun', *Hitler's Women*.

507 Beevor, Antony, *Berlin: The Downfall 1945*, Viking, 2002, p.343.

508 *Hitler's Downfall*, History Media GmbH for ZDF Enterprises and The History Channel, 2005.

509 Wolfgang Preiss.

510 *Hitler's Downfall*, 2005.

511 'Winifred Wagner', *Hitler's Women*.

512 Ibid.

513 *Hitler's Downfall*, 2005.

514 Wolfgang Preiss.

515 Deriabin, Peter, *Inside Stalin's Kremlin*, Brassey's Inc., 1998, p. 59.

516 Archive of the Chekhov house-museum at Melikhovo, V. V. Knipper Fond, file 22; also Beevor, Antony, *The Mystery of Olga Chekhova*, Penguin, 2005, p. 53.

517 Archive of the Chekhov house-museum at Melikhovo, V. V. Knipper Fond, file 22; also Beevor, p. 208.

518 Beevor, p. 211.

519 Archive of the Chekhov house-museum at Melikhovo, V. V. Knipper Fond, file 22.

520 Beevor, p. 226.

521 'Leni Riefenstahl', *Hitler's Women*.

522 Ibid.

523 *Harlan, In the Shadow of Jew Süss*.

524 Struan Robertson, 'Nos. 9–11 Hartungstraße', *Buildings Integral to the Former Life and/or Persecution of Jews in Hamburg – Rotherbaum II/Havestehude*, University of Hamburg, online.

525 Wolfgang Preiss.

526 The Berlin-Hohenschönhausen Memorial Foundation, online.

527 Niemi, Robert, *History in the Media: Film and Television*, ABC-CLIO, 2006, p. 6.

528 'Winifred Wagner', *Hitler's Women*.

529 Ibid.

530 Ibid.

531 Rentschler, Eric, *The Ministry of Illusion: Nazi Cinema and Its Afterlife*, Harvard University Press, 1996, p. 1.

BIBLIOGRAPHY

Adorno, Theodor, *In Search of Wagner*, Verso Books, 2009.

Andrew, Christopher & Gordievsky, Oleg, *KGB: the Inside Story of Its Foreign Operations from Lenin to Gorbachev*, Hodder & Stoughton, 1990.

Beevor, Antony, *Berlin: The Downfall 1945*, Viking, 2002.

Beevor, Antony, *The Mystery of Olga Chekhova*, Penguin, 2005.

Berezhkov, Valentin, *Diplomatic Mission to Hitler*, Allard, 1972.

Beyer, Friedemann, *Die Ufa-Stars im Dritten Reich: Frauen für Deutschland*, Heyne, 1991.

Brando, Marlon, with Lindsey, Robert, *Brando: Songs My Mother Taught Me*, Century, 1994.

Broder, Henryk M. & Geisel, Eike, *Premiere und Pogrom: der Jüdische Kulturbund 1933–1941*, Berlin: Wolf Jobst Siedler Verlag, 1992.

Browning, Christopher R., *The Origins of the Final Solution*, University of Nebraska Press, 2004.

Bullock, Alan, *Hitler: A Study in Tyranny*, Penguin Books, 1962.

Burleigh, Michael, *Death and Deliverance: 'Euthanasia' in Germany 1900–1945*, Cambridge University Press, 1994.

Butler, Ewan & Young, Gordon, *The Life and Death of Hermann Goering*, David & Charles, 1989.

Cecil, Robert, *The Myth of the Master Race: Alfred Rosenberg and Nazi Ideology*, Dodd, Mead, 1972.

Deriabin, Peter, *Inside Stalin's Kremlin*, Brassey's Inc., 1998.

Dollinger, Hans, *The Decline and Fall of Nazi Germany and Imperial Japan: A Pictorial History of the Final Days of World War II*, Gramercy, 1995.

Domarus, M., *Hitler: Speeches and Proclamations*, Vol. 3, Bolchazy-Carducci Publishers Inc.

Eisner, Lotte H., *The Haunted Screen: Expressionism in the German Cinema and the Influence of Max Reinhardt*, University of California Press, 1969.

Fest, Joachim C., *Hitler*, trans. Winston, Richard & Clara, Harcourt Brace Jovanovich, 1974.

Fischer, Thomas, *Soldiers of the Leibstandarte: SS-Brigadefuhrer Wilhelm Mohnke and 62 Soldiers of Hitler's Elite Division*, J. J. Fedorowicz, 2008.

Flanner, Janet, *An American in Paris*, Simon & Schuster, 1940.

Friedlander, Saul, *The Years of Extermination: Nazi Germany and the Jews 1939–1945*, Phoenix, 2008.

Friedman, Jonathan C. (ed.), *The Routledge History of the Holocaust*, Routledge, 2011.

Fröhlich, Elke (ed.), *Die Tagebücher von Joseph Goebbels: Teil I, Aufzeichnungen 1923–1941*, Saur, 1998–2006, 14 volumes.

Fröhlich, Elke (ed.), *Die Tagebücher von Joseph Goebbels: Teil II, Aufzeichnungen 1941–1945*, Saur, 1993–1998, 15 volumes.

Fry, Michael, *Hitler's Wonderland*, John Murray, 1934.

Geissmar, Berta, *The Baton and the Jackboot: Recollections of Musical Life*, Hamish Hamilton, 1944.

Giblin, James Cross, *The Life and Death of Adolf Hitler*, Clarion Books, 2002.

Gordon, Mel, *Hanussen: Hitler's Jewish Clairvoyant*, Feral House, 2001.

Görtz, Franz J. & Sarkowicz, Hans, *Heinz Rühmann 1902–1994: Der Schauspieler und sein Jahrhundert*, Beck, 2001.

Guderian, Heinz, *Erinnerungen eines Soldaten*, K. Vowinckel, 1951.

Gun, Nerin E., *Eva Braun*, Coronet Books, 1968.

Gutman, Robert W., *Richard Wagner: The Man, His Mind and His Music*, Harvest Books, 1990.

Gutman, Yisrael & Berenbaum, Michael (eds), *Anatomy of the Auschwitz Death Camp*, Indiana University Press, 1998.

Haggith, Toby & Newman, Joanna (eds), *Holocaust and the Moving Image*, Wallflower Press, 2005.

Haines, B. & Parker, S. (eds), *Aesthetics and Politics in Modern German Culture*, Peter Lang Publications, 2010.

Hamann, Brigitte, *Hitler's Vienna: A Dictator's Apprenticeship*, trans. Thomas Thornton, Oxford University Press, 1999.

Hanfstaengl, Ernest, *Hitler: The Missing Years*, Eyre and Spottiswoode, 1957.

Harlan, Veit, *Im Schatten meiner Filme: Selbstbiographie*, Mohn, 1966.

Heiber, Helmut (ed.), *Goebbels-Reden, Band I, 1932–1939,* Droste Verlag, 1971.

Heiden, Konrad, *Adolf Hitler*, Europa Verlag, 1936.

Herzstein, Robert Edwin, *The War that Hitler Won*, Putnam, 1978.

Hitler, Adolf, *Mein Kampf,* trans. Ralph Manheim, Sentry, 1943.

Hitler, Adolf, *My New Order*, Reynal & Hitchcock, 1941.

Huss, Pierre J., *The Foe We Face*, Doubleday, Doran & Co., 1942.

Isaacson, Walter, *Einstein: His Life and Universe*, Simon & Schuster, 2007.

Jenks, William Alexander, *Vienna and the Young Hitler*, Columbia University Press, 1960.

Jetzinger, Franz, *Hitlers Jugend*, Europa-Verlag, 1956.

Junge, Traudl, *Until the Final Hour: Hitler's Last Secretary*, Weidenfeld & Nicolson, 2003.

Kalat, David, *The Strange Case of Dr Mabuse: A Study of the Twelve Films and Five Novels,* McFarland & Co., 2005.

Karney, Robyn (ed.), *Cinema Year by Year 1894–2005*, Dorling Kindersley, 2005.

Kee, Robert, *Munich: The Eleventh Hour*, Hamish Hamilton, 1988.

Kershaw, Ian, *Hitler 1889–1936: Hubris*, Penguin, 1999.

Kirkpatrick, Sir Ivone, *The Inner Circle*, Macmillan, 1959.

Klee, Ernst, *Das Kulturlexikon zum Dritten Reich: wer war was vor und nach 1945*, Fischer, 2007.

Knipper, Vladimir Vladimirovich, *Pora Galliutsinatsii*, Spolokhi, 1995.

Knopp, Guido, *Hitler's Women*, Routledge, 2003.

Koonz, Claudia, *The Nazi Conscience*, Harvard University Press, 2003.

Kubizek, August, *Adolf Hitler, Mein Jugendfreund*, Stocker, 1953.

Langer, Walter C., *The Mind of Adolf Hitler: The Secret Wartime Report*, Meridian-New American Library, 1985.

Leiser, Erwin, *Nazi Cinema*, Macmillan, 1975.

Leview, Werner, 'Arbeitsbericht des Jüdischen Kulturbundes in Deutschland e.V. vom 1.10.1938 – 30.6.1939' activity report rendered on 12 July 1939, Berlin, published in Akademie der Künste (ed.), *Geschlossene Vorstellung: Der Jüdische Kulturbund in Deutschland 1933–1941*, Edition Hentrich, 1992.

Ludecke, Kurt George, *I Knew Hitler*, Scribner, 1937.

Ludwig, Hartmut, 'Das Büro Pfarrer Grüber 1938–1940', in *Büro Pfarrer Grüber Evangelische Hilfsstelle für ehemals Rasseverfolgte. Geschichte und Wiren heute*, Walter Sylten, Joachim-Dieter Schwäbl and Michael Kreitzer on behalf of the Evangelical Relief Centre for the Formerly Racially Persecuted, Berlin, 1988.

Maser, Werner, *Hitler: Legende, Mythos, Wirklichkeit*, Bechtle, 1971; trans. *Hitler: Legend, Myth & Reality*, Harper & Row, 1973.

Meissner, Hans Otto, *Magda Goebbels, First Lady of the Third Reich*, Sidgwick and Jackson, 1980.

Mend, Hans, *Adolf Hitler im Felde*, Huber Verlag, 1931.

Mitchell, Otis C., *Hitler's Stormtroopers and the Attack on the German Republic, 1919–1933*; McFarland & Co., 2008.

Murray, Williamson, *The Change in the European Balance of Power*, Princeton University Press, 1984.

Niemi, Robert, *History in the Media: Film and Television*, ABC-CLIO, 2006.

Oechsner, Frederick, *This is the Enemy*, Little, Brown & Co., 1942.

Phelan, Anthony (ed.), The *Weimar Dilemma: Intellectuals in the Weimar Republic*, Manchester University Press, 1985.

Pope, Ernest R., *Munich Playground*, G. P. Putnam's Sons, 1941.

Price, George Ward, *I Know These Dictators*, Harrap, 1937.

Rauschning, Hermann, *Gespräche mit Hitler*, Europa Verlag, 1940; *Voice of Destruction*, (US) G. P. Putnam's Sons, 1940; *Hitler Speaks*, (UK) Thornton Butterworth, 1939.

Rees, Laurence, *The Nazis: A Warning from History*, New York Press, 1997.

Reimann, Viktor, *The Man Who Created Hitler*, Doubleday, 1976.

Rentschler, Eric, *The Ministry of Illusion: Nazi Cinema and Its Afterlife*, Harvard University Press, 1996.

Richthofen, Felicitas Bothe-von, *Widerstand in Wilmersdrof* (*Memorial to the German Resistance*), Gedenkstätte Deutscher Widerstand, 1993.

Riefenstahl, Leni, *The Sieve of Time*, Quartet Books, 1992.

Rose, Paul Lawrence, *Wagner, Race and Revolution*, Yale University Press, 1992.

Rosenbaum, Ron, *Explaining Hitler: The Search for the Origins of His Evil*, Macmillan, 1998.

Sage, Steven F., *Ibsen and Hitler: The Playwright, the Plagiarist, and the Plot for the Third Reich*, Carroll & Graf Publishers, 2006.

Schönfeld, Christiane & Finnan, Carmel (eds), *Practicing Modernity: Female Creativity in the Weimar Republic*, Königshausen & Neumann, 2006.

Semmler, Rudolph, *Goebbels: The Man Next to Hitler*, Westhouse, 1947.

Seraphim, Hans Günther (ed.), *Das politische Tagebuch Alfred Rosenbergs*, Musterschmidt-Verlag, 1956.

Sereny, Gitta, *Albert Speer: His Battle with Truth*, Knopf, 1995.

Singer, Isidore & Adler, Cyrus (eds), *The Jewish Encyclopaedia*, Funk & Wagnalls, 1912.

Smith, Bradley, *Adolf Hitler, His Family, Childhood and Youth*, Hoover Institution on War, Revolution, and Peace, 1967.

Speer, Albert, *Inside the Third Reich*, Ishi Press International, 2009.

Strasser, Otto, *Flight from Terror*, R. M. McBride and Co., 1943.

Thacker, Toby, *Joseph Goebbels: Life and Death*, Palgrave Macmillan, 2010.

Tschechowa, Olga, *Meine Uhren gehen anders: Erinnerungen*, F. A. Herbig Verlagsbuchhandlung, 1973.

Voigt, Frederick Augustus, *Unto Caesar*, G. P. Putnam's Sons, 1938.

Wagner, Friedelind, *The Royal Family of Bayreuth*, Eyre and Spottiswoode, 1948.

Wagner, Gottfried, *Twilight of the Wagners: The Unveiling of a Family's Legacy*, Kiepenheuer & Witsch, 1997.

Wagner, Richard, *Art and Politics* Vol. 4, University of Nebraska Press, 1995.

Wagner, Richard, *My Life*, trans. Andrew Gray, Da Capo Press, 1992.

Wagner, Richard, 'Prose Works', *Das Judenthum in der Musik* (*Judaism in Music*), 1850.

Waite, Robert G. L., 'Afterword', in Langer, Walter C., *The Mind of Adolf Hitler: The Secret Wartime Report*, Meridian-New American Library, 1985.

Waite, Robert G. L., 'Hitler's Anti-Semitism', in Wolman, Benjamin B. (ed.), *The Psychoanalytic Interpretation of History*, Basic Books, 1971.

Waite, Robert G. L., *The Psychopathic God: Adolf Hitler*, Basic Books, 1977.

Wallace, Ian (ed.), *Feuchtwanger and Film*, Peter Lang Publications, 2009.

Waugh, Thomas, *Hard to Imagine*, Columbia University Press, 1996.

Weinberg, Gerhard, *The Foreign Policy of Hitler's Germany: Starting World War II*, University of Chicago Press, 1980.

Winkel, Roel Vander, 'Nazi Germany's Fritz Hippler', *Historical Journal of Film, Radio and Television*, vol. 23, no. 2, Carfax Publishing, 2003.

Wulf, Josef (ed.), *Musik im Dritten Reich: Eine Dokumentation*, Mohn Verlag, 1963.

Zalampas, Sherree Owens, *Adolf Hitler: A Psychological Interpretation of His Views on Architecture, Art, and Music*, Bowling Green University Popular Press, 1990.

Zoller, Albert, *Hitler privat: Erlebnisbericht seiner Geheimsekretärin*, Droste-Verlag, 1949.

NEWSPAPER AND MAGAZINE ARTICLES

Amberger, Cristoph, 'Feature on Hanns Heinz Ewers', *Einst & Jetzt*, 1991.

Behrend, Auguste, 'My Daughter Magda Goebbels', *Schwäbische Illustrierte*, 26 April 1952.

Boyes, Roger, 'Russia's Spying Stars Unmasked', *The Times*, 11 July 2003.

'Cocksure Dictator Takes Timid Soul Precautions', *Newsweek*, 6 April 1935.

Connolly, Kate, 'Hitler's Mentally Ill Cousin "Killed in Nazi Gas Chamber"', *Daily Telegraph*, 19 January 2005.

Conradi, Peter, 'Goebbels's Mistress Tells Tales from the Grave', *The Times*, 31 October 2000.

Hanisch, Reinhold, 'I was Hitler's Buddy', *New Republic*, 5 April 1939, 12 April 1939, & 19 April 1939.

Harding, Luke, 'Leni Riefenstahl: Hand-held History', *The Economist*, 13 September 2003.

High, Stanley, 'The Man Who Leads Germany', *Literary Digest*, 21 October 1933.

James, Clive, 'Reich Star', *New York Times*, 25 March 2007.

Langton, David, 'Letter Reveals Wodehouse's Pain at Being Branded a Collaborator', *The Independent*, 2 June 2007.

Macintyre, Ben, 'I Foresee a Troubled Future for Burmese Generals – a look at leaders who cling desperately to astrology and superstition', *The Times*, 28 September 2007.

Mitford, Deborah, 'My Sister and Hitler: Unity Mitford's War', *The Observer*, 8 December 2002

Moore, Charles, 'Leni Riefenstahl', *Daily Telegraph*, 10 September 2003.

Paterson, Tony, 'British Wagner Saves Jews from Her Friend Hitler', *Sunday Telegraph*, 25 June 2002.

Phayre, Ignatius, 'Holiday with Hitler', *Current History*, July 1936.

Potterton, Louise, 'Goebbels's Screen Goddess Dies Unforgiven', *The Times*, 31 October 2000.

Smith, David, 'Letter Reveals Wodehouse's Wounds over Nazi Broadcasts', *The Observer*, 3 June 2007.

Unger, Aryeh L., 'Propaganda and Welfare in Nazi Germany', *Journal of Social History* Vol. 4, No. 2, 1970–1971.

'Vom Wahne Besessen', *Pariser Tages Zeitung* no. 1212, 23 January 1940.

White, W.C., 'Hail Hitler', *Scribner 9*, April 1932.

Wiegand, Karl von, 'Hitler Foresees His End', *Cosmopolitan*, May 1939.

Williams, Val, 'Leni Riefenstahl', *The Independent*, 9 October 2003.

Wilson, Frances, 'The Eva Braun Story: Behind Every Evil Man', *The Independent*, 2 March 2006.

Yeoman, Fran, 'Did Unity Mitford Have Adolf Hitler's Love Child?', *The Times*, 12 December 2007.

DOCUMENTARIES

'Eva Braun: The Mistress', *Hitler's Women*, Stefan Brauburger and Oliver Halmburger, ZDF Enterprises, the History Channel, SBS, 2001.

Harlan, in the Shadow of Jew Süss, Felix Moeller, Zeitgeist Films, 2008.

Hitler – A Career, Joachim Fest, Werner Rieb Produktion, 1977.

Hitler's British Girl, Richard Bond, Blakeway Productions, 2007.

Hitler's Downfall, History Media GmbH for ZDF Enterprises and The History Channel, 2005.

'Hitler's Private World', *Revealed,* Channel Five, 2006.

'Leni Riefenstahl: The Film Director', *Hitler's Women,* Sebastian Dehnhardt & Friederike Dreykluft, ZDF Enterprises, the History Channel, SBS, 2001.

'Marlene Dietrich: The Opponent', *Hitler's Women,* Matthias Unterburg, ZDF Enterprises, the History Channel, SBS, 2001.

The Nazis: A Warning from History, BBC/A&E Network, 1997.

The Tramp and the Dictator, Kevin Brownlow and Michael Kloft, BBC, Photoplay Productions, Spiegel TV & TCM, 2002.

Wagner's Mastersinger, Hitler's Siegfried: The Life and Times of Max Lorenz (aka *Max Lorenz: Wagner's Mastersinger, Hitler's Siegfried*), a film by Eric Schulz and Claus Wischmann, EuroArts, SF, Südwestrundfunk, Österreichischer Rundfunk, 2008.

'Winifred Wagner: The Muse', *Hitler's Women,* Annette Tewes & Christian Deick, ZDF Enterprises, the History Channel, SBS, 2001.

'Zarah Leander: The Singer', *Hitler's Women,* Jörg Müllner & Ricarda Schlosshan, ZDF Enterprises, the History Channel, SBS, 2001.

ONLINE

(All websites last accessed 29 November 2011.)

The Berlin-Hohenschönhausen Memorial Foundation; http://en.stiftung-hsh.de

Calvin German propaganda archive; http://www.calvin.edu/academic/cas/gpa/goeb36.htm; http://www.calvin.edu/academic/cas/gpa/angrif11.htm

The Eternal Jew – a Blueprint for Genocide; http://www.holocaust-history.org/der-ewige-jude/millersville-19980427.shtml

'Film o tragičnom usudu dječje zvijezde', Nacional; http://www.nacional.hr/clanak/27554/film-o-tragicnom-usudu-djecje-zvijezde

Henriksson, Karin, 'Die Leander egentligen kamrat Zarah?', SvD KULTUR; http://www.svd.se/kultur/understrecket/die-leander-egentligen-kamrat-zarah_99666.svd

Interview Nina Gladitz über Leni Riefenstahl und ihren Film *Tiefland*; http://www.derfunke.at/nostalgie/hp_artikel/Interview_Riefenstahl. htm

Interview with Zeissler - Hollywood, California, June 24, 1943; Shofar FTP Archive File: people/h/hitler.adolf/oss-papers/text/oss-sb-zeissler; http://www.vex.net/~nizkor/ftp.cgi/ftp.py?people/h/hitler.adolf/ oss-papers/text/oss-sb-zeissler

Joods Monument, Online; http://www.joodsmonument.nl/person/473906

'Leni Riefenstahl', United States Holocaust Memorial Museum; http:// www.ushmm.org/wlc/en/article.php?ModuleId=10007410

Max Ehrlich Association; http://www.max-ehrlich.org/

Memorial Museum Auschwitz-Birkenau *Auschwitz and Shoah*; http://en.auschwitz.org

Memorial Museum Auschwitz-Birkenau *Imprisoned for Their Faith*; http://en.auschwitz.org.pl/m/index.php?option=com_content&task=vie w&id=370&Itemid=8

'More About Evi', *Time*, 18 December 1939; http://www.time.com/time/magazine/article/0,9171,763084,00.html

'Nazi Propaganda Book Reveals Charlie Chaplin Was on Hitler's Death List', MailOnline, 27 February 2008; http://www.dailymail.co.uk/news/article-520648/Nazi-propaganda-book-reveals-Charlie-Chaplin-Hitlers-death-list.html

PG Wodehouse – The Wartime Period; http://www.pgwodehousebooks.com/war.htm

Robertson, Struan, 'Nos. 9–11 Hartungstraße', *Buildings Integral to the Former Life and/or Persecution of Jews in Hamburg – Rotherbaum II/ Havestehude*. University of Hamburg; http://www1.uni-hamburg.de/rz3a035//hartungstrasse.html

Senses of Cinema, Issue 59; http://www.sensesofcinema.com/2002/book-reviews/goebbels/

'So wahr ich der liebe Gott bin', Zeit; http://www.zeit.de/2010/29/GES-Hans-Albers/seite-1

'Uneven Romance', *Time*, 29 June 1959; http://www.time.com/time/
    magazine/article/0,9171,86465,00.html
Larry Solomon, 'Wagner and Hitler';
http://solomonsmusic.net/WagHit.htm

INDEX

Auschwitz

A Doctor's Eyewitness Account

by Dr. Miklos Nyiszli

Foreword by Bruno Bettelheim

When the Nazis invaded Hungary in 1944, they sent virtually the entire Jewish population to Auschwitz. A Jew and a medical doctor, Dr. Miklos Nyiszli was spared from death for a grimmer fate: to perform "scientific research" on his fellow inmates under the supervision of the infamous "Angel of Death": Dr. Josef Mengele. Nyiszli was named Mengele's personal research pathologist. Miraculously, he survived to give this terrifying and sobering account.

$14.95 Paperback • ISBN 978-1-61145-011-8

With Hitler to the End

The Memoir of Hitler's Valet

by Heinz Linge

Introduction by Roger Moorhouse

Heinz Linge worked with Adolf Hitler from 1935 until the Führer's death in the Berlin bunker in May 1945. He was one of the last to leave the bunker and was responsible for guarding the door while Hitler killed himself. During his years of service, Linge was responsible for all aspects of Hitler's household and was constantly by his side.

Here, Linge recounts the daily routine in Hitler's household: his eating habits, his foibles, his preferences, his sense of humor, and his private life with Eva Braun. Linge also charts the changes in Hitler's character during their time together and during the last years of the war. In a number of instances—such as with the Stauffenberg bomb plot of July 1944—Linge gives an excellent eyewitness account of events.

Though Linge held an SS rank, he claims not to have been a Nazi Party member. His profile of one of history's worst demons is not blindly uncritical, but it is nonetheless affectionate. The Hitler that emerges is unpredictable and demanding, but not of an otherwise unpleasant nature.

$24.95 Hardcover • ISBN 978-1-60239-804-7

If the Allies Had Fallen

Sixty Alternate Scenarios of World War II

Edited by Dennis E. Showalter and Harold C. Deutsch

What if Stalin had signed with the West in 1939? What if the Allies had been defeated on D-Day? What if Hitler had won the war?

From the Munich crisis and the dropping of the first atom bomb to Hitler's declaration of war on the United States and the D-Day landings, historians suggest "what might have been" if key events in World War II had gone differently.

Written by an exceptional team of historians as if these world-changing events had really happened, *If the Allies Had Fallen* is a spirited and terrifying alternate history, and a telling insight into the dramatic possibilities of World War II. Contributors include: Thomas M. Barker, Harold C. Deutsch, Walter S. Dunn, Robert M. Love, D. Clayton James, Bernard C. Nalty, Richard J. Overy, Paul Schratz, Dennis E. Showalter, Gerhard L. Weinberg, Anne Wells, and Herman S. Wolk.

$14.95 Paperback • ISBN 978-1-61608-546-9